Anonymous

Industrial rivers of the United Kingdom

Anonymous

Industrial rivers of the United Kingdom

ISBN/EAN: 9783337134389

Printed in Europe, USA, Canada, Australia, Japan

Cover: Foto ©Andreas Hilbeck / pixelio.de

More available books at **www.hansebooks.com**

INDUSTRIAL RIVERS

OF THE

UNITED KINGDOM;

NAMELY:

*The Thames, Mersey, Tyne, Tawe, Clyde, Wear, Taff,
Avon, Southampton Water, The Hartlepools, Humber;
Neath, Port Talbot, and Caermarthen;
The Liffey, Usk, Tees, Severn,
Wyre, and Lagan.*

By VARIOUS WELL-KNOWN EXPERTS.

ILLUSTRATED

London:
T. FISHER UNWIN,
26, PATERNOSTER SQUARE, E.C.

1888.

CONTENTS.

	PAGE
The Thames	1
The Mersey	19
The Tyne	45
The Tawe	64
The Clyde	79
The Wear	108
The Taff: Cardiff	122
The Avon: Bristol	242
Southampton	158
The Hartlepools	175
The Humber: Hull	192
Neath, Port Talbot, and Caermarthen	203
The Liffey	218
The Usk	230
The Tees	241
The Lagan	256
The Wyre: Fleetwood	267
The Severn	275

LIST OF ILLUSTRATIONS.

———o———

		PAGE
The Liffey	*Frontispiece*	
Roman London	*Facing*	3
Old Temple Stairs, London	,,	17
Liverpool in 1520	,,	24
The Brown Free Library, Liverpool	,,	27
The Sailors' Home, Liverpool	,,	30
Corn Warehouse, Liverpool	,,	35
Watts' Engine in West End Park, Glasgow	,,	85
Glasgow Royal Exchange	,,	97
Low Water Pier, Cardiff—Penarth Head	,	128
Entrance to Bute Docks...	,,	130
Clifton Suspension Bridge	,,	144
Harbours, Docks, &c., at the Hartlepools ...	,,	176
A Bit of Hull	,,	193
Neath Harbour Improvements	,,	203
The Bank of Ireland, Dublin	,,	224
Newport	,,	231
The Cleveland Hills	,,	242
The Port of Middlesborough	,,	246
Middlesborough Railway Station	,,	252
The Severn from Worcester to Bridgnorth ...	,,	281

PREFACE.

THIS volume is composed of chapters dealing with the leading Industrial Rivers and Ports of the United Kingdom. The different articles were written at first for THE SHIPPING WORLD by acknowledged authorities, such as Mr. James Deas, the able and well-known engineer of the Clyde; Mr. Richard Welford, whose literary abilities, and intimate acquaintance with shipping and commerce are so well illustrated in the article on the Tyne; Mr. William Duncan, of Sunderland; Mr. Steel, of Hartlepool; Mr. J. G. E. Astle, of Cardiff; the accomplished "Irvonwy," whose death in Swansea Bay was so universally regretted, and mourned by his friends in South Wales; Mr. Consul Lathrop, of Bristol; and others, selected by the Editor of THE SHIPPING WORLD as possessing special fitness for the work.

The chapters are not confined to the commerce and industries which characterise the great rivers: the history of each stream is traced from the earliest times. The foundation of the trade and manufactures which distinguish the several ports and districts are noticed; and the improvement of the rivers and harbours, and the develop-

PREFACE.

ment of the trade and commerce, up to the latest possible period, are dealt with at length.

The article devoted to each river constitutes a commercial and industrial history of the district traversed by the stream. The greatest possible pains were taken by the contributors, and by the Editor of THE SHIPPING WORLD, to make the statistical portion of each chapter absolutely correct. Facilities were afforded to the Trusts and Authorities to correct inaccuracies, and supply omissions. And judging from the commendation of those concerned in the great industries, and by the comments of the press, the articles gave entire satisfaction, while they certainly widened the scope and increased the popularity of THE SHIPPING WORLD.

It was felt by many that contributions of such a valuable and authentic character should be brought together and reproduced in a single volume. In response to that feeling, arrangements were made for the publication of the present volume. Pamphlets have appeared dealing with single rivers. The Tyne, Wear, and Tees have been incorporated in one book; but, so far as we are aware, the present volume is the first attempt to give in compact form the leading Industrial Rivers of the United Kingdom. And the book is now given to the public, in the belief that it supplies a want, and in the hope that it will be well received.

THE EDITOR OF THE SHIPPING WORLD.

INDUSTRIAL RIVERS.

THE THAMES.

'This is indeed old Father Thames, in the overwhelming wonders of his wealth; and the ships and the warehouses that we see contain the stimulus and the reward of those men who have made England the queen and London the jewel of the world."—BABYLON THE GREAT.

It would be an interesting task to dilate on the influence which rivers have ever exerted upon the settlement, trade, and prosperity of a country; the natural instincts which led the primitive inhabitants to erect their rude dwellings by the banks of streams, and the gradual development whereby these ancient villages have grown into mighty centres of commerce. To trace the evolution of these influences for one river alone would be instructive no less than interesting; and still more tempting would it be were the theme the Thames, that famous stream whose only competitor in historic interest is the "yellow Tiber, to whom the Romans prayed!" But antiquarian researches are beyond our scope, as are historic associations. For well-nigh every footstep by the banks of the Thames is planted on classic ground. The windings of the silver river, presenting a succession of the fairest sylvan scenes, embrace many a famous spot before reaching the busy mart of London. Oxford, the ancient citadel of learning, the second capital, the bulwark of the king when his unfaithful commons ruled in the metropolis; Windsor, the stately home of the English sovereigns; Runnymede, where the charter of our liberties was forced from a reluctant monarch; Hampton Court, the monument of Wolsey's pride; Richmond Hill, with its fairy landscape, would all woo us for a while from the contemplation of that marvellous commerce to which the spirit of the day commands attention.

The founders of London were probably little influenced by any question of scenery, and certainly not at all by historic associations, when they first settled on the banks of the Thames. Their reasons were thoroughly utilitarian. They found there a collection of hills, bathed at the foot by a river rich in salmon and other fish, expanding into a wide estuary at high water, and bounded south, east, and west by marshes forming a defence against the attacks of other tribes. Behind stretched dense forests teeming with wild boar and other beasts of the chase. On these hills they erected their fortified dwellings, whither they could in troublous times withdraw their families and flocks. They soon, as by a natural instinct,

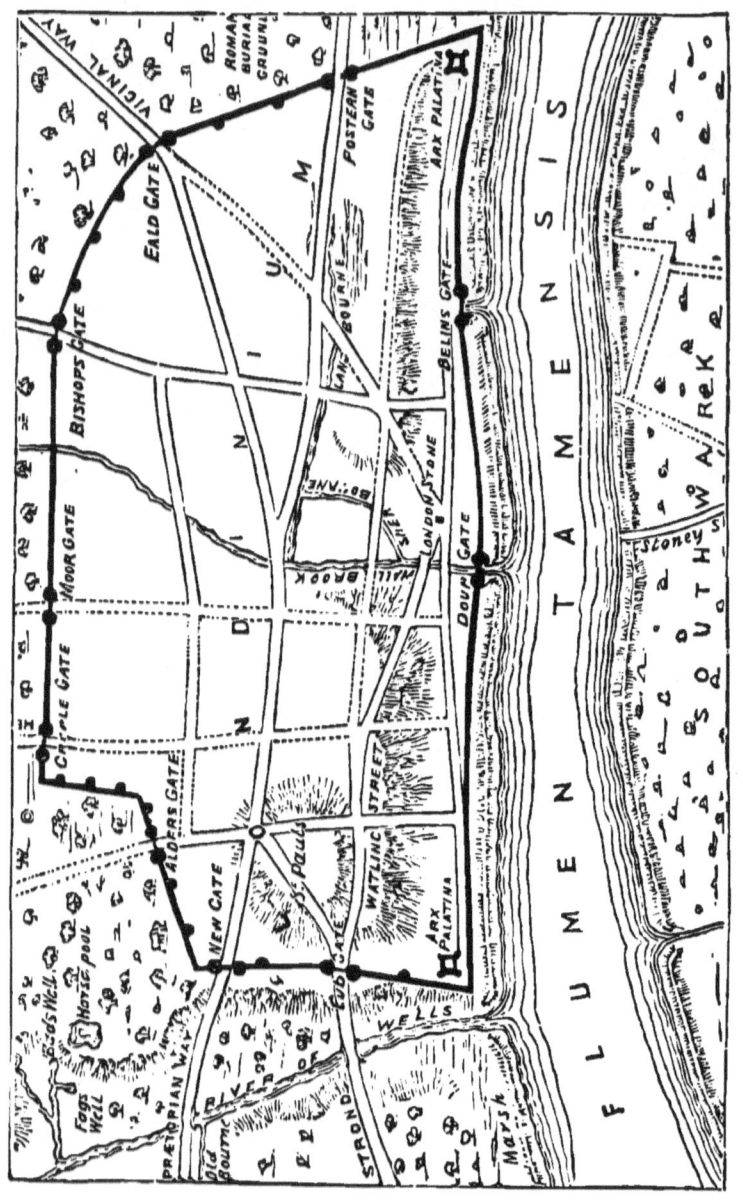

ROMAN LONDON.

became great traders, their proximity to the Continent contributing to the spread of their commerce. During the wars between Cæsar and the Gauls the latter were kept largely in supplies by the Britons, and it seemed to be this fact, together with the rumours of its general wealth, that urged Cæsar to attack the island. The principal exports hence in these days were cattle, hides, corn, and slaves; the imports being chiefly salt, earthenware, works in brass and glass goods. The conquest by Cæsar introduced Roman civilisation, and led to the construction of the Roman town, the main features of which, even to the names, remain to this day in the modern city. At this time, too, do we first find the town called by the name of London, which the best authorities consider to mean "the ship town," thus exhibiting its early importance as a mart of trade.

This importance it has maintained and increased, aided by its noble river. From Thames Head to the Nore it would be impossible to find a single manufacture of the slightest importance. London, it is true, contributes a little to all trades, but it is to the river, gathering to its bosom the mercantile navies of the world, that we must turn for the source of London's great commercial activity. None know this better than Londoners. "May it please your majesty," said a Lord Mayor, in response to the threats of James I., in want, as usual, of money, "you are at liberty to remove yourself and your courts wherever you please; but, Sire, there will always be one consolation to the merchants of London; your majesty cannot take the Thames along with you."

The industrial history of the Thames cannot thus be said to extend beyond a history of the trade and port of London, of the river below London Bridge. The first merchants of whom we have note after the Roman period were the "Easterlings," a band or guild of German traders whom we find at Billingsgate, the first legal dock, so early as 979. The Easterlings, whose quarters were at the Steelyard, in Thames-street, controlled if they did not monopolise the foreign trade of London for more than five centuries, even to the extent of fixing and stamping weights and measures. The Londoners became so jealous of these privileges that in 1493 they attacked the Steelyard, and the agitation was so successful that during the succeeding century the monopolies of the guild were all by degrees abolished. Meanwhile, not a few Venetians and Genoese had taken up their quarters among us, and in the time of Henry III. (1236) the practice was introduced of landing the goods on wharves, docks, or quays, instead of buying them and paying dues, &c., on board the import ship and thence transporting them direct to the premises of the merchant. Billingsgate, Queenhithe, and Dowgate were the chief of the early docks, and there is a record of the unloading at Dowgate, in 1345, of timber, firewood, coals, stone, chalk, and *avoir-du-pois* (fine wares). There are also sundry regulations for Dowgate Dock which shows that the sewage question was not unknown in those early days. The various wards were charged with the protection of the shipping in their districts, to protect them not alone from foreign foes, but from river thieves and the " pirates of Southwark," over against which vessels were on no consideration allowed to lie between sunset and sunrise. Indeed, the shipping was considered of such importance to the City that we have repeated mention of special steps taken for its protection. Thus, in 1397, on a rumour that enemies' ships were off the mouth of the river, it was ordained that four Aldermen, each with one hundred men-at-arms and archers from his ward, should keep watch over the shipping, each set of four taking a day and night in rotation.

In 1559 the Legal Quays were appointed. They were twenty two in number, extending from London Bridge seawards on the north side of the river, with a combined frontage of 1,464 feet. They were for long the only legal landing places for dutiable goods, and most of them remain with their original names and serving their original purpose to the present day. The trade now began to grow rapidly. In 1590 the whole of the Customs dues for England and Wales amounted to £50,000, in 1613 they had increased to £148,000, of which London contributed £109,572. The privileged guilds of foreigners were replaced by great chartered trading companies. Among these may be mentioned the Russia Company, chartered in 1555; the Eastland or North Sea Company, 1579; the Levant or Turkey Company, 1581; the East

India Company, whose charter bore date 1599, whose original capital was £369,891 5s., and whose first venture was with four ships in the year 1600; the African Company, 1663; and the Hudson's Bay Company, 1681. So successful were the efforts of these and private adventurers that by the year 1700 the value of goods entered inwards exceeded ten million sterling, and before 1800 was reached attained thirty millions sterling.

Meanwhile, accommodation for ships and goods had not increased in proportion. As a matter of fact, absolutely no step in advance had been made either by public or private bodies. So early as 1674 complaints culminated in a petition to Parliament, but nothing came of it, and things went from bad to worse. Indeed, until 1790 there was but one wet dock on the river. This, known in 1660 as Mrs. Howland's Great Wet Dock, and afterwards as the Greenland Dock, was situated on the south side of the river, on the site of the present entrance to the Grand Surrey Canal. It was 1,000 feet long, 500 feet broad, and 17 feet deep. It was fitted for the accommodation of the Greenland whalers, with conveniences for preparing the oil, but when that trade left the Thames it became a timber dock. But this was naturally useless for general trade. Such was all confined to the legal quays and to a few sufferance quays, where non-dutiable goods might be landed. The legal quay warehouses were quite unequal to the demands made on them; as an instance, they possessed storage room for 32,000 hogsheads of sugar, whereas the import about 1790 amounted to 140,000 hogsheads. Only a fraction of the ships could get alongside the quays, the majority had to lie about at mooring chains from London Bridge to below the Pool, and the crush was often such that one could cross the river by passing from deck to deck. The cargoes had to be unloaded into lighters and other small craft, and weeks were frequently wasted in the work. This state of things, coupled with the high customs duties, gave rise to a disgraceful state of plunder and rapine. The Thames pirates became proverbial, they worked in recognised gangs under such titles as "Night Plunderers," "Light Horsemen," "Heavy Horsemen," &c., and their depredations were calculated to amount to at least half a million sterling yearly. Of 37,000 persons employed on the river about 1790, 11,000 were known to be thieves and receivers. Vessels had to be regularly garrisoned; a 500-ton East Indiaman required a staff aboard of thirty customs' officers, themselves not unfrequently confederates of the various gangs. The old plan, too, of "kedging" made the voyage up the crowded river most tedious, four days being sometimes occupied in getting round from Blackwall point.

The honour of making the first dock is due to Mr. Perry, a shipbuilder, who in 1790 opened the Brunswick Dock for East Indiamen on the site of the present East India Export Dock. The immediate popularity of this dock, in spite of its—

in those days of no railways—immense distance from the business centre, showed how severe were the hardships to which the shipping community were subjected. Though it afforded such a very small relief, it gave practical enforcement to the public indignation now fairly aroused. In two days the West India merchants subscribed £800,000 for a dock in the Isle of Dogs, Parliament was petitioned, inquiries were held, and schemes innumerable were proposed by engineers and others. Many of the last are extremely interesting, and some show a grandeur of conception which causes many now-a-days to regret that some such comprehensive and uniform scheme was not carried out once for all by the Government or the Corporation of London. But prejudice, vested interests, and all the other forces that fight against progress, were too strong, and the docks of London had to grow up a system of patchwork, due solely to the enterprise of private individuals. It was not until July 12, 1799, that the Act authorising the construction of the West India Dock was passed, and then Parliament did all it has ever done for the port by paying out of the Consolidated Fund £1,600,000 as compensation to the owners of legal quays and sufferance wharves, lightermen, watermen, and all the host of hangers-on, who declared that they and London as well would be ruined by the new wet dock.

The West India merchants having succeeded in their endeavour, and having also obtained a monopoly for twenty-one years, the friends of the

Corporation and other interests who had opposed the Bill resorted to competition. In 1800 Parliament authorised the formation of the London Docks, with a concession for twenty years that all vessels laden with wine, brandy, tobacco, and rice, should unload therein; and, in 1803, the East India Dock Company was incorporated with a similar monopoly of the East India and China merchantmen. When the monopolies fell through, St. Katherine's Docks were started as free docks. The London and St. Katherine's subsequently coalesced, and now form an immense corporation, with a total capital of £9,370,981. The East and West India Dock Companies having united their forces in 1838, their joint capital now amounts to £3,351,651.

Space will not permit us to do more than give a very curt account of the admirable docks which these companies have from time to time given to the port of London. The export freight of the City is to a large extent miscellaneous, while that imported is mainly produce, including vast quantities of dutiable goods, which have to be landed and warehoused under the eyes of the Customs, and on which operations have often to be performed in bond. The business has therefore to be conducted under very different conditions from that at a coal or iron port, and by no means the least interesting features of the river are the marvellous arrangements for loading, unloading, storing, sampling, racking, despatching, and performing other multifarious operations.

Taking the docks on the north bank in order, as we leave London Bridge, we come first to St. Katherine's Docks, lying under the shelter of the Tower and close to the City. They were opened in October, 1828, and cost £195,640 per acre for eleven acres of water, the total area being twenty-three acres. They and their warehouses are specially adapted for housing, working, and showing wool, coffee, indigo, manufactured tobacco, sugar, and other valuable goods. The London Docks adjoin these, and still retain, to a great extent, the feature of their old monopoly, the Eastern trade. The Western Dock, opened in 1805, cost £140,654 per acre. The whole space covered is now about 100 acres, of which forty are water. There are three entrances from the river, the principal being the Shadwell new entrance, 350 ft. long and 60 ft. wide, with a depth of water over the sill of 28 ft. at high water. A favourite sight for strangers at these docks are the warehouses. These include the tobacco warehouse, covering 5 acres, and holding 24,000 hogsheads; the wool warehouses, with a capacity of 124,000 bales; and the $18\frac{1}{4}$ acres of vaults with storage room for 65,000 pipes of wine, 50,000 hogsheads of brandy, 18,000 puncheons of rum, and 6,500 tons of oil.

Proceeding down the river, we find the next great bight of land, the Isle of Dogs, bounded by Limehouse, Greenwich, and Blackwall reaches, occupied by the West India Docks. These comprise three parallel docks, with basins and entrances at each end, called the Export Dock, the Import

Dock, and the South Dock. The two former were opened by William Pitt in 1802; they have a water area of 55 acres, costing £17,000 per acre, and were the first docks where the important practice of separating the export and import ships was adopted. The guard-houses still remain, originally erected for the soldiers sent by Government to protect the dock from the attacks of the river pirates, exasperated at the loss of their occupation. The South Dock, opened so lately as 1870, and largely devoted to mahogany and other fine timber, was formed out of a canal, which, by the original Act, the Corporation of the City were permitted to construct and levy toll on all ships passing through to avoid Greenwich reach. But little used, it was eventually purchased by the Company. The whole land and water space covered by these docks is 295 acres. The southern extremity of the Isle of Dogs is occupied by the Millwall Dock, opened in 1864 at a cost of £7,000 per acre, which attracts a fair share of miscellaneous trade.

The East India Docks, opened in 1806, and incorporating Perry's original dock, are opposite Blackwall point, and have a water area of 30 acres. They are remarkable for a noble quay, 700 ft. long towards the river, and for the depth of water, which is 33 ft. in the dock, 31 ft. on the sill at spring tides, and never less than 23 ft. They were also the direct cause of the construction of two of the finest thoroughfares of Eastern London, the Commercial and East India Dock Roads.

The next great bend, bounded by Bugsby, Woolwich, and Galleons Reaches, is cut clean across by the Victoria and Albert Docks. The Victoria Dock Company, formed in 1850, leased the dock to Messrs. Peto, Betts & Brassey, but it was subsequently transferred to the London and St. Katherine's Dock Company. The Victoria Dock covers seventy-four acres of water, while it is approached on the Blackwall side through a semi-tidal basin of sixteen acres. It has six jetties, a four-acre tobacco warehouse, and storage room for 100,000 tons of guano; while the Thames Hydraulic Graving Dock Company's Docks open into it on the south side. At the eastern end, a passage eighty feet wide leads into the Albert Dock, opened on the 28th June, 1880, with an entrance into Galleons Reach. The combined length of these magnificent docks is $2\frac{3}{4}$ miles, with a water space of 175 acres, and a depth over the sill of the eastern dock of thirty feet at Trinity high water. The use of this entrance, which admits not only the largest merchantmen but any ironclad of the Navy, saves four miles of intricate river navigation. The whole of the apparatus connected with these docks and their warehouses is worked by hydraulic machinery, and the complete system of railways laid down connects the docks with all the main lines in the Kingdom, so that trains from the manufacturing districts run direct to the sheds and *vice versâ*.

On the south side of the river the great network of the Surrey Commercial Docks covers a water area of 370 acres. These were formed by a combination of the Commercial Docks—started in 1807, with a dock of forty-five acres, on the site of Messrs. Howland's Dock—and of the Grand Surrey Canal and Docks. These were not made legal quays until 1851, and are but rarely used as such. There is very little traffic from London southwards, and therefore the freight coming to these docks is mainly such as London itself consumes,—timber, gas and steam coals, bricks, stone, cement, grain, and so forth.

But all these docks left an inconvenience unremedied, an inconvenience which has grown as the progress of marine construction, and the introduction of compound engines, have increased the length, beam, and draught of vessels. Our new type of vessels can only, as a rule, enter the docks at or about high water, and if they arrive in the river have to wait at buoys at Gravesend until the tide serves. Indeed, if a ship just miss the morning tide she has to wait till the next morning, thus losing a day. For the same reason outward-bound steamers, such as the P. and O., cannot fix a definite time of departure, and are compelled to adopt a tidal time-table. Moreover, with long ships the sharp corners, and with deep ships the numerous shallows, render the navigation up the river difficult as well as tedious. To remedy this, the East and West India Dock Company conceived the project of forming docks which should admit, immediately on arrival, vessels of all sizes, at all states of the tide. This project they are now executing by the construction of docks at Tilbury, opposite Gravesend, twenty-four miles from London, and at the very entrance of the port. This bold enterprise will, it is expected, not only intercept a portion of the tonnage now proceeding up the river, but attract much which at present prefers other ports to the troublesome navigation of the River Thames.

Considerable activity is imparted to the southern banks of the river by the large Government establishments, which distribute annually little short of a million sterling in wages. They include the Victualling Yard at Deptford, Woolwich Dockyard and Arsenal, the Dockyard at Chatham, on the Medway, and that at Sheerness, on Sheppey Island, at the junction of the Medway and Thames. There is at present nearly 40,000 tons of naval shipping building or fitting at these two last-named places. Private shipbuilding on the river has, since the introduction of iron into the construction of vessels, been of the most limited dimensions. It is confined to two or three firms, and to vessels of war for our own and foreign Governments, to small passenger steamers, and of recent years to torpedo boats and launches. The marine engine works of the Thames are, however, famous, and the names of Maudslay, Humphreys, Penn, and Russell are known throughout the world.

The following Tables, which accompanied a petition presented to Parliament to sanction the new wet dock at Wapping, show as accurately as can be now ascertained the progress of the shipping trade of London during the 18th century :—

Outward from Great Britain.

Years.	Tons English.	Tons Foreign.	Total tons.	Value.
1688......	190,533	95,207	285,800	£4,086,087
1792......	1,396,003	101,152	1,565,154	24,905,200

British Trade of London.

Years.	Inward Ships.	Tons.	Outward Ships.	Tons.
1751......	1,408	198,023	1,139	140,792
1792......	2,409	451,188	1,708	310,724

Foreign Trade of London.

Years.	Inward Ships.	Tons.	Outward Ships.	Tons.
1751......	184	36,346	152	33,051
1792......	1,186	152,243	501	87,708

Shipping belonging to the Port of London.

Years.	Ships.	Tons.	Under 200 tons.	200 to 500 tons.	500 to 700 tons.	700 to 1,300 tons.
1732...	1,417	178,557	1,212	203	2	—
1792...	1,860	374,000	1,102	634	22	95

At this period, as may be imagined, from the inefficiency of land carriage, the coasting trade formed a very important item in the totals. In 1796, 625 coasters made 6,500 voyages between London and home ports, and it is curious to note that the traffic with Hull was more than double that of any other town in the Kingdom. In that year 100 vessels made 900 voyages to Hull, while, excluding ports in the estuary of the Thames itself, we find the next most important to be Ipswich, with 420 voyages; Newcastle and Stockton, with 108 apiece; and far-away Aberdeen with 120.

The enterprise of the petitioners has been amply rewarded by the extraordinary development of trade shown by the 19th century. If we take the proportion exhibited by the first Table as a fair criterion for London, which it includes, we shall see that between 1688 and 1792 the volume of oversea tonnage multiplied between six and seven-fold. In the somewhat similar period, 1792 and 1882, it has multiplied above forty-fold. For the third Table shows the total foreign, or over-sea trade, outwards and inwards, to have been 239,951 tons for the former year; for the year 1882, the outward clearances of ships with cargoes for foreign ports were 6,436 vessels, with a tonnage of 3,775,986, of which 4,408 vessels, of 2,795,545 tons, were steamers; the outward clearances for foreign ports, in ballast, 1,995 vessels, of tonnage, 942,753. The entrances inward from foreign ports were 11,094, with a tonnage of 6,119,523 tons, of which 6,557 were steamers, carrying 4,375,995 tons. The discrepancy between the entrances inwards and clearances outwards is accounted for by vessels proceeding in ballast coastwise to look for the freight they cannot find in London, a fact illustrating the peculiar nature of London trade.

> "Where has commerce such a mart,
> So rich, so thronged, so drained, and so supplied
> As London—opulent, enlarged, and still
> Increasing London? Babylon of old
> No more the glory of the world than she,
> A more accomplished world's chief glory now!"

No account of the Thames, however brief, would be complete without a reference to the great work which has within the last twenty years transformed the river aspect of London above Bridge. The great embankment, extending from

C

OLD TEMPLE STAIRS.

Blackfriars to Westminster, and again at Chelsea on the north bank, and from Westminster towards Battersea on the south side, may be justly termed one of the great engineering achievements of the century. The foreshore of the river, left bare by every receding tide, was generally a noxious stretch of mud, while the banks were lined with antique wharves and rotten buildings, always liable to sudden flooding, and the refuge often of trades ill-suited for the centre of a town. Our illustrations exhibit the contrast. On the one hand we have the old Temple stairs, whence the Templars could, as in the "Fortunes of Nigel," step into their wherries and proceed up or down stream to similar landing places. On the other hand we have a view, partly in section, of the embankment at Charing-cross, showing its main front, its steamboat pier, and its internal construction, with its galleries for sewers, water and gas pipes, and the underground railway. The total area of land reclaimed from the river by the Victoria Embankment alone amounts to $37\frac{1}{4}$ acres, of which 19 are devoted to the carriage and footways, 8 to public gardens, and the remainder to the Temple, the Crown, and other riparian proprietors.

The subway for gas and water pipes is 7 ft. 6 in. in height, and 9 ft. in width, and the diameter of the sewer averages 8 ft. The level of the rails of the railway is $17\frac{1}{2}$ ft. below the surface of the road, the upper face of the arches being 18 inches below. The embankment contains, among other material,

650,000 cubic feet of granite and 1,000,000 cubic yards of earth filling. It cost nearly two millions sterling, and not only forms a worthy memorial to the enterprise of the public bodies of the Metropolis, but imparts to the city more than all the artistic beauty predicted for it by its first projector, John Martin, the painter.

THE MERSEY.

In a former number we gave a description of the Thames as our first "Industrial River." In portraying her rival sister, the Mersey, the writer who aimed at the picturesque would find himself at a considerable disadvantage. On the Thames, we come upon green "aits," sloping lawns, pleasant villas, and all the life and colour which a crowd of pleasure-yachts and their gay crews can so readily lend to the most sluggish of streams. But following the Mersey from her source in the Switzerland of Derbyshire for a similar distance, what do we find?

It is permissible to imagine that the ashes of Sodom and Gomorrah immediately after the destruction of those wicked cities emitted no more pestiferous vapours, or were more devoid over all their wide area of one single green leaf or sign of vegetation, than those twin-sister towns of the Mersey—Widnes and Runcorn. The latter have, however, this advantage: they are by no means *dead* cities of the plain. Great and busy industries are carried on day and night in both, and in each large fortunes have been, and are still being made; it must be admitted, however, that the process is, in their case, neither picturesque nor odoriferous. Indeed, some miles before the railway passenger arrives at that graceful and wonderful structure "Runcorn Bridge," he is made aware of the vicinity of Widnes by experiences beside which the "twenty-nine separate stenches" of Cologne appear as so many odours of Araby. The Mersey may claim, however, even in this respect, one advantage over her southern sister. When the latter approaches the more industrial portion of her course, she loses, to most eyes, the greater part of her beauty; with the former it is when her broad stream is fulfilling to its utmost its beneficent duties, as she passes onward to the sea, that she presents herself in the most charming aspect. The oarsman who nears London on the Thames from Richmond, sees the river at her most beautiful points. Probably the finest view of the Mersey is obtained from the hurricane-deck of some homeward-bound ocean "liner," passing between the North and Rock lights. The passenger then sees on the one hand the bristling fort and long sweep of sea-wall, and on the other the Rock Battery backed by the green Cheshire hills. But we are treating of both noble streams as *industrial* rivers, and the presence or absence of pretty scenery on their course is—from that view-point—of little consequence. It will, however, be well before attempting to describe the Mersey at the proud consummation of its career, when the wealth of nations is entrusted to its keeping, and the mercantile navies of half the world float upon its broad bosom, to follow it in a panoramic manner from its humble source to its responsible maturity.

The Mersey, in its Derbyshire home, is born of the union of the Goy and the Thame—both insignificant streams—and pursues its very unimportant way until it arrives at Stockport, and it remains unimportant until past Flixton, where, being joined by the Irwell, the augmented stream flows on to Warrington, passing between Widnes on the Lancashire side and Runcorn on the Cheshire bank. After this, being joined by the waters of the Weaver and the Bollin, it widens out between Hale Head and Weston Point to become that important estuary of the sea which is known all the world over for its great "Port of Liverpool." Although Warrington is twenty-one miles east of Liverpool it is on the Mersey, and being an undoubted factor in the industrial history of the river, must have a word or two of description. It has a population of some 50,000, and is the centre of the tanning trade of the North for heavy sole leather, there being some thirty, or more, tanneries for that description of leather, using from 8,000 to 10,000 hides per week. Almost all the soles supplied in Army and Police contracts are tanned there. Widnes and Runcorn—which we have passed on the way—may be dismissed with the remark that they produce alkali, good soap, and bad smells. Sailing onwards in the wider portion of the river, the Weaver having now joined its waters to those of the Mersey, we come, on the Lancashire side, to Garston, where there are extensive docks and excellent railway communication, and where the vessels connected with the Rouen trade are generally berthed. From this point the grand series of docks of the Mersey Dock and Harbour Board commence on the Lancashire side, and which are to be described in detail later on.

We will now pass over to the Cheshire side, where we pass Eastham—with its picturesque woods and Zoological Gardens—Rock Ferry, Birkenhead, Seacombe, Egremont, and New Brighton, and are then on our way to the Irish Sea, and the Black Rock Light, which marks the opening to the Victoria Channel, as the entrance to the Mersey is called. Birkenhead, the principal place of interest on the Cheshire side, will have to be spoken of further on, but it will be in order here to record the importance of one great industry connected especially with Cheshire.

As the names, Nantwich, Saltwich, Northwich, &c., indicate, Cheshire is a very saline country; indeed, in many parts the villages have "caved in" in consequence of the salt-making operations. During the month of June last 121,726 tons of salt were exported from the Mersey, probably all, or nearly all, the production of Cheshire salt works, and it is interesting to note the proportion imported by our various customers: the United States took 13,095 tons; British North America, 13,350 tons; and the East Indies, 23,314 tons.

Having followed the Mersey from its mountain

home to that "wide sandy estuary on which are built the magnificent docks of Liverpool," it will be well to give a few lines to that "good old town" and quite modern city. In the "metropolis of Wales," as it is often called by the members of its Welsh colony, it would wound susceptibilities to inquire whether the word "Liverpool" was derived from the words Lle'r-pwl, *i.e.*, place of the pool, or refers to the pool which was the favourite haunt of that legendary bird, the "Liver," or "Lever," with the supposititious representation of which aquatic fowl the civic "Liverpudlian" of to-day delights to ornament his corporate property. Whether christened by Taffy, or dedicated to an extinct species of heron, the present city of Liverpool owes its origin principally to stout old Roger of Poictiers, who chose it as a site for his castle, though the place is mentioned in deeds of much earlier date. In 1173 Henry II. granted its first charter, in consequence of its importance as a port of communication with Ireland. King John gave it a second charter in 1207, and twenty years later Henry III. constituted it a "free borough for ever." In 1272 Liverpool consisted of only 168 houses, and was then in so much the opposite of a flourishing condition that in 1561 the number was but 138, and the merchants of the town only owned twelve ships. During the French war, under Edward III., the town could only contribute one ship to the carrying on of the same, but during that reign "the Stanleys, who owned land in the neighbourhood," built a tower, where Water-street now ends, for the defence of the town. What may be considered the commencement of the present splendid dock system took place in the reign of " good Queen Bess," when a mole was formed to protect shipping in winter, and a quay for loading and unloading the ship's cargoes. The port, however, still remained a very insignificant one, as shown by the amount of "ship money" levied by Charles I., namely £25, while, at the same time, Bristol was rated £1,000.

During the Civil Wars Liverpool had quite her share of vicissitudes, being at one time in the hands of the Parliamentary party, and at another period occupied by Royalists under Prince Rupert. In fact, about 1644-5 it had quite a changeful history of fire, siege, and *compensation*. Liverpool's exceptional success in securing the latter item may have been a foreshadowing of that peculiarly keen eye to the main chance which has honourably distinguished her sons in later years. In the early part of the preceding century Liverpool was constituted a separate parish, having previously been a chapelry of Walton—a position about as anomalous as if Saint Paul's Cathedral were a Chapel of Ease to some church at Greenwich. We give an illustration of Liverpool in 1520, which will speak for itself. Even towards the end of the seventeenth century the town consisted merely of Castle-street and a few narrow streets adjoining on the north and north-east of that thoroughfare. During the reign of William III.,

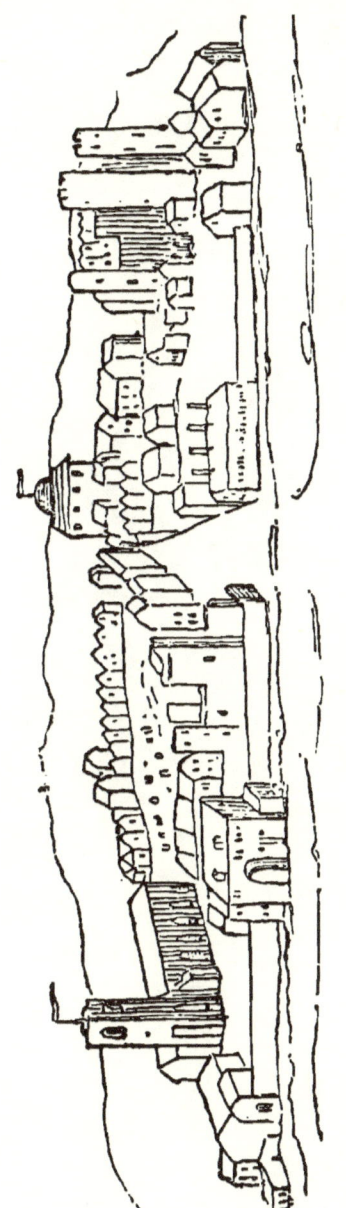

LIVERPOOL IN 1520.

however, the town and its importance increased so rapidly that it obtained the distinction before mentioned, and became a distinct and separate parish.

If one chose a date to be for ever held as a red-letter day in the calendar of Liverpool, it should be that in 1708, when it is recorded that her first "wet dock for commercial purposes" was established. Although that dock has long since been filled up, and its site occupied by the buildings of the Customs House and Inland Revenue Offices, its formation was, no doubt, only the first step in that career of shipping prosperity, which has rendered necessary the miles of magnificent docks which line the Mersey of to-day. Two points noted by the same chronicler may here find a place. The Customs House is described as a handsome building, "with an octostyle" of an Ionic character in the centre of its north front. Our space does not permit a representation of the building, but very few ancient mariners using the port of Liverpool would, we venture to say, recall the *beauty* of so dismal an edifice. The second point is more satisfactory, viz., that the rapidly-increasing prosperity of the port was due to the substitution of the trade in cotton and other raw material for the Slave Trade, by which in past years Liverpool had profited so much. It is not necessary or kindly to repeat here the well-known taunt hurled by a tipsy actor at a displeased audience, many years ago, in the great seaport. But that many fortunes were made in this odious traffic remains, unhappily, an undoubted truth.

Some figures connected with the influence of the cotton trade upon the prosperity of the port, will not be out of place here before we enter on a description of the modern city and docks which that prosperity has produced. In 1831 the tonnage of vessels frequenting the port of Liverpool was 1,592,436 tons. In 1861 it had increased to 4,977,272 tons, while in 1881 it was 7,893,948 tons. To show the rapidity of the growth at certain times, we take the following figures from the "Liverpool Year Book" for 1856:

Vessels belonging to Liverpool.

Dec. 31, 1850............	1,808 vessels	514,635 tons.
,, 1853............	2,144 ,,	737,559 ,,
,, 1856............	2,235 ,,	890,288 ,,
Increase in six years...	427 vessels...	375,653 tons.

The subjoined statement of Liverpool transactions in cotton for the last five years will give, better than any descriptive words, an idea of the magnitude which the dealings in that material have assumed. We are indebted for this interesting table of quantities to Mr. John Jones, of Brown's-buildings, Liverpool Exchange, who publishes the "Weekly List of Cotton Ships at Sea," annual handbook of "Daily Cable Records," &c.

THE BROWN FREE LIBRARY.

	Total transactions which include sales, and forwarded direct from the ship's side.	Average weekly.	Total actual export during year.	Average weekly.	Total import during year.	Average weekly	Largest weekly transactions during week ending.
	Bales.	Bales.	Bales.	Bales.	Bales.	Bales.	Bales.
1878	3,083,370	59,295	294,455	5,662	2,885,579	55,492	Aug. 1 107,360
1879	3,074,340	59,122	276,398	5,315	3,081,420	59,258	March 20. 97,480
1880	3,385,160	65,099	340,423	6,546	3,390,683	65,205	Jan. 8. 104,770 Dec. 16. 104,670
1881	3,580,780	68,861	324,609	6,242	3,536,573	68,011	Nov. 10. 107,800
1882	3,765,250	72,409	422,710	8,129	3,857,659	74,186	June 22. 123,100
1883 Jan., June 30	2,000,680	76,949	160,284	6,165	2,280,633	87,717	Jan. 25. 127,970
1882 Jan., June 30	2,030,100	78,081	166,299	6,395	2,330,513	89,627	—

It is unnecessary, in the case of the commercial reader, to say that so rich a "coign of vantage" as Liverpool had been made the most of by the directing powers of railway and canal companies. The London and North Western Railway Company have their terminus at Edgehill, whence by three branches their lines reach the heart of the City (at Lime-street Station, fronted by one of the finest hotels in the world) and the northern and southern extremities of the dock system. The railway companies which form the Cheshire Lines Committee have their terminus in Ranelagh-street (Central Station), and the Lancashire and Yorkshire Railway, by which are reached many of the most popular residential spots between Liverpool and Southport, runs into Exchange Station, closely adjacent to the " Flags " of that commercial hunting ground, the stones of which so frequently form the stepping-stones to the comfortable mansion " down the line."

The Canal Companies, too, are in strong force, the Leeds and Liverpool, Bridgewater, and Shropshire Union Canals having most complete and convenient connection with the port, and thence by their several systems providing water communication with all the leading industrial centres of the Kingdom. Our illustration of the Shropshire Canal Basin gives also a glimpse of the tower of St. Nicholas' Church, and the tower on which are hoisted the cone and drum betokening the weather to be expected.

The most imposing building in Liverpool—indeed it would be difficult to name so fine a structure of its kind in the three kingdoms—is St. George's Hall, an edifice which covers three and a half acres of land, and displays its classic outlines upon one of the finest sites in Europe. Erected from the designs of the late Harvey Lonsdale Elmes, it was not completed until after the premature and lamented death of that gifted young architect, while abroad, whither he had been sent at the Corporate expense, with a desire to prolong a life which promised so much. The Hall contains the Courts in which are held the Sessions and Assizes, the Court of Passage, and Courts in which the inquiries instituted by the Board of Trade are carried on, beside a large and small concert room, and a bewildering labyrinth of passages in which are a great number of rooms utilised in different ways in the conduct of the business of the building.

Probably no city in the world can boast so unique a block of buildings, or one of which her citizens have more just right to be proud, than that which we give in our illustration of the "Brown Library" and "Picton Reading Room," our artist having unfortunately been unable to include in his view the concluding edifice of the series, the "Walker Art Gallery." The first of the three is due to the munificence of the late Sir William Brown, Bart., who erected it at a cost of over £40,000. In 1851 its contents were enriched by the late Earl of Derby's bequest of his wonderful collection of specimens of natural history, and still further in 1867, when Mr. Joseph Mayer, F.S.A., presented to the citizens his unique antiquarian collection. The circular building which forms the centre of these civic "three graces" is the "Picton Reading Room," and was erected in 1880 by the City Council at a cost of £23,000, and is so named in compliment to Sir J. A. Picton, a local architect, and leading spirit in all art matters. The "Walker Art Gallery" is entirely the gift of Sir A. B. Walker, and cost over £60,000. The exterior of the building is elaborated if not beautified by some bas-reliefs of a distressingly modern and realistic character, in which "plug" hats and coach wheels preponderate, and three white marble statues, which, however praiseworthy in themselves, effectually destroy the architectural symmetry of the structure. In this building the Corporation Art Gallery is located, and the annual exhibitions of pictures are held.

The "Sailors' Home," of which we give a picture, is one of those necessary centres of accommodation required in a great seaport where so many sailors are so far from *home*. Although in itself a handsome and commodious structure, it is not what can be described as externally attractive; its value and uses are, however, known to and appreciated by numbers of seamen of every nationality under the sun, and although the fact of their presence has attracted to its neighbourhood an undesirable colony, and its existence and mode of management have provoked some little jealousies among neighbouring tradesmen, there can be no doubt of its achieving a great amount of useful work.

The one feature, however, of attraction and interest in Liverpool is undoubtedly that wondrous line of docks, presenting a quayage, to wet docks and tidal basins alone of $22\frac{1}{2}$ miles, and a water space of $333\frac{1}{2}$ acres, and which with land, sheds, yards, quays, and warehouses, cover an area of $1,039\frac{1}{4}$ acres.

These wonderful figures, however, only apply to the Lancashire side of the Mersey Dock and Harbour Board's Estate. On the Cheshire shore at Birkenhead, there are docks with a water area of $164\frac{1}{2}$ acres, with $9\frac{1}{2}$ miles of quayage, thus making in all a water area of 498 acres, and a total

THE SAILORS' HOME.

quayage of 32 miles, in addition to 22 graving docks for repairing vessels, with an aggregate length of floor of over 14,000 ft., the whole estate being studded with more or less imposing buildings, such as dock-masters' residences, customs and police depôts, clock-towers, dockyard offices, and so on, and on the Lancashire side traversed by a double line of railway five miles in length.

As a matter of seniority and central position we should no doubt commence our brief details of the various docks with those of the George's Dock, but it will, on the whole, be preferable to take the docks as they appear on the river's banks. The first dock of the estate reached as we approach Liverpool on our way to the mouth of the Mersey is the Herculaneum Dock, which, with its branch dock, has a water area of 10 acres, and quayage of 1,309 yds. New docks are fast approaching completion between the Herculaneum and Brunswick Docks. The particulars of the rest of the docks will be best given in a tabular form. We may, however, note here that at this point the river has widened out into a broad expanse known as the "Sloyne," where lie the man-of-war acting as guardship to the port, the training ships *Indefatigable*, *Clarence*, and *Akbar*, and, nearer to Eastham, those perpetual sources of anxiety and alarm to the good people who reside in Southern Liverpool—the floating powder magazines.

Water Area and Quayage of Principal Docks on Liverpool shore north of Toxteth Dock.

Dock	Acres	Yds.	Yds.
Brunswick Half Tide	1 acre	3,388 yds.	491 yds.
Brunswick	12 „	3,010 „	1,086 „
Coburg	8 „	26 „	1,053 „
Queen's	10 „	1,564 „	1,214 „
Queen's Half Tide	3 „	3,542 „	445 „
King's	7 „	3,896 „	875 „
Wapping Basin	1 „	3,151 „	454 „
Wapping	5 „	499 „	815 „
Salthouse	6 „	2,019 „	784 „
Albert	7 „	3,542 „	885 „
Canning Half Tide	2 „	2,688 „	429 „
Canning ("old dry dock")	4 „	376 „	585 „
Manchester Dock and Chester Tidal Basin	1 „	3,478 „	684 „
George's (begun 1767)	5 „	164 „	645 „
Prince's	11 „	1,490 „	1,178 „
Prince's Half Tide	4 „	3,250 „	429 „
Waterloo Corn Dock	2 „	3,375 „	506 „
Waterloo Dock West	3 „	2,146 „	533 „
Victoria	5 „	3,559 „	755 „
Trafalgar	6 „	2,643 „	1,020 „
Clarence	6 „	273 „	914 „
Clarence Graving Dock Basin	1 „	1,056 „	291 „
Stanley	7 „	120 „	753 „
Collingwood	5 „	244 „	553 „
Salisbury	3 „	2,146 „	406 „
Nelson	7 „	4,786 „	803 „
Bramley Moore	9 „	3,106 „	935 „
Wellington Half Tide	3 „	813 „	400 „
Wellington	7 „	4,120 „	820 „
Sandon	10 „	100 „	867 „
Huskisson Branch, No. 2	8 „	780 „	890 „
„ „ „ 1	7 „	592 „	910 „
„	14 „	3,451 „	939 „
Canada	17 „	4,043 „	1,272 „
Canada Tidal Basin	9½ „	„	846 „
South Carrier's	1 „	4,515 „	615 „
North Carrier's	2 „	3,423 „	641 „
Brocklebank	11 „	„	1,000 „
Langton	18 „	„	1,322 „
Langton Branch	2 „	4,549 „	671 „
Alexandra (with its three branches)	44½ „	„	1¼ mile.

BIRKENHEAD—
West Float	2 miles	210 yds.
East Float	1 mile	1,506 ,,
Alfred Dock		482 ,,
Egerton Dock		754 ,,
Morpeth ,,		1,299 ,,
,, Branch		637 ,,

By the foregoing table it will be seen that the course of dock construction in Liverpool tends northwards: in other words, the docks of the Mersey, like those of the Thames, are tending towards the sea.

The Alexandra, opened and christened by the Princess whose name it bears, in September, 1881, is certainly a splendid dock. It is frequented by the great Atlantic liners, and surrounded by its capacious sheds, 80 ft. or 90 ft. in width, with all the attendant noise, bustle, and industry of loading and unloading ships of from 5,000 to 7,000 tons burden, and the arrival and departure of the engines connected with the Dock railway, which places it in direct communication with all the railway lines having depôts in Liverpool: the scene it presents is one long to be remembered as an exhibition of commercial life and activity.

A series of mineral docks to the north of the Alexandra, for which excavations are in progress, will conclude the dock system to the northward; the sea, and not a lack of enterprise, arresting further progress. At the Langton Dock, a new hydraulic crane capable of lifting 100 tons is erected, and relieves that old servant of the Dock Board the 50-ton crane at Sandon Dock, which so successfully manipulated the "Infant" guns for the new "Seaforth Battery," which guards, with its sister fort on the Cheshire shore, the entrance to the Mersey.

The Carriers' Docks, are, as their names imply, principally used for the distribution inland of goods arriving at the port.

The Canada Docks, and their immediate neighbourhood, may well be termed "Lumberland," so redolent of the backwoods are their spacious quays, and so suggestive of backwoodsmen are the muscular men who there ply their calling. Figures will, however, again serve better than words to show the extent of the lumber-trade of Liverpool. We take the same from Messrs. Duncan, Ewing & Company's annual circular:

Arrivals of Timber in Liverpool from the 1st February to 30th June in the last two years—

From	1883		1882	
Quebec	12 Vessels	4,750 tons	13 Vessels	5,800 tons
St. John, N.B.	19 „	22,661 „	25 „	26,917 „
Other North American Ports	16 „	8,888 „	25 „	6,169 „
North of Europe	102 „	40,203 „	81 „	32,950 „
Pitch Pine Ports	34 „	26,320 „	68 „	53,953 „

Connected with the Canada Tidal Basin, which forms the river entrance to the Canada and Brocklebank Docks, there is an elaborate system of sluices for maintaining a sufficient depth of water to enable vessels of the largest class and draught to enter the adjacent docks at any state of the tide. Did our space permit we do not doubt that a description of this intricate yet simple triumph of engineering skill would afford our readers as much pleasure as the examination of

CORN WAREHOUSE.

it has afforded the distinguished visitors who have witnessed its workings. The entire network of sluices and the unique application of engineering knowledge which their creation has necessitated are due to Mr. G. F. Lyster, C.E., who for the last twenty years has been Engineer-in-chief to the Mersey Dock and Harbour Board.

The Huskisson Dock is given up principally to the American and Mediterranean trades; the Bramley-Moore Dock to ships trading with the United States of America; and the Nelson Dock to those trading with the West Indies, Holland, and Ireland. Each dock has its speciality in the matter of the ships which frequent it and the special merchandise they carry.

The Waterloo Corn Dock and its warehouses are especially fitted for the reception of grain ships and grain; and a visit to the corn warehouses and their elevators is made a point of duty with distinguished foreigners who come to Liverpool. The corn warehouses are capable of storing 165,000 quarters of corn, and the elevators will lift from the ships and put into their respective places, 250 tons of corn per hour, which is distributed over the entire block, to any floor, by a system of endless bands worked by hydraulic machinery: the visitor seeing literally a stream of grain flowing from the hopper at the top of the building.

On the Cheshire side the principal dock is the Floating-Dock, or "Great Float," as it is called, which has an area of 150 acres, and was formed by closing the entrance to a natural pool called Wallasey Pool. There are also tidal and graving docks and extensive and convenient wharves. Birkenhead, in which "city of the future," as it is jocularly termed by the inhabitants of its big sister across the ferry, these docks are situated, may be described as residential and industrial, the industrial part being principally connected either with the engineering trade, as at the Britannia works, or the shipbuilding trade, as at Messrs. Laird's great yards,* or beef slaughtering, as at the extensive "abattoirs" connected with the "lairages" established for the reception and *despatch* of our bovine American cousins. Both centres of industry present at busy times and in their different ways striking, though in the one case not very pleasant pictures, and when the Mersey Tunnel is completed it may be that the "future" of the Cheshire borough is not so remote as scoffing "Liverpudlians" would suggest.

The "landing-stage" on the Liverpool side is, without doubt, the largest floating structure of the kind in the world, being 2,063 ft. in length by 80 ft. in width, and, supported by pontoons, has upon its broad promenade, besides customs offices, stage-master's offices, police depôt, and so forth,

---

* From the yard of Messrs. Laird Brothers the longest vessel ever built on the Mersey was launched on the 4th of August last. She is constructed entirely of steel, is 450 ft. long, 47 ft. beam, and 5,500 gross tonnage, with 4,000 indicated horse power. Christened the *Western Land*, she is intended to carry the mails between Antwerp and New York for a Belgian company.

capacious refreshment rooms, until lately managed by the late Mr. Wm. Simpson. The name and figure of Mr. Simpson are so inseparably connected with any mention of the Prince's landing-stage, that a line placing on record a kindly inspiration upon which he acted will not be without interest.

In various seasons of distress, it occurred to Mr. Simpson that an appeal to the hundreds of wealthy merchants and others who daily cross the ferry and took or left the boats almost immediately opposite his chief restaurant, could not fail to enlist their aid on behalf of the sufferers, and there are very few frequenters of the "stage," either English or foreign, who have not heard of "Simpson's bowl," which was placed outside his restaurant, in aid of the distressed whenever occasion required, by which means several thousand pounds were collected in the cause of charity. The sum of £203 1s. 3d. was collected for the Indian Famine Fund in this way; £1,079 19s. 11d. for the distress in South Wales; for the Haydock Colliery explosion, £574 8s. 11d.; the Abercarne Colliery explosion, £526 0s. 6½d.; and for distress in Birkenhead and Seacombe, £815 7s. 11½d. The bowl was out sixty days for the distress in the West of Ireland early in 1880, and Mr. Simpson himself went across to Connemara to distribute the amount received—namely, £521 13s. 8d.—amongst the poverty-stricken peasantry. The bowl was displayed, and its contents, various and valuable, left quite unguarded, yet such was Mr. Simpson's faith in the respect that would be paid to any undertaking of his by the lower classes, for whom he had laboured on several occasions so successfully, that not a single instance of theft occurred.

Any attempt to describe the Mersey which omitted a notice of the wonderful "floating palaces" which undertake and carry out with such admirable safety and facility her great passenger traffic, would indeed be inadequate. The most marvellous part of any preface to a description of almost the smallest passenger-carrying vessel that now leaves the Mersey would be the necessity of recording and rendering credible the short space of time which has sufficed for the transformation effected between 1840 and to-day. A perusal of the "Liverpool Steam Packet Circular," published in the former year by one Robert Cantrell, Redcross-street, Liverpool, and purporting to set forth all the dates and hours of sailing of all the steam packets leaving the port of Liverpool, and a glance at the "library of useful information," which is now handed to you, should you venture the mildest inquiry as to dates of sailing at a Liverpool shipping office of to-day, will of themselves suggest a history so startling as to come almost within the range of stories told by the mendacious Baron himself. It was, too, in 1840 that that revolutionary craft, propelled by a screw, and named the *Archimedes*, made its appearance on the Mersey, and called forth the pious forebodings of the onlookers. Only so few years ago, and yet we have already become quite accustomed to such graceful and wonderful forms as those of the *Servia*, *Britannic*, and *Alaska*, entering port after their rapid trips across the Atlantic, with everyone on board enjoying the comforts and benefited by the discipline which rules a first-class hotel, or leaving, luxuriously equipped, for their distant destination.

The Cunard line, for several reasons, claims priority of notice. The reasons are its seniority, the absence of fatalities which has characterised its career, and the large number of passengers that have been conveyed by the vessels forming its fleet. Last year between 60,000 and 70,000 passengers were carried by Cunard vessels; and about 17,000 were cabin passengers.

As examples of the changes in passenger vessels since that eventful year 1840, we may take the *Britannia*, the first Cunard mail (paddle) steamer and the latest addition to the Cunard fleet. The *Britannia* measured: Length, 207 ft.; breadth, 34 ft. 2 in.; depth, 22 ft. 4 in.; tonnage, 1,139 tons. The *Aurania*, the last steamer put upon the Line, measures: Length, 470 ft.; breadth, 57 ft.; depth, 39 ft.; tonnage, 7,500 tons.

On the boats of all the many lines now leaving Liverpool for the various American ports, and carrying saloon and steerage passengers, the wants of all are studied so closely as to leave little or nothing to be desired. It would be invidious to particularise, where all aim so generously to attain excellence. In each and all we find the saloons, smoking saloons, ladies' saloon, bath-rooms, barber shops, culinary arrangements, and daily "bills of fare," equal, if not superior, to those items as found in the leading hotels of *terra firma*. It is, however, in the arrangements of the steerage and intermediate portions of the different vessels carrying emigrants that we find most ground of congratulation. Not as a matter of comparison with the boats of other lines at all, but because we have before us a picture, recalling to us many personal experiences of such a scene, we would, were it possible, describe the steerage of those splendid vessels, the *Britannic,* or *Germanic,* of the White Star Line. Ample room, free ventilation, and every requisite arrangement to ensure health and cleanliness, as compared with the steerage of the past, where dirt, squalor, overcrowding, and intermixing of grades and sexes combined to produce a scene and an experience scarcely to be exaggerated by the florid pen of a Dickens.

To continue our brief notes of the leading steamship companies, we must mention the National Steamship Company, which, started 20 years ago, at a time which would scarcely have been pronounced a favourable one, has so far prospered that its fleet at the present day consists of 12 splendid ships, with a combined tonnage of 50,384 tons, to which is shortly to be added the steel vessel, being constructed by Messrs. Thomson, of Glasgow, to be called the *America,* of 6,500 tons burden. The White Star Line possesses a fleet of vessels of such exceptional beauty, not only in their external outlines, but in their luxurious internal embellishments, that they must, on the principle of avoiding temptation, be passed over with a hurried but hearty line of admiration. Perhaps no greater proof of the popularity of the Inman Line of steamers can be afforded than by the following figures. Between 1851 and 1882 the steamers of the Inman Line have carried no fewer than 1,161,272 souls. The vessels of this line are named after the leading cities of the world, and when we see such figures as the foregoing they are presented to us as floating cities indeed. The latest addition to their fleet is the *City of Chicago*, which, like the porcine emporium from which it takes its name, is the "biggest thing" of its kind belonging to the Company.

The Allan Line owes its inception to the requirements of our cousins in the Dominion of Canada, who, animated by that spirit of enterprise for which they are celebrated, as early as 1852 entered into a contract with the Messrs. Allan, which has led to the formation of the present splendid fleet. As representative boats of the Company, the *Sardinian* and *Sarmatian* may be named. The latter was frequently patronised by our Princess Louise and her noble husband during their official life in the Dominion.

To the Guion Line, one of the most rapidly prosperous of all the Atlantic Companies, we owe "the Greyhound of the Atlantic," the *Alaska*, that wonderful vessel of 7,500 tons. To her the honour belongs of accomplishing the voyage from Queenstown to New York considerably under seven days, thus earning the blue ribband of the "Herring Pond." Not satisfied, however, with either the speed or dimensions of this splendid ship, Mr. Guion has just eclipsed both in his *Oregon*, which was launched on June 23, 1883, and which on its trial trip recently made twenty knots per hour. The *Oregon* is 12,382 horse power, being thus 3,000 horse power greater than the *Alaska*.

To the "Mississippi and Dominion" Line, we owe, besides its safe carriage of thousands of passengers during last year, the safe conveyance of 10,261 head of cattle, and 26,967 sheep, which numbers should have produced an appreciable effect upon that important item, the price of steaks and chops. A Company which deserves, not only by courtesy, but as a matter of considerable interest, a friendly notice, is the American Line of steamers. It was not to be expected that Brother Jonathan would leave to the enterprise of the Britisher whatever benefits might be reaped by steaming the ocean blue, without a decided and energetic attempt to prove his own capacity to compete. Accordingly, on the 18th of April, 1871, under a charter of the Legislature of Pennsylvania, the Company was started. The success which has attended it may be best shown by the following figures. The fleet now consists of nine splendid steamers (the first four exclusively of American material and construction, and supplied with engines of

American manufacture) having an aggregate measurement of 30,910 tons, and being impelled by machinery of 5,200 horse power nominal. To this list is to be added the new arrival, *British Princess,* a steel steamer, 420 ft. long.

The Pacific Steam Navigation Company is probably one of the most flourishing commercial undertakings of later years; the wide ramifications of its extensive system prevents us, however, describing a most interesting and admirably managed fleet. The River Plate Line to the Brazils and South American ports; the West India and Pacific, as well as the " Harrison " and various Spanish Lines to the West Indian and Gulf ports; the Booth and Singlehurst Lines to the River Amazon; the " Harrison," " Star," " Hall," " City," and " Anchor " Lines to India; the " Leyland " and " Moss " Lines to Egypt; Mr. Alfred Holt's China steamers, and the many and various private Lines trading with every known portion of the Globe, render themselves by their number and diversity beyond our scope.

The Mersey has not sustained its early pre-eminence in shipbuilding. It is, however, the greatest shipping river in the world. Twenty-three ships, measuring something over 25,000 tons, were constructed on the river in 1881, and twenty-two ships, representing 33,597 tons, in 1882. These are modest figures when compared with the Clyde, Tyne, and Wear. But in shipping Liverpool takes the premier position, as follows:—

Number and tonnage of sailing and steam vessels entered and cleared with cargo and in ballast foreign and coastwise, 1882.

	No.	Tonnage net.
Liverpool	16.625	7,550,948
Tyne	17,038	6,360,243
London	19,891	6,120,970
Cardiff	12,955	4,641,940
Dublin	7,742	2,125,803
Hull	4,638	1,915,436
Belfast	9,310	1,803,262

The Mersey takes the first position in the American trade. The declared exports are greater for the Thames, because large quantities of goods declared to in London and therefore credited to the southern river, are shipped from the Mersey. The following interesting particulars are taken from the report of the much-esteemed American Consul at Liverpool, Governor Packard: "The total amount of declared exports for the United States for the year ending September 30, 1882, amounted to £6,956,304, of which tin plates furnished £1,801,453; chemicals, £1,011,939; pig iron, £466,686; wool, £434,356, and indiarubber, £402,811."

The advantages of the Mersey for traffic with the West are a guarantee that Liverpool shall long continue to enjoy the trade and title as the "great emporium of American trade."

THE TYNE.

The Tyne is not the longest river in the United Kingdom, nor the broadest, nor the deepest, but, historically, it is one of the most interesting; naturally, one of the most diversified; commercially, one of the most important.

Historically considered, the Tyne carries us back to the very infancy of the Christian era. Upon the northern bank of this river, within a century and a half from the birth of Christ, imperial Rome had erected that famous barrier of stone which protected her conquests and divided her civilisation from the barbarism beyond. Upon the opposite shore, when Rome had departed and the milder rule of the Saxon prevailed, the light of Christianity, fading elsewhere after brief splendours, was kept alive, and the wonderful story of religious progress in Britain was written down for the instruction and admiration of posterity. Later, still, when Norman and Plantagenet strove against the irrepressible Scot, this river side was the rendezvous of all the chivalry and service of the realm; the arena of battle, truce, and treaty; the scene of imperial homage, favour, and punishment. In the Wars of the Roses, the civil commotion against the Stuarts, and the first of the abortive attempts to overthrow the house of Hanover, the eyes of all Europe were attracted to the valley of the Tyne, for it was to Hexham that York finally crushed the pretensions of Lancaster, at Newcastle that Charles I. was delivered over to the victorious Parliament, and at Hexham again that the adherents of the old Pretender assembled their forces and went forth to defeat, exile, and death.

From a natural point of view the Tyne presents itself in most varied aspects. The two branches in which the river takes its rise commence their journey—the one in the morasses of the Scottish border, the other in the hilly ranges of east Cumberland. Each of them, aided by numerous burns and streamlets, runs a rapid and tortuous course to the "meeting of the waters," about thirty-six miles from the North Sea. In these wide-gathering affluents, and in the upper reaches of the united river, Nature holds her own. There the angler throws his line, the fisherman casts his net, and the artist plies his pencil, amid rugged rocks and verdant slopes, where no sound breaks the stillness of nature louder than the bleating of sheep, the lowing of kine, and the revelry of birds. For the greater part of its course the Tyne runs in picturesque channels, through pleasant meadows and corn land, by lonely hamlets and busy villages, rippling over stony bottoms and filtering through sandy beds, widening here and curving there, and ever gaining strength and volume as it rolls along. By and by the river meets the tidal flow, and then its commercial life begins. Thenceforward its shores are occupied by docks, shipyards, engine works, foundries, factories innumerable, and populations that spread themselves out far into the adjoining country. Shriek of locomotive, clatter of coal staith, roar of machinery, clang of hammer and crash of adze replace the rural sounds of the higher waters; tapering masts and towering chimneys supplant the waving woods and rugged crags, through which it continues its ceaseless journey; while over all hovers the smoke fiend, whom science cannot exorcise nor legislation suppress. From Newcastle to Shields is a veritable Pandemonium, through whose fire and smoke the river bears on its bosom in mighty ships the commerce of great nations, and finally loses itself in the all-absorbing ocean.

It is in this latter part of its course, and in its more prosaic character of a commercial river, that the Tyne is best known and most widely appreciated. A venerable local proverb informs us that "a Scottish man and a Newcastle grindstone travel all the world over." The proverb might now be altered to read that "a Tyneside man and a Newcastle grindstone travel together the wide world over." For it is undeniably true that wherever the railway system has penetrated, and machinery needs skilled and skilful guidance, Tyneside men are encountered, and that Tyneside grindstones, coals, and bricks, locomotives, steamships, and artillery, are seen in every civilised, and in many of the uncivilised, portions of the habitable globe.

The commerce of the Tyne was originated, grew, and is maintained by the coal trade. Underlying the two counties of Northumberland and Durham, which the river geographically divides but commercially unites, are vast fields of mineral fuel, and it is to the raising, distribution, and economical utilisation of these treasures that we owe the huge enterprises which distinguish the Tyne district, and the teeming populations that inhabit and surround it. From the necessities of transit for north country coal arose the great shipbuilding industry of the Tyne, with its affiliated trades and callings. From the building and employment of ships proceeded the great development of ocean navigation, which made this river a nursery for seamen. From the wants of both these enterprises came the application of steam to locomotion, which was first successfully demonstrated on Tyneside, and thence have flowed innumerable discoveries that contribute to the national wealth, and promote the comfort and happiness of the people.

Let us try to make plain how all this wonderful traffic has grown up. Five centuries and a half ago, during the night of the 31st of July, in the year 1325, when Edward II. had about exhausted the patience of the nation, Thomas Rente, a merchant of Pontoise, was sailing in the North Sea, homeward bound. Suddenly he found himself surrounded by armed ships, and taken, as a French prize, into the harbour of Yarmouth. Rente petitioned the King and Parliament for the recovery of his goods, affirming that he was a liege man, who had been to Newcastle with a cargo of wheat, and was returning with a cargo of coals, and had nothing to do with the King's troubles in France. The petition was preserved, and printed in the Rolls of Parliament; and thus we know that so early as the first quarter of the fourteenth century there was not only a coal trade on the Tyne, but a foreign coal trade, however limited it may have been in its scope and character. At that period the Tyne was a crooked stream, with an entrance that was shallow and perilous, and an inland navigation of a tortuous and difficult nature. There was only one town upon its shores—the largest and strongest between York and Edinburgh—that of Newcastle, and the burgesses there claimed exclusive jurisdiction over the river and all its affairs. The priors of Tynemouth, who wanted to encourage the growth of a community under shelter of their monastery, and the prince bishops of Durham, who tried to preserve their rights of fishing and navigating the stream that washed their domains from Ryton to the sea, were everlastingly at war with Newcastle. And when mace and mitre came into conflict it was generally the mitre that went to the wall; for the burgesses had friends at Court, and made good use of them. Time after time, during the wars with Scotland, Newcastle entertained the sovereign within her walls, and time after time royal favours and trading privileges were conferred upon the town, in recognition of local patriotism, and in requital of local service. Thus, with the passing years, the trade of the river grew, and Newcastle became as famous in the peaceful pursuits of commerce as in martial display and mural strength. Within a quarter of a century from the date of Thomas Rente's disastrous voyage, the Tyne was able to contribute more ships for the service of the nation than any port on the north-east coast, except Yarmouth. The number of Tyneside vessels that formed part of the English fleet at the siege of Calais was seventeen, while London itself contributed only twenty-five, though no doubt the latter were of greater burthen, and more numerously manned. And in proportion as the commercial value of coal forced itself into recognition, Tyneside trade expanded. By the time that the first Stuart monarch in England was established on his throne, four hundred English ships were engaged in carrying coals from this river to various parts of His Majesty's dominions, besides foreign vessels that came "in fleets of fifty sail at once," as often and as rapidly as wind and weather permitted, to convey the staple produce of the district beyond the seas. At the commencement of the eighteenth century the exportation of coals from the Tyne had risen to nearly half a million tons a year, and at its close shipments had doubled, and were made at the rate of a million tons per annum.

Meanwhile other industries, fostered by the apparently inexhaustible resources of the coal trade, established themselves alongside the river. Shipbuilding grew up side by side with the demand for mineral fuel, till, in 1800, forty-seven vessels, of an aggregate tonnage of over eleven thousand tons, equal to two hundred and thirty-six tons each, were launched into the coaly stream. The manufacture of glass, introduced from Lorraine in 1619, became an important element in local trade, and it is said that a hundred years ago more glass was made on Tyneside than in the whole of France. Metal workers, chiefly in iron and lead, found cheap fuel, a home market and ready means of exportation for their produce among the collieries, shipyards, and loading places of the Tyne; while the various handicrafts that minister to the daily wants of a mining, maritime, and manufacturing community increased and multiplied. When the present century came in, the Tyne had risen to a high place among the ports of the kingdom, employing annually in the conveyance of its mineral produce and associated manufactures, nearly two million tons of shipping. Great progress had undoubtedly been made in a hundred years, but still greater progress was coming, still greater achievements were approaching, still greater triumphs were at hand.

An industrial revolution had begun. The inconsiderable forces of wind and water in mechanical operations were being replaced, and the power of hand and hammer infinitely multiplied by the agency of steam. Rapid adoption of steam as a motive power opened up wide prospects of expansion for the coal trade, and expeditious transit from the collieries to the shipping places became a matter of first necessity. On the Tyne, where the want was most pressing, men's minds were concentrated upon the problem of supplying it. And it was upon the shores of this river that the problem was solved, that all difficulties were overcome, and that the first successful locomotive steam-engine saw the light. All the world has read the story of the Wylam coal-owner and his ingenious co-workers, William Hedley and George Stephenson; all the world knows how great and beneficent was the revolution which their genius and enterprise produced, not merely in the industrial arts, but in the conditions of life upon the earth, and in the political and social status of mankind. Locally, the change was most rapid, and most striking. The resources of the coal trade were developed with surprising energy, and marvellous success. "Staiths" and "drops" reared their weird and grisly frames upon either shore; "colliers" filled the harbours and shipping places, and keels and wherries covered the navigable channel. Capacious engineering works were established to meet the increased and increasing demand for locomotives and steam machinery. Furnaces, foundries, and forges; ovens, kilns, and gas works lighted up the river with a ruddy glare, and filled the atmosphere with superabundant smoke. The manufacture of chemicals was introduced, throve, and expanded. The utilisation of vast seams of fire clay, overlying and interlacing the coal measures, was rendered possible, and a wide-spreading industry in retorts, pipes, and other fire-resisting articles sprang up. In fifty years the trade of the Tyne had made greater progress than in the preceding two centuries.

Then came another crisis in the history of the river, and again the necessities of the coal trade were the moving and impelling influence. Rapid transit from the collieries to the shipping places had been secured, but a fresh demand was created by the very agency that secured it. All over the kingdom railways were uniting town with town, and county with county, and at the same time concentrating both town and county upon the metropolis. Coalfields had been opened out in other parts of England; Wales was pressing its mineral fuel into prominence, and from every colliery district south of Northumberland and Durham, railways were taking coal to London at a price and with a regularity that north-country owners found it difficult to equal and impossible to excel. A deeper water-way, with larger and faster ships, and ample means of despatching them, became to the collieries on the Tyne a matter of life or decay. And the hard-headed men of the North, who had created the railway system, were equal to the occasion.

Chief among the obstacles that barred the way was the condition of the Tyne itself. The Corporation of Newcastle had been rulers of the water from time immemorial, deriving large revenues from the traffic which local enterprise brought to their doors. Yet they did nothing, or next to nothing, for the river; disregarded the crying wants of the trading community, and resented, rather than welcomed, the settlement of industrial populations between them and the sea. So long as Newcastle controlled the navigation, improvements commensurate with the important interests involved appeared to be impossible of attainment. River reform, therefore, became the pressing question of the day. The Corporation found that they had no longer to contend with bishop and prior, but with free towns and great industries, and at the close of a sharp and bitter struggle they were beaten. On the 15th of July, 1850, the control of the river passed into the hands of an elective body; the "River Tyne Improvement Commission" was inaugurated, and a new epoch in local progress and prosperity began.

While the transference of the Tyne to its new rulers was taking place, the other great want of the coal trade was earnestly considered, and within two years after the transfer, a means of accelerating traffic by sea, second only in commercial importance to the introduction of railways, was designed and carried to a successful issue by a Tyneside man. Availing himself of the experience already gained in the construction of iron ships, driven by the motive power of steam, and the mechanical agency of the screw propeller, Mr. Charles Mark Palmer built an iron screw steamer for the carrying of coals alone. The difficulty of bringing back an empty vessel was overcome by the wonderful contrivance of water ballast, which involved no delay and incurred no expense. Thus equipped, this vessel, the first "screw collier," did in one year the work of a dozen or more of the old sailing craft. Speed and regularity of transit compensated for extra cost of construction; the railway competition was made less formidable; and the coal trade of Northumberland and Durham was enabled not only to maintain its supremacy in the London market, but to secure new markets across the seas. From the "screw collier" sprung the "cargo steamer," and thus Tyneside, where the problem of steam locomotion on land had been successfully solved, contributed to the establishment of the mercantile marine on a new basis, and assisted to revolutionise ocean navigation.

The improvement of a crooked and neglected river is a work of time and patience. When Mr. Palmer launched the "screw collier" from his yard at Jarrow in 1852, very little had been done by the new governing body of the Tyne. As soon however, as they settled down fairly to work, and commenced in earnest to grapple with the difficulties of the position, the condition of the river began slowly to mend. Two docks were constructed: one of them placed on the northern shore, about three miles from the sea, and enclosing about fifty-five acres of water space, was made by the Commissioners themselves for the accommodation of the steam coal trade of Northumberland; the other, on the opposite shore, with a water space of fifty acres, was constructed by the North Eastern Railway Company, as an outlet for the Durham coalfield and for general merchandise. Piers were commenced at the sea entrance to the river with the object of checking the in-flow of the ocean, which, in tempestuous weather, was a source of great danger; and in the hope of removing by natural process the formidable " bar " that for so many generations had obstructed navigation and imperilled the safety of the mariner.

Concurrently groynes and training walls were advanced into the stream at various places between Shields and Newcastle to facilitate the tidal flow, and systematic efforts were made by dredging to widen and deepen the navigable channel. In 1861 Parliamentary sanction was given to a comprehensive scheme of improvement that embraced nearly the whole river, from " Spar Hawk to Hedwin Streams," and since then the development of the Tyne has been rapid and unremitting. The piers now extend, on the north side about 2,500 feet, and on the south side about 4,500 feet, and the harbour has become a veritable harbour of refuge. Tynemouth " bar " has been removed, and the place it occupied with only six feet depth at low water has been deepened to twenty feet, while at Shields, vessels can moor in more than thirty feet of water at low tide for a distance of a mile and a half. Between Shields and Newcastle the channel has been so vastly improved that a depth of above twenty feet at low tide is secured for the whole distance; while "above bridge," for about two and a half miles, the deepening extends to eighteen feet. Bill Point, a lofty and dangerous obstruction to navigation, where in former times vessels continually came to grief, has been removed, and the foreshore set back about four hundred feet. In the higher part of the river a cutting has been made through Lemington Point by which the navigation has been shortened three-quarters of a mile, and at Elswick a group of islands—one of them known as the King's Meadows, of considerable size—is fast disappearing. The old bridge at Newcastle, which prevented vessels from passing the town westward, has been replaced by a remarkable swing bridge of iron, which weighs 1,450 tons, and is moved to and fro in a few seconds by hydraulic machinery. A dock of twenty-four acres, making the third in the river, is approaching completion at Coble Dene, near North Shields; while coal sfaiths, timber ponds, wharves, warehouses, river walls, and landing places have been constructed, until the river itself, from the sea to Scotswood, may be considered as one great tidal dock, available in all weathers, and at all times of tide, for the largest cargo steamers in the merchant navy.

Time would altogether fail to tell of the varied industries that are clustered along the banks of the Tyne; from the leviathan establishment at Elswick, past the busy towns of Newcastle and Gateshead to the gigantic undertaking at Jarrow. The very names of Stephenson, Palmer, Armstrong, Hawthorn, Hawks and Crawshay, Cowen, Pattinson, Allhusen, and one or two others. suggest of themselves vast enterprises and widespread activities that have given the Tyne its position and character as a commercial and manufacturing centre.

Nor is it easy to grasp the extent of the traffic of the river. It is only by resorting to the aid of dry and uninviting statistics, and by comparing the present of the Tyne with its past, and its commerce with that of other maritime communities that we are able, so to speak, to focus the trade which it floats in, sustains, and carries away; and obtain a reasonably clear idea of the position which it occupies in the commerce and navigation of the country.

Turning to the "Annual Statement of the Navigation and Shipping of the United Kingdom for the year 1882," we find that in respect of the total tonnage of vessels that enter and leave in cargo and in ballast, the Tyne is exceeded by the Mersey alone; while in the number of vessels employed it yields only to the Thames. Whether, therefore, we regard numbers or tonnage, the Tyne is the second commercial river in Great Britain. But the figures shall speak for themselves:—

TABLE XIX.—Number and tonnage of sailing and steam vessels, including their repeated voyages, that entered and cleared with cargoes, and in ballast, from and to foreign countries, British possessions, and coastwise (fourteen principal ports) :—

Ports.	With cargo.		With cargo and in ballast.	
	Vessels.	Tonnage.	Vessels.	Tonnage.
Liverpool	12,765	6,487,764	16,225	7,550,948
Tyne Ports	15,369	5,926,067	17,038	6,360,243
London	17,936	5,178,217	19,891	6,120,970
Cardiff	12,238	4,455,201	12,955	4,641,940
The Clyde { Glasgow	8,183	2,430,830	8,633	2,634,561
{ Greenock	2,828	504,212	5,192	846,685
Sunderland	8,966	2,459,632	9,228	2,616,095
Dublin	3,864	1,134,675	7,742	2,125,803
Hull	4,063	1,520,549	4,638	1,915,436
Belfast	5,411	1,168,740	9,310	1,803,262
Newport	9,237	1,565,855	9,810	1,778,745
Swansea	7,652	1,304,401	8,025	13,90,670
Bristol	4,736	621,342	8,946	1,186,836
Leith	2,563	734,682	3,550	957,266

The entries and clearances for the whole of the United Kingdom in the year 1882 amounted to 66,526,092 tons, distributed as per the following table:—

United Kingdom.	With cargo.		With cargo and in ballast.	
	Vessels.	Tonnage.	Vessels.	Tonnage.
England and Wales	168,646	39,735,901	234,669	50,654,740
Scotland	37,998	7,401,614	49,903	9,323,013
Ireland	17,671	4,141,022	30,397	6,548,339
Total	224,315	51,278,537	314,969	66,526,092

The Tyne, therefore, represents an eighth of the entries and clearances with cargo, and ten per cent. of the entries and clearances with cargo and in ballast, throughout the United Kingdom.

From another table it is easy to see what progress the traffic of the Tyne has made in the last five years, so far, at least, as its shipping is concerned.

TABLE XXXIII.—Number and tonnage of British and foreign vessels, including their repeated voyages, that entered and cleared from and to foreign countries, British possessions, and coastwise, with cargoes and in ballast from the Tyne each year during five years:—

Year.	Ships.	Tonnage.
1878	15,808	5,118,047
1879	16,943	5,712,610
1880	17,990	6,299,507
1881	17,060	6,218,223
1882	17,038	6,360,243

showing an average rate of increase per annum amounting to 248,439 tons. In other words, an average of nearly a quarter of a million more tonnage has been employed in the trade of the Tyne every year during the five years ending last December.

Turning again to the "Annual Statement," we find that the total amount of net tonnage of iron, steel, wooden, and composite sailing and steam vessels built at each port in the United Kingdom during the year 1882 was, on home account, 667,712 tons, and on foreign account, 115,776 tons, making a total of 783,490 tons. In that department of industry the Tyne ranks second, being exceeded by the Clyde alone. Thus:—

	No. of vessels built. 1882.	Net tonnage. 1882.
The Clyde (Glasgow, Greenock, &c.)	259	247,612
The Tyne ports	140	134,407
Sunderland	108	121,064
The Tees (including both Hartlepools)	72	83,060

No one needs to be told that the greater part of the traffic indicated by the figures from Table XIX. consists of coal. In this respect the Tyne has always occupied first place, and although Welsh ports are treading close upon its heels, the northern river has, so far, maintained its supremacy. By the kindness of Mr. Urwin, secretary to the River Tyne Improvement Commissioners, we are able to give comparative statements of the exportation of coals, coke, and patent fuel, from the leading ports of the United Kingdom in 1882 as follows:—

Exportation of Coal, Coke, &c.

Ports.	Tons. 1882.
The Tyne Ports	8,303,843
Cardiff	6,954,092
Sunderland	3,570,405
Newport	2,269,226
Swansea	1,989,790
Liverpool	1,201,807
The Clyde (Glasgow and Greenock)	853,004
Hull	661,924

An approximate idea of the exportations of merchandise, other than coal and coke, from the Tyne is afforded by the following figures, which represent the leading productions of the district, shipped from the Tyne in 1878 and 1882, a five years' interval.

Exportation of Local Manufactures.

	1878. Tons.	1882. Tons.	Increase. Tons.
Cement	25,852	41,668	15,816
Chemicals	242,057	289,810	52,247
Copper	7,765	9,228	1,463
Fire-clay goods	75,091	120,264	45,173
Grindstones and millstones	8,258	11,434	3,176
Iron and steel	91,802	221,546	129,744
Lead Goods	36,523	38,326	1,803

As an importing river the Tyne occupies a position of less pretension. Lines of steamers run regularly to all the principal ports on the Continent, and to the United States and Canada, bringing in supplies of food and general produce. The cattle trade is, in particular, large and important, and is growing year by year. But as yet the Tyne is not a considerable *entrepôt*. Most of the produce imported goes into local consumption, and is not, as in the Thames, the Mersey, and the Humber, merely on its way to wider destinations. The populations of Tyneside proper number about 500,000, while outlying the shores of the river, in the Northumberland coalfield on the one hand, and among the mining districts of the county of Durham on the other, are vast aggregations of people whose chief supplies come from the Tyne, and go no further. A few statistics from the annual returns of importation, both foreign and coastwise, for 1842, 1881, and 1882, will show the progress made in forty years, and indicate the present rate of progression :—

IMPORTATION OF FOOD AND GENERAL PRODUCE.

		1842.	1881.	1882.
Box and bale goods	Pckgs.	None.	39,961	43,660
Fruit (raw)	Pckgs.	24,068	173,256	198,433
Flour and meal	Tons.	8,375	47,460	54,548
Grain	Qrs.	270,294	776,353	752,440
Glass	Cases.	None.	9,020	12,284
Live Stock	Head.	76	130,419	171,040
Manures	Tons.	2,628	28,901	35,268
Minerals and Metals	Tons.	740	814,259	830,090
Provisions	Tons.	9,607	29,753	20,939
Eggs	Hund.	238	Cases 36,311	37,893
Vegetables	Tons.	305	15,449	20,870

Twenty years ago, when the Tyne was but commencing to develop its resources, Mr. Gladstone visited the river, and said of it: " I know not where to seek, even in this busy country, a spot or district in which we perceive so extraordinary and multifarious a combination of the various great branches of mining, manufacturing, trading, and shipbuilding industry; and I greatly doubt whether the like can be shown, not only within the limits of the land, but upon the whole surface of the globe."

If Mr. Gladstone revisited the Tyne to-day he might repeat those words with equal force and added meaning.

THE TAWE.

It is wonderful how the Welsh mountain streams have been utilised in several signal instances at their outlets. The river Tawe, even at Swansea, can scarcely be considered a navigable stream, any more than the Taff at Cardiff: and yet on either side of its banks great works have grown up—notably the Landore Siemens, Hafod (silver and copper), Middle Bank, Morfa (copper), White Rock (lead), Hafod Isha (nickel and cobalt) works, and a host of others, while, mountain torrent as it practically is, it has been the means of concentrating at its confluence with the Bristol Channel, first a town, and then an extended port, with numerous busy docks and railways. Of course we refer to Swansea. Several of the ports of the Bristol Channel have, it is true, lately risen into just prominence, and their advantages and shortcomings, real or supposed, have been dwelt upon in a hundred different ways. And yet, as we consider the part played by these ports, the subject never seems to lose its interest. On the contrary, refreshing instances of the remarkable progress which has been made, of the difficulties which have been overcome by enterprising and persevering men; and the weighty propositions of further development, exist in almost boundless store. Swansea is one of the most interesting of Welsh ports, and, without going deeply into the records of this historical centre, we may be allowed to note one or two points that will tend to demonstrate the remarkable change which has occurred in the character and constitution of the place even so late as the present century. The name of Swansea is well known: and the town—which, by the by, has had very numerous charters and appellations, and was in remote years the scene of Danish depredations —is of considerable antiquarian interest (its name has been spelt in eighty-one different ways). But ancient Swansea has, nevertheless, been outgrown by the modern: the mediæval town exists only by inference, and "Swansee as a bathing place," has, figuratively speaking, been lost in its own celebrated sands—now the location of its docks—just as were previously lost in a more literal manner the forests which Donovan said, in 1805, were reputed to lie beneath the adjacent shores of an encroaching sea: "That the shores of Swansea Bay have suffered greatly by the encroachment of the sea, at no distant period, is extremely obvious. A wide extent of forest land now lies buried beneath its sands. It is confidently asserted by the natives that there was formerly a direct road from the Mumble Point to Briton Ferry, and that during one of the rebellions, the country people were afraid to pass through the woods from that point to Swansea, lest they should be surprised by a banditti of freebooters who infested it." In confirmation of this event, branches of trees are not unfrequently washed out of the sands by the sea, and numbers are dredged up, with buffalo horns, &c., by the large deep-sea dredgers of the Harbour Trustees. Coidbank Forest, standing between Swansea and Briton Ferry, in the time of Speed (1610), seems to have been in a great measure, if not entirely lost since that period.

"Early in the last century," one of the best things that could be said of the town was that "by its advantageous situation it is enabled to hold an extensive and profitable correspondence with the City of Bristol," and it was not until the beginning of this century that a decided attempt was made to commence "the harbour improvements, of which so much can now be said." This was Donovan's reference to the place eighty years ago, and which will explain the nature of the early improvements which preceded the remarkable expansion of the trade of the district. Writing at that time, he also said: "There are other improvements in the condition of the town to which we should advert; those which have been accomplished for the convenience of its extensive commerce. In speaking of these, the amendments at the entrance of the Tawe are not to be forgotten. About thirteen years ago an Act of Parliament was obtained for the purpose of enlarging and amending the entrance into the harbour and immediately carried into execution. The expense of this important public work was to be defrayed by an easy tax of twopence per ton on all the ships admitted into the port. Vessels bring, besides many other articles of trade and commerce, vast quantities of copper, tin, and iron, for the works carried on upon the eastern banks of the Tawe. Coal, store coal, and culm from the adjacent collieries, together with copper, brass, spelter, wrought or prepared for use, are among the principal articles of exportation." What a contrast between the Swansea of that day and this! Then, practically a river-side port with a population of about 10,000 persons, and governed in an antiquated fashion, she is now a great seaport of 100,000 inhabitants, and confessedly the metallurgical centre of the world—a district abounding in large and capable works at which some twenty thousand hands are employed in the producing in marketable form of iron, patent fuel, copper, tin plates, steel spelter, silver, lead, zinc, nickel, cobalt, sulphate of ammonia, oxalic acid, ultramarine, &c. The coal exports are also very considerable, and when it is borne in mind that behind Swansea there is a coal-field computed to contain 192,278,000,000 tons of minerals, it will be understood how great the resources of the district are, and how vastly the mercantile traffic of the port may yet be increased when the coal basin is more fully developed. The Swansea people very pertinently observe, "they have no Taff Vale Railway like Cardiff," but the conveyance of minerals to the port from the Rhondda Valley will be greatly facilitated by the opening of the Rhondda and Swansea Bay Railway, more especially as, under the administration of Mr. Yeo, Chairman, and the practical guidance of Mr. Capper, the esteemed General Superintendent and Harbour-master, the docks themselves are in a high state of efficiency. The new line to which we have referred is the project of a Company, of which the Earl of Jersey is chairman and Sir J. Jones Jenkins, M.P., deputy-chairman, the directors being Sir H. Hussey Vivian, Bart., M.P., Mr. Charles Bath, Mr. Thos. Cory, Mr. T. D. Daniel, Mr. J. R. Francis, Mr. M. B. Williams, with Mr. H. S. Ludlow as secretary. With the opening up of a Transatlantic trade in tin plates, the development of the dock system and the improvement of railway facilities, the Swansea people are deeply concerned; and they are to be congratulated on the progress they are making in these matters. The export of tin plates last year was 35,000 tons; this year it has reached a rate of 10,000 tons a month. The locality has ceased to be satisfied with a profitable trade with Bristol. Nothing short of a world-wide commercial renown is appreciated by the Swansea men of to-day. They recognise modern changes; they see the advance that is taking place around them, and they are keenly alive to the necessity of keeping abreast with the times. Actuated by such feeling and possessing so good a geographical position, they are bestirring themselves with especial vigour, and great though recent progress has been it may be signally eclipsed by what is yet to come. As to the advantages of site, it may be repeated that the compilers of Admiralty surveys observed that, "of all ports in the Bristol Channel there are perhaps none more favourably situated than Swansea; for it is an important fact that Swansea Harbour is accessible to any stranger that may arrive in the Bay, when blowing too strong for pilots to get off." One hundred and fifty years ago, the port of Swansea extended as far up the Bristol Channel as Chepstow. It is still intimately associated with the House of Beaufort, but, strangely enough, it was, before the Reform Act, a contributory borough to Cardiff—which, as has often been pointed out in local controversy, is $45\frac{1}{2}$ miles distant, Now, however, it is a Borough, and Neath, Loughor, Aberavon, and Kenfig are its contributories. The Corporation estate is valued at about three-quarters of a million sterling, and most of the leases, let for 99 years, will expire in some 15 years. The Corporation is therefore regarded as the largest landed proprietary of any Corporation in the Kingdom. The Swansea Harbour Trust consists of the following trustees and leading officers, with the year of the first election of each: Mr. Frank Ash Yeo (1871), chairman. Ex-Officio Trustees: Owner of the Briton-Ferry Estate, the Earl of Jersey (1880); Coroner of Seigniory, Edward Strick (1862);

Steward of Seigniory of Gower, the property of His Grace the Duke of Beaufort, Charles Baker (1861); nominated by Lord of Seigniory, Francis Holborrow Glynn Price (1883) and John Gaskoin (1855). Proprietary Trustees, elected for periods of six years, in batches of four every second year: Sir Henry Hussey Vivian, Bart., M.P. (1847), Sir John Jones Jenkins, Kt., M.P. (1872), Thomas Cory (1872), Lewis Llewelyn Dillwyn, M.P. (1840), William Harries Francis (1864), John Glasbrook (1850), John Crow Richardson (1855), George Burden Strick (1858), Charles Bath, Chairman Finance Committee (1861), Thomas Ford (1866), John Richardson Francis (1876). Corporation Trustees (elected annually by the Corporation out of their own body): Edward Bath (1881), Edward Henry Bath (1880), Robert Dickson Burnie (1880), John Cady (1881), Edward Rice Daniel (Mayor, 1871), Thomas Davies (1877), William Thomas (1876), Daniel Jones (1883), Lawrence Tulloch (1875). Officers, &c.: Robert Capper, Assoc. Inst. C.E., General Superintendent of the Docks, Railways, and Estate; Clerk and Solicitor, Francis James; Treasurers, the Glamorganshire Banking Co.; Engineer-in-Chief, James Abernethy, F.R.S.E., Pres. Inst. C.E., 4, Delahay-street, Westminster; Resident Engineer, Augustus James Schenk. It will be seen from the above particulars that several of the leading men of the locality are very old friends of Swansea.

The Harbour is governed much upon the same principle as that which obtains at Liverpool under the Mersey Docks and Harbour Board, excepting that in the case of the latter there is no one responsible head to whom all can refer. At Swansea, Mr. Capper, who has now superintended the harbour for nearly seven years, is invested with managerial responsibility, and we are only repeating a fact when we state that during his term of office many improvements in shipping and pilotage matters have been effected by the Board, and that the gross revenue has increased 67 per cent., the exports have increased 64 per cent., and the imports 77 per cent., results that are well worthy of record, as they can scarcely be equalled in any other port.

In glancing over the dock works as they exist to-day, at the mouth of the Tawe, we may bear in mind the following order of progression: The first works were a small tidal inlet with two piers quay walls; then, in 1836, the trustees went to Parliament, with the idea of making a new cut and floating the river. This was only copying what has already been done in Bristol. A bend of the river was cut off—as shown by some comparative plans drawn by Mr. James Abernethy, F.R.S.E., who has been connected with Swansea Harbour for forty years—and turned into the North Dock or town float. This so-called dock is therefore really the old bed of the river locked and floated. It was opened in 1852. The town float proper has a water area of $10\tfrac{1}{4}$ acres, with a half-tide basin of $2\tfrac{1}{2}$ acres, between which there is a lock, 160 ft. long by 56 ft. wide. This style of dock was, it may be observed, very popular in the early part of this century—witness that of Bristol, and the "Pent" at Dover by way of example. Next followed the South Dock—the first sod of which was cut by his Grace the Duke of Beaufort, K.G., then Marquis of Worcester—which is built at the west of the entrance channel, and at right angles to the line of the North Dock. It was opened in 1859 by Miss Talbot, the daughter of the Lord-Lieutenant of the county, Mr. C. R. M. Talbot, who has represented the county in Parliament from before the passing of the Reform Bill. The water area of this dock is 13 acres, with a half-tide basin of 4 acres. It is 1,600 ft. long, and the connecting lock is 300 ft. long by 60 ft. wide. The old high water-mark runs right through the centre of the dock and lock. More than half of the dock has therefore been reclaimed from the sea. The fashionable sands, to which we have referred, occupied a site here, and it ought to be put on record that it was hotly debated at one time whether the docks should be on the west or the east side of the river. One of the advocates of the east side was the late Mr. Starling Benson, who was for many years Chairman of the Harbour Trust. It was this same gentleman who, after the lapse of a generation, moved that the most recent dock—the Prince of Wales, or East Dock—should be placed on the east side of the river. He lived long enough to see his original policy adopted, but in the meantime the establishment on the west side of the South Dock had for ever destroyed the reputation of Swansea as a fashionable resort. The Prince of Wales Dock was advocated as early as 1872, by the then Mayor of Swansea, Mr. James Livingston, and the necessary Act of Parliament was obtained in 1874. The central stone of the lock was laid by Sir H. Hussey Vivian, Bart., M.P., the oldest continuous proprietary trustee, amidst great public rejoicings, in March, 1880. Said Sir Hussey Vivian on this occasion: " The geographical position of Swansea is manifestly as good as it possibly can be. The distance from Lundy Island to the Pierhead at Swansea is 40 miles, while to the Bute Docks it is 65, and 75 to Newport. Taking into consideration the time of the tide flowing, and presuming a vessel to sustain a speed of 10 knots from Lundy, one-third of the vessels passing up the Channel would save a tide by coming to Swansea. A vessel coming into Swansea would leave Swansea seven hours sooner than Cardiff, and be that much further on her way. I hope we shall soon have an improved light at the Mumbles. When that is done there will be very few nights in the year when a ship would not be able to make the Port of Swansea without anchoring at all." The dock was christened in October, by the Princess of Wales, while, amid considerable ceremony, the Prince of Wales opened the sluices. The first vessel that presented itself for admission was the *Atlas;* the lock for her was made by Mrs. Yeo, wife of the Chairman, and Mr. Capper, who happened quite casually to meet at the dock-head. The construction of this dock involved the removal of 2,000,000 cubic yards of earth, and over 80,000 cubic yards of masonry, and its total cost has been half a million sterling. The engineer was Mr. Abernethy (who designed the Alexandra Docks, Newport), and the contract was carried out by Mr. T. A. Walker, who is at the present moment engaged in completing the dock extension at Penarth, the Severn Tunnel, and the Inner Circle Railway of London. The water area is 23 acres, and there are 156 acres of land adjoining. The length is 2,320 ft., breadth 500 ft. to 340 ft., and the depth 36 ft. There is on the outer cill of the lock a depth of 32 ft. at ordinary tides, and on the inner cill of 27 ft. The length of the dock giving the depth of 32 ft. is 500 ft., and the tidal basin has an area of $4\frac{1}{2}$ acres. The floors of all docks are higher than their approaches, vessels have therefore to be locked up to the higher level. If docks were made as deep as the sea approach, they would form a sort of well, and the walls would not only have to be built much higher, but their thickness throughout would, consequently, have to be greater, adding very largely to their cost ever so much more than amateur engineers can guess. What has therefore to be aimed at is economy and efficiency—two points of especial interest to the shipowning world. Upwards of £100,000 have been spent in productive works out of surplus revenue, and the income of the trust has grown from £5,000 in 1852 to £87,000 in 1883.

Among recent incidental improvements is the establishment of a Telephonic Ship Signal Station at the Mumbles, and the consequent connection of the same with Cardiff, thanks to the enterprise of the Harbour Trustees, and their able Superintendent. Three railways, viz., the London and North-Western, the Midland, and the Great Western, the latter shipping coal equal to a million tons per annum since the opening of the Princes Dock, have independent access to the town and docks, and, as we have already pointed out, there are projects on foot for increasing both the railway and dock facilities, so that there shall be the fullest accommodation for the growing requirements of the port. From the published returns of the Harbour it will be seen that the working and maintenance does not exceed 41 per cent. of the gross receipts :—

The Increase Nett Tonnage of Shipping frequenting the Port during the last 7 years, bringing the figures down to December, 1883, has been ... ... 54·10%
Increase of Steam Ship Tonnage in the same period ... 136·10%
The Gross Revenue of the Trust for the last financial year was £87,167

The following statement of five years' trade of Swansea Harbour demonstrates the shipping progress that has been made :—

Year.	No. of Vessels.	Register tonnage.	Imports. Tons.	Exports. Tons.
1878	4,689	701,783	450,180	1,051,860
1879	4,745	761,708	470,777	1,158,711
1880	5,126	885,362	648,799	1,333,093
1881	4,790	838,107	623,115	1,341,710
1882	5,010	1,017,006	669,318	1,640,099

The Mayor of Swansea in December, 1883, publicly observed that during the past few years a large expenditure of money had been made on the harbour, and the prospects were of a very encouraging nature, the profit made on the new dock alone within a period of two years being unprecedented in the history of docks. The dock had cost over £300,000, and the trustees had not only managed to pay expenses, but they were in possession of a large surplus accruing from that dock.

A few further trade particulars will not be without interest in this connection. During last year the quantity of copper smelted in the local works was 21,000 tons, of the value of £1,631,250. In the same period, the value of gold, silver, yellow metal, and lead was £237,000. At the Landore Siemens' Steel Works, 1,300 men are engaged in the manufacture of armour-plates. The spelter and zinc manufactured in Swansea form one-twentieth of the whole production of the United Kingdom, and the total value is £360,000. Tin and terne plates made within a radius of four miles of Swansea were valued at two and a half millions sterling last year; and within a radius of twelve miles, 4,800,000 boxes are turned out yearly. There are one hundred works of thirty-six varieties within a radius of four miles, and villages which were once entirely separated by country tracts from Swansea are now amalgamated with it. Colonel Grant Francis has sketched very ably in his work on "Copper Smelting in the Swansa District" the leading historical features of local trades, and he has thrown considerable light on the transactions of the founders of Swansea's greatness. He says: "It is in a great degree due to the facilities for shipping in Swansea, that the copper trade has established itself there; these facilities have from time to time been greatly improved upon, otherwise, in all probability, or as may be said to be the rule, the trade would have taken to itself wings and have established itself elsewhere. The necessity for docks in Swansea has always been unquestionable, but the port seems to have enjoyed in times past the questionable advantage of being the subject of numerous consultations, at times of a very warm character. The father of the Baths of Swansea lost his seat in the Corporation for advocating the building of docks on the site of the new Prince of Wales' Docks; at the same time the want of the gift of clear prevision, as shown by the Swansea Harbour Trustees, has caused Bristol to lose its chance and its position among the great ports of the country, and on the opposite coast the time was when Bideford was the largest western port in England, in the days of the Armada sending more ships to fight the Spaniards than any other in Her Majesty's dominions."

It is not our purpose, however, on the present occasion, to delve into these matters. We have referred briefly to what has lately been accomplished at the rising port of Swansea; we have indicated its importance; we have admired it in its geographical, mercantile, trade, and residential aspects, and we await with interest the results of the labours of earnest men who are seeking to push forward day by day the various enterprises that are destined to render Swansea yet more famous as a great port.

THE CLYDE.

"I had never seen before, and I have never seen since, any river for natural beauty that can stand in competition with the Clyde; never did stream glide more gracefully to the ocean through a fairer region."—*Cyril Thornton.*

"Nowhere as at Glasgow is there revealed in such luminous traits all that can be done by the efforts of man, combined with patience, energy, courage, and perseverance, to assist nature, and if necessary, to correct her. To widen and deepen a river previously rebellious against carrying boats, to turn it into a great maritime canal, to bring the waters where it was necessary to bring the largest ships, and finally to gather a population of 750,000 inhabitants, all devoted to commerce and industry, upon a spot where only yesterday there was but a modest little town, almost destitute of every species of traffic—such is the miracle which in less than a century men have performed at Glasgow."—*Glasgow and the Clyde,* by M. L. SIMONIN, in "*La Nouvelle Revue,*" *November,* 1880.

So wrote the eminent French engineer, after a visit of inspection of and inquiry into the ports of Great Britain.

And no wonder that he wrote thus when he learned that only eighty years ago the quayage of Glasgow Harbour was only 382 yards in length, the water area of the harbour only four acres, the annual revenue of the Clyde Trust, £3,400; the Customs revenue £427, and the population of the city 77,385, and that when he wrote in 1880, the length of the quayage was 8,422 yards, now increased to 10,623 yards, that the water area of the harbour was 120 acres, now increased to upwards of 150 acres, that the Trust revenue was £223,709, now risen to £283,998; that the Customs revenue was £1,071,587, and the population nearly 700,000, including suburbs.

All honour to the shrewd, far-seeing men who not only conceived the grand idea of bringing the sea to Glasgow, and making its harbour in the heart of the city, but resolutely set about accomplishing these ends, and to their successors in office, who have carried, and are still carrying on the great work, without ever having received a single penny of Government aid.

What would Glasgow, now the second city of the empire, to-day have been, but for this gigantic enterprise—a mere inland provincial town.

There would have been none of these extensive shipbuilding yards and marine engineering works, giving employment to tens of thousands, and which have made the Clyde famous throughout the whole world.

The deepening and widening of the Clyde have increased the value of the land on its banks an hundredfold, created the Burghs of Patrick, Govan, Hillhead, Crosshill, and the other burghs which environ Glasgow, given wealth to thousands, and the means of life to hundreds of thousands, and what has been the total expenditure up to 30th June, 1883, only £9,908,000, of which

£2,757,000 has been paid for interest on money borrowed.

The Clyde rises in the south of Lanarkshire, in the same hill range, on the confines of Dumfriesshire, near Moffat, that gives birth to the Tweed and the Annan, hence the couplet—

> "The Tweed, the Annan, and the Clyde,
> All rise from one hill side."

It is 98 miles long, drains an area of 945 square miles, and until a century ago was chiefly known for its famed falls near Lanark. In its upper reaches it flows through rich pastoral lands, in its middle reaches through fertile holms and prolific orchards, and in its lower reaches through valuable mineral fields and busy seats of industry and commerce, passing in its progress seaward the towns of Lanark, Hamilton, Rutherglen, Glasgow, Renfrew, Dumbarton, Port Glasgow, Greenock, Helensburgh, and Gourock, and numerous villages, among others, above Glasgow, being Bothwell, Blantyre, where the celebrated African traveller, Livingstone, worked as a mill spinner—and Uddingstone; and below Glasgow, Kilpatrick, Bowling, Langbank, and Cardross.

The panorama below Greenock is one of exquisite grandeur, the serrated peaks of the Argyleshire hills rising in sublimity towards heaven on the north, the island of Bute and the two Cumbraes guarding the entrance from the sea, while still further seaward Goatfell, in the island of Arran, rears its lofty head proudly to the sky, and away in the far distance, in mid ocean, stands Ailsa Craig in all its lonely isolation.

The numerous watering-places, with their infinite variety of architectural design, close shaven lawns and expanses of foliage which fringe both sides of the estuary, in some places continuous for miles, the white-winged yachts innumerable, skimming its surface in all directions, the outward or inward-bound Atlantic liner ploughing its way through its azure waters, the full-sailed Indiaman gliding slowly along, and ever and anon the swift passenger steamers dashing from pier to pier, make in the summer months a scene which once gazed upon must ever be remembered.

Unlike London, Glasgow cannot boast of a Roman origin. Its foundation is ascribed to a monk named Kentigern or Saint Mungo, the patron saint of the city, who, in the sixth century, settled on the Molendinar Burn, a tiny tributary of the Clyde, on the side of which Glasgow Cathedral was subsequently erected.

Roman legions must, however, have camped on the banks of the Clyde while they were engaged in the construction, under Agricola, 80-81 A.D., of the chain of forts between the Clyde, near Bowling, and the Forth, near Bo'ness, and under Antoninus Pius, in 140 A.D., in connecting these forts by a rampart of earth and stones, with a deep and wide ditch outside, and a paved military road along the inner or south side, to check the inroads of the Caledonian barbarians.

In pre-historic timès savages must have paddled their "dug-outs" on the spot where, in the latter part of 1883 the s.s. *City of Rome* lay berthed, for canoes have been unearthed on the banks of the river at Glasgow and Bowling, and even at the Cross of Glasgow, fully 500 yards from the present margin of the stream.

Geologists say that at one time the Clyde at Glasgow was an arm of the sea, and the finding of canoes twenty-five feet under the surface of the ground seems to confirm that statement. Be that as it may, the Clyde in 1566 was so shallow and insignificant a stream, and so choked up with sand-banks, that even twelve miles below Glasgow it was forded by carts and carriages; and Thomas Tucker, "one of Cromwell's servants," as he calls himself, appointed by Cromwell to arrange the customs and excise in Scotland, says of Glasgow and the Clyde in his report dated November 20, 1656, "The situation of this towne in a plentiful land, and the mercantile genius of the people, are strong signs of her increase and growth, were she not chequed and kept under by the shallowness of her river, every day increasing and filling up, soe that noe vessels of any burden can come nearer up than within fourteene miles, where they must unlade and send up theyr timber and Norway trade in rafts or floates; and all other comodityes by three or foure tonnes of goods at a time, in small cobbles, or boates, in three, foure, five, and none above six tonnes a boat. There are twelve vessells belonging to the merchants of this port, viz., three of 150 tonnes each, one of 140, two of 100, one of 50, three of 30, one of 15, and one of 12, none of which come up to the towne."

While vessels of moderate draught could get up to about fourteen miles below Glasgow, the nearest deep water was, as it still is, at Greenock, upwards of twenty miles below Glasgow.

In 1658, two years after the date of Commissioner Tucker's report, the magistrates of Glasgow, despairing of getting the sea brought up to Glasgow, determined to go towards the sea, and made overtures to the magistrates of Dumbarton for the acquisition of ground there, about fourteen miles from Glasgow, for the construction of an extensive harbour, which the latter declined to entertain, on the ground "that the great influx of mariners and others would raise the price of provisions to the inhabitants." Disappointed, they turned their attention to a suitable site on the other side of the river about five miles lower down, and in 1662 purchased thirteen acres of ground, on which they built harbours, and subsequently constructed, from the designs of James Watt, the first graving dock in Scotland, naming the place Port Glasgow.

The union of England and Scotland, consummated on 25th March, 1707, though violently opposed and leading to riots of a serious character, gave to the commerce of Glasgow its first great stimulus, which has increased in volume down to the present day. It opened up to Scotland its trade with the Colonies, led its merchants to go

WATT'S ENGINE IN WEST END PARK.

into shipowning on their own account, instead of, as hitherto, chartering vessels from the port of Whitehaven and elsewhere in the North-West of England, and ultimately gave them the largest share of the foreign export trade, and an almost national monopoly of the tobacco trade of the Kingdom.

They had still the shallow, sanded-up river to contend with, and it was not until 1759 that the first Act for its improvement was obtained, on the advice of Smeaton, to construct a dam seven feet in height across the river four miles below Glasgow, with a lock in it " 18 ft. in the clear, and to take in a vessel of 70 ft. long, or to let pass a sloop or brig of 100 tons when there is water in the river to admit it."

Fortunately for Glasgow no dam and lock were constructed, but acting on the advice of Golborne, a civil engineer, of Chester, an Act was obtained in 1770 to contract the river by jetties and deepen it by dredging " between the lower end of Dumbuck Ford and the Bridge of Glasgow, so as there shall be seven feet of water in every part of the said river at neap tides."

The previous year James Watt made a survey of the river, and found the depth in Glasgow Harbour at low water to be 14 in., and at Dumbuck Ford 2 ft.

In 1773 Golborne took a contract to make Dumbuck Ford 6 ft. deep and 300 ft. wide at low water, and in 1781 reporting to the magistrates, who were " desirous to know if a greater depth of

H

water could be brought to the Broomielaw Quay, so as to receive vessels trading to England and Ireland," said that on sounding Dumbuck Ford with the magistrates, on the 8th day of August, at low water, "we had the pleasure to find no less than 14 ft."

Thomas Telford, in reporting on the further improvement of the river on 24th May, 1806, notes as an interesting circumstance, "that on the 14th February last, Mr. Archibald Wilkie, master of the *Harmony*, of Liverpool, then lying at the Broomielaw, informed me that he came up with ordinary spring tide, drawing 8 ft. 6 in. of water." He adds, "this was a vessel of 120 tons burthen."

This report of Telford fixes very clearly the maximum draft and size of vessel that could reach Glasgow. So recently as 1812 the *Comet*, drawing only 4 ft., required to leave Glasgow and Greenock, respectively, at or near high water to prevent it grounding in the river. In 1821, vessels drawing 13½ ft. could come up. Now we have had the *Alaska*, the *Servia*, the *Austral*, the *Aurania*, and the *Oregon*, built on its banks; and the *City of Rome* coming to Glasgow for graving dock accommodation.

This marvellous increase in the magnitude of the river is due almost entirely to persistent and unremitting dredging, first by large rakes wrought by hand capstans, which drew the material from the bed of the river on to the banks; then by dredgers with small buckets on a ladder wrought by hand, and subsequently by horses. In 1824 the first steam dredger was started. It dredged only to 10 ft. 6 in.; in 1826 it was altered to dredge to 14 ft.; now several of the dredgers employed work to 30 ft. The dredging plant of the Clyde Trustees now consists of five steam dredgers, one steam digger, eighteen steam screw-hopper barges, two diving-bells, and one tug-steamer.

Some very interesting results have followed the deepening, widening, and straightening of the river, a few of which we will shortly notice.

In 1755 the Clyde at Glasgow was only 15 in. deep at low water, and 3 ft. 8 in. at high water, thus giving a range of tide of only 2 ft. 5 in.; it is now 15 ft. deep at low water, and 26 ft. at high water, giving a tidal range of 11 ft.

High-water level has risen 9 in. since 1853, and low-water level has fallen 23 in. within the same period, and 7 ft. 10 in. since 1755.

The bed of the river from Glasgow to Port Glasgow is now virtually level throughout, and 6 ft. 7 in. of the increased range of tide and the whole present depth of 15 ft. at low water, together 21 ft. 7 in., have been obtained by dredging out the bottom of the river.

In 1800 the time of high water was three hours behind Port Glasgow, now it is only one hour. Even so lately as the summer of 1858 a float put into the river at Glasgow Bridge at the first of ebb took 537 hours, or $43\frac{1}{2}$ tides, to reach Port Glasgow, a distance of 19·4 miles, while in the summer of 1881 a float under exactly similar conditions reached Fort Matilda, below Greenock, a distance of 23·5 miles, in 86 hours 20 minutes, or 7 tides, and the average of six trials was 23½ miles in 123 hours 40 minutes, or 10 tides.

The Queen's Dock, and the "Anchor Line" berthage on the north side of the harbour, and the quayage on the south side of the harbour, are connected with the railway system of the Kingdom, the Trustees possessing nine miles of private railways in connection therewith.

The spiritual and temporal wants of the seamen frequenting the port have not been overlooked by the shipping community. A sailors' church, or Bethel, has existed for many years on the north side of the harbour, and a mission-hall on the south side has succeeded so well that some time ago the foundation-stone of a church to take its place was laid by Alexander Allan, Esq., of the "Allan Line."

A Sailors' Home has long been a prominent feature on the Broomielaw, with its pleasing tower surmounted by a time ball, not now in use; and a few months ago, by the liberality of the leading shipowners, underwriters, and others, a Sailors' Restaurant, built on ground granted rent free by the Clyde Trustees, was opened at the Queen's Dock. This restaurant is unique of its kind, both in arrangement and design, and is not surpassed at any port of the country. The following description of the structure may be useful to the authorities of other ports who may desire to minister somewhat to the comfort of all connected with shipping, from the shipowner and shipmaster down to the A.B. and the hard-wrought lumper. The building is in the Swiss style of architecture, and is two storeys in height, a wooden balcony running round three of the sides, with a verandah overhead. The building occupies an area of 96 ft. by 50 ft., and the ground floor is occupied as a large dining hall for seamen and harbour workmen, the tables accommodating 150 at a time. The walls of the apartment are finished with white, red, and brown bricks, and it has been finely furnished in every respect.

The quayage of Glasgow Harbour has increased along with the increasing depth of the river.

In 1792 it was	382	yards in length.
,, 1823 ,,	865	,, ,,
,, 1840 ,,	1,973	,, ,,
,, 1850 ,,	3,391	,, ,,
,, 1860 ,,	4,376	,, ,,
,, 1870 ,,	5,604	,, ,,
,, 1880 ,,	8,422	,, ,,
,, 1883 ,,	10,623	,, ,,

The water area of Glasgow Harbour was—

In 1800	4	acres.
,, 1840	23	,,
,, 1850	51	,,
,, 1860	70	,,
,, 1870	75	,,
,, 1883	151¾	,,

Up till within twenty years ago the river banks between Glasgow Bridge and the River Kelvin, two miles down, and the western boundary of the harbour, gave scope for the extension of the quayage.

In 1867, Kingston Dock, on the south side of

the river, with 5⅓ acres of water space, and 830 lineal yards of quayage, was opened; in 1882, the Queen's Dock, on the north side of the river, with 33¾ acres of water space, and 3,334 lineal yards of quayage, was added to the harbour, and in the last Session of Parliament an Act was obtained for docks on the south side of the river, with 38½ acres of water space, 3,786 lineal yards of quayage, and two graving docks 600 ft. long each. In the space of the last fourteen years the water area and length of quayage of Glasgow Harbour have been more than doubled, and the area of quayage, the area of sheds, and the revenue nearly doubled. There are now 23½ acres of sheds for the accommodation and protection of goods in the harbour.

The Clyde Trustees have four passenger steam ferries, and one horse and carriage ferry across the river within the precincts of the harbour, and carried last year upwards of 10,000,000 passengers. They have also two row-boat ferries across the river, outside the harbour boundaries.

The revenue of the Clyde Trust was:—

	£	s.	d.
From July, 1752, to July, 1770	147	0	10
In 1771	1,044	10	0
,, 1780	1,515	8	4
,, 1800	3,319	16	1
,, 1820	6,328	18	10
,, 1840	46,536	14	0
,, 1850	64,243	14	11
,, 1860	97,983	18	1
,, 1870	164,093	2	10
,, 1880	223,709	0	8
,, 1883	283,998	8	5

The sources of the Trusts' Revenue for the year ending June 30, 1883, were, according to the published accounts, as follows:—

	£	s.	d.
Tonnage dues on vessels	64,114	11	5
Dues on goods	164,375	14	2
Crane dues	8,989	17	5
Weighing	1,639	9	0
Planks	1,309	0	7
Water	3,319	2	6
Rents for timber yards and offices	1,604	0	11
Graving dock	7,592	1	2
Coaling and mineral cranes	5,437	15	3
Lower stages of the river	1,632	5	8
Ferries	15,390	13	3
Rents	6,456	10	7
Miscellaneous	2,137	6	6
Total	283,998	8	5

The Trust have no warehouses, and, unlike Dock Companies, they do not load and unload goods; those duties, with their consequent profits, are left to the shipowners to perform. They, however, by means of 32 steam and hydraulic cranes, ranging from 30 cwt. to 75 tons, load coal and heavy machinery, discharge ore, and place the boilers, engines, &c., on board the majority of the numerous steamers built on the river in Glasgow and neighbourhood. Several of the largest shipbuilders and marine engineers, such as John Elder & Co., A. and J. Inglis, and Alex. Stephen & Sons, put the boilers, engines, &c., on board themselves by means of shears and cranes in their own yards.

The total expenditure of the Clyde Trust from 1770 to June 30, 1883, amounts to £9,908,592. The chief items of expenditure are:—

General management, officers' salaries, &c...	£351,700
General expenditure, repair, and upkeep of works, &c.	465,519
Ferries, wages, and repair of boats	151,800
Ground annuals and feu duties	304,362
Taxes	153,662
Interest on borrowed money	2,757,282
Dredging in river and harbour	723,795
Dredgers, tugs, hopper barges, punts, and repair of same	650,944
Land purchased for enlargement of harbour	1,070,016
Construction of harbour works	1,076,199
Kingston Dock works	97,338
Queen's Dock works	818,456
Graving Dock works	151,565
Land purchased for widening of river	177,666
River works	437,793
Acts of Parliament, Parliamentary oppositions, and extraordinary repairs	112,314
Engineering and surveying	19,643

The total debt as at June 30, 1883, was £4,259,685.

The arrivals of sailing vessels at, and departures from, the harbour of Glasgow for the year ending June 30, 1883, are stated in said accounts as under:—

	Inwards.				Outwards.			
	Loaded.		In Ballast.		Loaded.		In Ballast.	
	No.	Tonnage.	No.	Tonnage.	No.	Tonnage.	No.	Tonnage.
Scotland	358	12,164	416	95,276	586	19,765	64	5,268
England	254	47,696	48	38,304	235	25,155	5	4,577
Ireland	491	34,035	36	16,575	571	46,156	—	—
Coasting	1,103	93,895	500	150,155	1,392	91,076	69	9,845
Foreign	178	73,754	13	9,882	315	216,988	16	8,220
Total	1,281	167,649	513	160,037	1,707	308,064	85	18,065

	Inwards.			Outwards.	
	No.	Tonnage.		No.	Tonnage.
Loaded	1,281	167,649	Loaded	1,707	308,064
In Ballast	513	160,037	In Ballast	85	18,065
Total	1,794	327,686		1,792	326,129

The number and registered tonnage of steam vessels which arrived during same period from—

	No.	Tonnage.
Scotland	11,510	889,628
England	1,323	604,476
Ireland	2,063	576,245
Foreign	961	901,665
Total	15,857	2,972,014

And the number and registered tonnage of steam vessels which sailed during the same period for—

	No.	Tonnage.
Scotland	10,791	661,840
England	994	387,587
Ireland	2,201	589,560
Foreign	1,088	1,087,814
Total	15,074	2,726,801

The total tonnage of goods for the same period was as follows:—

Imported—Foreign	1,087,282	
Exported „	1,161,523	
Total Foreign		2,248,805
Imported—Coastwise	685,087	
Exported „	790,786	
Total Coastwise		1,475,873
Grand Total		3,724,678

	Imports.	Tons.
Foreign	1,087,282	
Coastwise	685,087	
		1,772,369

	Exports.	Tons.
Foreign	1,161,523	
Coastwise	790,786	
		1,952,309
Total		3,724,678

The Chief Exports were :—

Ale, beer, and porter	33,661
Bale and box goods	132,678
Bricks	51,788
Castings	32,904
Cast-iron pipes	81,318
Coal	801,473
Coal Tar Pitch	12,370
Earthenware	10,258
Flour	26,588
Iron; Bar and Rod	40,846
Iron; Pig	261,239
Machinery	51,203
Oatmeal	9,086
Oil	18,713
Railway Chairs	59,828
Soda Ash	11,099
Spirits	17,490
Steel	13,170
Stones	16,182
Timber	16,324
Tubing; Malleable Iron	9,628
Wrought Iron Railway Sleepers	5,950

The Chief Imports :—

Bacon	12,611
Bale and box goods	30,787
Barley	24,266
Beans	17,829
Beef	10,858
Brimstone	9,561
Cheese	8,655
Chrome Ore	10,829
Clay	31,111
Flour	213,787
Fruit	22,140
Herrings	12,028
Indian Corn	99,742
Iron Ore	328,976
Jute	6,323
Lead	4,998
Linseed	5,496
Linseed Oil Cakes	7,793
Logwood	7,275

Nitrate of Soda	7,670
Oats	11,785
Oil	15,533
Pease	13,748
Phosphate Rock	6,642
Pyrites	24,384
Rice	5,666
Rosin	14,564
Sand	18,389
Seeds	5,449
Slates	9,412
Soda	7,407
Spirits	11,754
Stones	18,433
Sugar	31,114
Timber	128,173
Wheat	118,548

The first commerce of Glasgow was the capture, curing, and exporting of salmon caught in the river, and the curing and exporting of herrings, brought by wherries from the West Highlands. After the Union came the tobacco trade, which the enterprise of Glasgow merchants made almost entirely their own, so that in the year 1772, out of 90,000 hogsheads imported into Great Britain, Glasgow alone imported 49,000, and in the year preceding the American War of Independence the imports into the Clyde were 57,143 hhds., the property of forty-two merchants who realised princely fortunes. The Declaration of Independence changed all this, and pastures new had to be sought for. Trade with the East and West Indies was opened up, and cotton spinning was started.

At this time the vast mineral deposits of the West of Scotland still lay many fathoms deep, waiting the genius of James Watt to supply the mighty power to bring them to the surface, and to raise the strong blast to fuse them into use.

The power-loom introduced into Glasgow in 1773, and driven by a large Newfoundland dog, also awaited his master hand, which was at length so well applied, that in 1846 the consumption of cotton in Scotland was 119,225 bales, the greater part being absorbed in Glasgow.

All this is now altered; little tobacco is imported direct, the consumption of cotton is much reduced, and what is used comes by Liverpool, while London has carried off the tea trade, but in place of these the imports of American and other produce, in their infinite variety, has largely increased in late years, and Glasgow has become a large distributing centre for the south-west of Scotland and the north of England, while a trade in Spanish and other ores, and in fruit, has sprung up in recent years, which has more than made up for the loss of the tobacco, cotton, and tea; the mineral wealth of the district in coal, iron, lime, shale oil, &c., has been largely developed, and the making and exporting of sugar machinery, locomotives, and miscellaneous ironwork, has taken such deep root in Glasgow that it will not easily be displaced.

At the present moment the Singer Sewing Machine Company are erecting Works on the north side of the Clyde, about six miles below Glasgow, which will cover forty-six acres of ground, and give employment to several thousands of men, women, and children.

Glasgow Royal Exchange.

In no instance have river improvement works been attended with such beneficent results, commercial, industrial, and social, as those of the Clyde, which has in recent years been indeed a gold producing stream. It is a familiar saying in Scotland, if not beyond its borders, that "Glasgow has made the Clyde, and the Clyde has made Glasgow." As already noted, in 1801 the population of that city was 77,385, in 1881 it was, including its suburban burghs, which are part and parcel of it, 674,095. Need more be said to prove the saying true?

Glasgow is the birth-place of the "Allan Line," the "Anchor Line," the "City Line," the "State Line," and the "Clan Line" of first-class steamers, by which constant communication is kept up with Canada, the United States, Africa, and India, while the famed "Burns' Line" of steamers to Belfast cross nightly in all sorts of weather with such regularity, that the town clocks of Greenock might safely be set by their arrival and departure. Aitken, Lilburn & Co.'s Lines of sailing ships to Melbourne and Sydney leave nothing to be desired. Various other Lines maintain frequent communication with other colonial and foreign ports, while the connections with English, Irish, and continental ports are numerous and regular.

Nowhere can such a fleet of handsome and commodious river passenger steamers be seen as on the Clyde; the names of many of them have become household words for all that is luxurious and comfortable in pleasure sailing.

While Glasgow is the chief port on the Clyde, the minor ports must not be overlooked.

RENFREW, about five miles below Glasgow Bridge, comes first in order. A royal burgh, its proximity to its great neighbour has overshadowed it. From time to time its authorities have made laudable efforts to give it a harbour, but have as yet had to be content with renewing the short stretch of quayage on the town-side of a burn called the Pudzeoch.

PAISLEY comes next; situated on the River Cart, about $3\frac{1}{2}$ miles from the junction of that river with the Clyde, and 7 miles by rail from Glasgow. It allowed Glasgow to take the lead in river improvement, and beyond spasmodic efforts now and again to deepen, straighten, and widen its river, resulting in but slight amelioration, it has not yet been able to get more than vessels of shallow draft up to its town quays.

BOWLING HARBOUR, about 11 miles below Glasgow, is next in order; it is a tidal basin of 12 acres, the joint property of the Clyde Trustees and the Caledonian Railway Company, and used by the latter in connection with the Forth and Clyde Canal, is largely used by the former in the laying up, for the winter, of the extensive fleet of passenger steamers plying in summer on the waters of the Clyde and adjoining lochs. Here, side by side, may be seen, dismantled and silent, the famed *Iona*, *Columba*, *Lord of the Isles*, and *Ivanhoe*, which during the summer months are crowded with tourists from all parts of the world, viewing, with admiration, the enchanting scenery of the Western Highlands.

THE FORTH AND CLYDE CANAL.—The Forth and the Clyde are joined by this ship canal, now the property of the Caledonian Railway Company, the junction with the Clyde being at Bowling, 11 miles from Glasgow. The canal is 35 miles long, with a branch to Port Dundas, Glasgow, 2¾ miles long. It was begun in 1768, and opened between sea and sea on July 28, 1790. Vessels 68 ft. keel, 19 ft. beam, and 8 ft. draught, can pass through its locks. A considerable trade is carried on by it between Glasgow and London *viâ* Grangemouth, and in timber from the Clyde to Port Dundas, while it has played a not inconsiderable part in the development of the mineral trade of the West of Scotland.

DUMBARTON.—The present authorities are inspired with much broader views on the harbour question than were their predecessors of 1658— already referred to—and in 1881 carried a Bill through Parliament for the improvement of the River Leven, on which the town is situate, and for the providing of quay accommodation, and the works will shortly be commenced.

PORT GLASGOW.—The old harbours were acquired by the municipal authorities of that Port in 1864 from the magistrates of Glasgow on payment to the latter of five shillings per pound on the amount of the debt on them, and since then they have lengthened the graving dock and effected other improvements. The harbour accounts for the year ending 30th June last show that the receipts were £4,257 2s. 5d., and the surplus for the year £1,099 18s.

GREENOCK, Glasgow's greatest rival and former superior, and the birthplace of James Watt, has, in recent years, through the enterprise of its leading men, been engaged in harbour extension of an important character. Its harbour revenue, while not showing the elasticity of Glasgow, has yet largely advanced.

For the year ending the 3rd September last—

The total ordinary revenue was	£66,699
Extraordinary ditto	10,698
	£77,397

On the completion of the James Watt Dock within the next eighteen months or two years, a return should begin to come in for the large outlay of the last few years. Greenock has an almost complete monopoly of the sugar refining trade, and its imports of American timber are very large, extensive ponds being provided for its storage, both above and below Port Glasgow.

Of the numerous industries which flourish on the banks of the "busy Clyde," the palm must be given to shipbuilding and marine engineering. These, as much as its commerce, have spread its fame over every portion of the habitable globe; its floating palaces traverse every sea.

The Clyde took the lead in introducing the

steamboat to the Old World, which in the short space of seventy years has revolutionised the carrying trade of the world, and brought about that commercial intercourse between the nations which has so vastly increased the comfort and happiness of the whole human race.

It began by setting afloat the *Comet* on its then shallow stream, and it still leads the van of progress by giving to the world the *Alaska*, the *Servia*, the *Aurania*, and the *Oregon*.

The inventions of James Watt, the application of these to steam navigation by Patrick Miller, William Symington, and Henry Bell, and the improvement of the Clyde most singularly synchronised, and the further development of them still go hand in hand.

But for the deepening of the Clyde, shipbuilding above Dumbarton would have been impossible; the *Comet* of 1812, although engined in Glasgow, was built at Port Glasgow in a yard still flourishing, and for several years thereafter, while the engines of the pioneer steamers were constructed in Glasgow the hulls were built elsewhere. Now the majority of the yards are within six miles of Glasgow, five, including that of the well-known firm of Robert Napier & Sons, being within the precincts of the harbour, and the largest of all, John Elder & Co.'s, within sight thereof.

One yard, that of T. B. Seath & Co., where have been built many of the beautiful steam-yachts and pleasure steamers which are on our English lakes, on our Scottish lochs, and on foreign waters, is at Rutherglen, three miles above Glasgow.

The river all the way to Greenock is studded with shipyards, the Glasgow and Whiteinch district embracing thirteen, Renfrew and Dalmuir four, Paisley five, Bowling one, Dumbarton five, Port Glasgow and Greenock twelve, in all forty, from which and from one yard at Troon, one at Ayr, one at Campbeltown, one small yard at Maryhill on the Forth and Clyde Canal, and one at Blackhill on the Monkland Canal, and a yacht yard at Fairlie, were launched in 1883, 413 vessels, of an aggregate tonnage of 415,694 tons, the amount by each firm being as follows :—

	Steam.		Sailing.		Total.	
	No.	Tons.	No.	Tons.	No.	Tons.
John Elder & Co.	12	40,093	1	20	13	40,113
Russell & Co.	9	1,848	19	28,763	28	30,611
R. Napier & Sons	6	23,873	—	—	6	23,873
A. Stephen & Sons	11	22,450	—	—	11	22,450
W. Denny & Brothers	10	22,240	—	—	10	22,240
London & Glasgow Co.	9	19,793	—	—	9	19,793
D. & W. Henderson & Co.	7	14,724	72	2,990	79	17,714
Scott & Co.	9	17,685	—	—	9	17,685
Aitken & Mansel	8	16,890	—	—	8	16,890
R. Duncan & Co.	6	4,244	12	12,335	18	16,579
Barclay, Curle & Co.	7	13,214	1	1,986	8	15,200
J. & G. Thomson	7	15,010	—	—	7	15,010
A. & J. Inglis	8	14,741	—	—	8	14,741
A. McMillan & Sons	3	4,376	5	8,751	8	13,127
Caird & Co	7	12,258	—	—	7	12,258
Connell & Co.	5	12,002	—	—	5	12,002
Dobie & Co.	9	7,913	1	1,367	10	9,280
Napier, Shanks & Bell	3	8,796	1	298	4	9,094
W. B. Thompson	4	6,545	1	2,278	5	8,823
Blackwood & Gordon	8	8,616	1	25	9	8,641
Lobnitz & Co.	13	6,647	—	—	13	6,647
H. Murray & Co.	6	6,645	—	—	6	6,645
Carried forward...	167	300,603	114	58,813	281	359,416

THE CLYDE.

	Steam.		Sailing.		Total.	
	No.	Tons.	No.	Tons.	No.	Tons.
Brought forward	167	300,603	114	58,813	281	359,416
J. Reid & Co.	2	994	6	5,752	8	6,746
Murdoch & Murray ...	8	6,308	—	—	8	6,308
H. M'Intyre & Co. ...	10	6,262	—	—	10	6,262
R. Steele & Co.........	4	4,015	2	1,805	6	5,820
D. J. Dunlop & Co....	7	5,559	—	—	7	5,559
Burrell & Sons	5	4,255	—	—	5	4,255
W. Hamilton & Co....	3	1,828	1	2,093	4	3,921
M'Arthur & Co.........	12	1,438	3	1,178	15	2,616
W. Simons & Co.......	6	2,544	—	—	6	2,544
Birrell, Stenhouse & Co.	1	1,439	1	1,081	2	2,520
T. B. Seath & Co.....	9	1,681	7	630	16	2,311
Fullerton & Co.	7	2,212	—	—	7	2,212
Campbeltown S. Co...	4	1,826	—	—	4	1,826
Abercorn S. Co.	4	851	1	25	5	876
Scott, Bowling	3	846	—	—	3	846
Murray Bros.............	3	403	—	—	3	403
Troon S. Co.............	—	—	2	379	2	379
Swan & Co.	—	—	4	285	4	285
M'Knight & M'Creadie	1	237	—	—	1	237
W. S. Cumming	2	80	6	100	8	180
W. Fyfe	1	65	5	47	6	112
M'Adam	1	10	—	—	1	10
M'Allister	1	50	—	—	1	50
Total	261	343,506	152	72,188	413	415,694

The tonnage given underneath is the Board of Trade gross register, with the exception of a few vessels launched within the last few days, the official tonnage of which not being recorded, builder's measurement is given:—

	1879.		1881.		1882.		1883.	
Steamers.	Vsls.	Tons.	Vsls.	Tons.	Vsls.	Tons.	Vsls.	Tons.
Govt. vessels....	—	—	—	—	2	7,546	2	5,048
Paddle.............	18	6,730	11	3,109	18	11,854	26	13,446
Screw	95	135,204	181	279,269	191	289,762	208	316,202
Hoppers	7	1,696	3	462	14	5,666	19	7,309
Dredgers.........	7	3,400	4	3,458				
Sailing vessels:								
Iron and steel.	14	15,531	24	35,796	44	67,768	42	64,156
Wood	—	—	3	603	1	198	2	380
Barges	20	4,130	55	6,522	13	4,321	103	7,652
Yachts:								
Steam	12	1,428	18	2,290	8	1761	6	1,300
Sailing	18	341	14	362	4	124	5	201
	191	168,460	313	331,876	295	389,000	413	415,694

For the two foregoing tables we are indebted to the *Scotsman* newspaper.

This is the largest amount of tonnage built on the Clyde in one year. Twenty-five years ago the total tonnage was only 35,709 tons.

The following table, giving the yearly launching since then, cannot fail to interest our readers:—

TONNAGE FOR THE LAST TWENTY-FIVE YEARS.

Year.	Tonnage.	Year.	Tonnage.
1883	415,694	1870	180,401
1882	389,000	1869	192,310
1881	331,868	1868	169,571
1880	239,015	1867	108,024
1879	168,460	1866	124,513
1878	222,353	1865	153,932
1877	169,710	1864	178,505
1876	174,824	1863	123,262
1875	211,824	1862	69,967
1874	262,430	1861	66,801
1873	232,926	1860	47,833
1872	230,347	1859	35,709
1871	196,229		

Compare this with the work done in the early days of the steamboat, which happily we can do, thanks to the careful recording of James Cleland, Superintendent of Public Works of the City of Glasgow, who, in his "Annals of Glasgow," published at the end of 1816, gives a list of steamboats built on the Clyde, and how they were disposed of, which will be found on the next page.

Steel is every year more and more displacing iron in the construction of the hulls of vessels on the Clyde. In 1879, 18,000 tons were of steel; in 1880, 42,000 tons; in 1881, 66,500 tons; in 1882, 108,250 tons; and in 1883, 129,500 tons.

port and haven of Sunderland the boundaries of the River Trust are—from Souter Point 2½ miles from the bar towards the North-East, and so into the sea at five fathoms at low water; and from thence in a direct line until it falls opposite to Ryhope Dene, about four miles towards the South. The average breadth of the harbour half a century ago was 350 feet, its actual capacity not exceeding 80 acres. It will thus be seen that the Commissioners had strong inducements to provide ampler accommodation for mooring the large fleets of colliers which even then resorted to the port to load the output of the important collieries in the neighbourhood. Brigs and schooners of a type now rapidly disappearing from the port crowded the harbour berths, and making their twelve or thirteen voyages to the Thames and back in a twelvemonth they generally yielded to their owners an excellent return on the twelve or fifteen hundred pounds invested in each bottom.

Occasionally, however, serious disasters overtook those fleets as they lay at what might have been regarded as safe moorings, and when thaws set in after heavy frosts and snowstorms, ponderous masses of ice were floated down the Wear, causing an immense amount of damage to the colliers. One season the destruction was so great that the river could actually be crossed by a sort of bridge formed of the shattered hulls of vessels driven against each other by an ice-rush. The local marine insurance clubs suffered so severely through the devastation of that winter's day, that an agitation which had long been in progress for the formation of wet docks received an impulse that never altogether ceased to make itself felt until the great want of the port was fully met. Scheme after scheme for the construction of docks had been propounded from the year 1794, and in 1831 the project had so far succeeded that plans by the afterwards famous Brunel, and Giles, the engineer to the Wear Commissioners, were submitted to Parliament, but only, after all, to be rejected. Again, in 1832, another effort was made in the same direction, when the Commissioners deposited plans by Rennie and Walker for the formation of a small dock on either side of the Wear. The question of site had, however, aroused much bitterness between the inhabitants on the north side and those on the south, and in consequence of a wish expressed by the original promoters of a dock on the north side, the Commissioners agreed to abandon that part of their scheme, and ultimately, under the sanction of a charter, the "Wearmouth Dock Company" constructed a dock of six acres, which was opened for traffic in 1838. As far as the south side scheme was concerned the opposition encountered by the Commissioners compelled them at last to abandon it, and for a time it seemed as if the North Dock was to be all that the port was to witness of so indispensable a requirement in the equipment of a prosperous seaport. The North Dock was not a success financially, and in an engineering point of view its failure was conspicuous, exposed as its entrance was to the heavy seas that rolled up the harbour in stormy weather. But the troubles of the shareholders came to an end in the year 1847, when the York, Newcastle, and Berwick (now the North-Eastern) Railway Company purchased it, and in their possession it still remains.

By that time the battle of the South Docks had ceased to be waged, a strong Joint-stock Company having been formed, with Mr. George Hudson (then M.P. for Sunderland) at its head, for their construction. In the Parliamentary session of 1847 an Act was obtained, and under its provisions a commencement was made with the long-debated works. In the summer of 1850 the South Docks were formally opened, their entire water area, including a half-tide basin, being $21\frac{1}{2}$ acres. One remarkable feature of the scheme was the formation of an outlet, which led direct from the docks to the sea, and altogether independent of the river. This great undertaking was not completed until the year 1856, by which time an addition of thirteen acres had been made to the docks, the total cost of docks and outlets being about three quarters of a million sterling.

But while the dock agitation had been running its course, the Commissioners were steadily applying themselves to the improvement of the Wear. So far back as the year 1819 Sir John Rennie had laid down a quay line, but, as far as that identical scheme was concerned, it never became more than a piece of engineering drawing; and in 1853 the Admiralty, at the request of the Commissioners, sanctioned an important departure from Rennie's plan. The chief object which the Commissioners had in view by asking for permission to abandon the original quay line was a desire to add to the available area lying along the riverside for the accommodation of shipbuilders, iron vessels being by that time gradually growing in favour. The dredging of the stream was carried on with great persistency, serious obstacles to navigation were removed from the upper reaches, a silting basin was formed at the mouth of the river to aid in diminishing the sea disturbance in the harbour, and the bar had been greatly improved. With the opening of the South Docks, and their outlet to the sea, a keen rivalry had sprung up between the Commissioners and the Dock Company. The docks had proved less remunerative to their proprietors than had been anticipated, and this disappointment soon began to produce rather strained relations between the two bodies. But while they agreed, apparently, to hate each other for the love of the port, Sunderland, which, speaking metaphorically, had long been swaying at its old moorings, began to make sail on a new tack.

In wood shipbuilding, its great staple, the Wear had long occupied the leading place in the United Kingdom. For many years before the opening of the docks, shipowners from all parts of the country had resorted to Sunderland when bent on adding to their tonnage. In 1839 the number of new vessels launched on the Wear was

247; in 1840 the launches numbered 251, this being the highest total ever reached on the river. The average tonnage per vessel did not, however, exceed 250 tons in the two years named; but when the South Docks were opened a larger class of vessels began to make their appearance. In 1851, the year after the completion of the docks, only 146 vessels were launched, but their average tonnage had risen to 355. In 1852 there were 142 launches, with an average tonnage of 339; while in 1853 the launches had risen to 153, with an average tonnage of 449½. The shipment of coals, the Wear's chief export, also received a considerable impetus from the docks, for while, in 1849, the quantity of coal and coke exported amounted to 1,519,354 tons, it had reached, in 1850, 1,718,427 tons; and in 1856 the quantity had increased to 2,204,898 tons. Driven, by the impatience of their shareholders, to devise some mode of augmenting their receipts, the Dock Directors, in 1856, adopted the impolitic resolution of charging the dock rates on ships upon the ton burthen, instead of the ton register. Great public dissatisfaction followed, but the Directors justified the step by pointing to their low dividends, and the refusal of the River Commissioners to help them in any way, notwithstanding that the opening of the dock had largely increased the receipts of the Commissioners, who, under their Act, were entitled to dues on coals shipped in the docks, as well as in the river.

Out of this unsatisfactory state of things there

arose an agitation in favour of the Commissioners acquiring the docks, and in the end the supporters of an amalgamation of the river and docks as one concern, administered by a public board solely in the interest of the whole community, triumphed. In the Parliamentary session of 1859 a Bill was promoted by the Commissioners seeking legislative sanction to the scheme, and after a brief conflict with the municipal corporation, which sought to place six of its own members in the remodelled Board, the Commissioners at last became the owners of a fine dock property.

From this date the Trust made a new departure, and instead of its affairs being managed by a body of self-elected Commissioners, as had been the case since the year 1717, it became a popularly elected body. The shipowners, the coalowners, and the merchants were severally empowered to elect their own representatives, and the river-side landowners' representatives were to be elected by the Commission itself. The Admiralty and the Customs were to have each one representative, the North-Eastern Railway Company (as North Dock owners) one, and the Corporation of Sunderland one. The new *régime* rapidly commended itself to the favour of the shipping and mercantile interests, but for several years after their purchase of the Docks the Commissioners were compelled to encounter an unexpectedly heavy outlay in order fully to equip them for the work which was looked for from the new possession of the port. Undaunted, however, by the magnitude of its vastly increased obligations, the Trust proceeded to extend the water area both of the docks and the sea outlet. Additional graving-dock accommodation was provided for the larger class of vessels which were then finding their way to Sunderland; the direct outlet from the docks to the sea was deepened and otherwise improved; the harbour at the Narrows was cleared of a series of sunken rocks, and spirited efforts were made to foster the iron shipbuilding trade, which by that time—and chiefly through the enterprise of Mr. James Laing, the present Chairman of the Commission—was seriously threatening entirely to supplant the trade in wood. The revenue of the Board in due course received the impulse which had naturally been looked for as the result of the amalgamation, and while the total yearly receipts between the years 1840 and 1850 had averaged about £14,000, they amounted in 1863 (four years after the purchase of the docks) to £35,000 from the river and £52,000 from the docks, but out of this aggregate of £87,000 a sum of £18,000 had to be paid as interest to the dock shareholders. The subjoined table shows the gross revenue of the Trust from both sources from 1860 to 1883:—

Year.	Port. £	s.	d.	Dock. £	s.	d.	Total. £	s.	d.
1860	31,970	0	9	45,874	12	9	77,844	13	6
1861	35,489	10	0	50,907	2	9	86,396	12	9
1862	36,279	18	6	52,391	9	3	88,671	7	9
1863	35,542	5	3	52,036	12	3	87,578	17	6
1864	34,373	9	4	49,733	14	8	84,107	4	0
1865	34,925	14	3	53,972	17	8	88,898	11	11
1866	33,110	2	11	49,401	4	2	82,511	7	1
1867	34,207	11	11	51,965	7	2	86,172	19	1

Year.	Port.			Dock.			Total.		
	£	s.	d.	£	s.	d.	£	s.	d.
1868	35,307	3	2	52,985	6	11	88,292	10	1
1869	34,023	8	6	55,473	18	3	89,497	6	9
1870	35,772	1	8	53,797	5	8	89,569	7	4
1871	37,527	17	0	62,715	19	7	100,243	16	7
1872	35,362	16	2	65,570	19	5	100,933	15	7
1873	34,688	15	7	64,054	1	5	98,742	17	0
1874	36,431	7	9	67,479	1	9	103,910	9	6
1875	39,079	3	4	70,751	11	9	109,830	15	1
1876	41,269	4	3	66,297	14	5	107,566	18	8
1877	44,798	2	5	75,125	7	5	119,923	9	10
1878	46,454	9	1	75,090	3	6	121,544	12	7
1879	43,725	0	3	64,699	5	7	108,424	5	10
1880	49,100	7	6	74,143	16	6	1232,44	4	0
1881	50,064	14	8	76,242	7	6	126,307	2	2
1882	52,484	2	6	76,318	10	4	128,802	12	10
1883	56,289	3	4	82,892	17	6	139,182	0	10

While their exchequer was thus gradually strengthening, the Commissioners persevered in their course of judicious expenditure. Two additional warehouses were built, mainly for the storage of the increased importation of grain. Chain Cables and Anchor Testing Works were erected at a cost of £18,000, and improvements were effected in the deep-water channel at the docks for the development of the fish trade.

Towards the close of 1875 the attention of the Board began to be earnestly directed to a still greater undertaking than any of these, with the view of avoiding the detention caused to screw-colliers when they were compelled to wait for the tide; and to remedy this, so that vessels could enter direct from the sea at any time of the tide, it was proposed to construct a Lock at the Sea Outlet. The engineer to the Commissioners (Mr. H. H. Wake) in due course laid before the Board the plans he had been instructed to prepare, and the estimated cost of whose execution was £100,000. These plans were ultimately adopted, and a commencement was made with the works in 1877. In the autumn of 1880 the Lock was formally opened by the Earl of Durham (who is the largest shipper of coal in the port), the undertaking having been completed within a few pounds of Mr. Wake's estimate. This Lock is 481 ft. in length, 90 ft. in breadth, and at ordinary spring tides it has a depth of $29\frac{1}{2}$ ft., with, at the same time, a depth of 27 ft. on the outer cills. This work has proved to be most advantageous to the great fleets of screw-steamers, which are now, in very many instances, passed into the dock, loaded, and got ready for sea again, within the time during which they had formerly to wait for the tide. There is, at present, accommodation in the docks for 200 of the largest class of vessels, and the departure of steamers drawing 24 ft. is by no means an uncommon occurrence. The total water area of the docks (including the Sea Outlet, New Lock, tidal, and half-tidal basin) is a little over seventy-eight acres. There are nineteen coal-spouts in the docks, at which 15,000 tons per day can easily be shipped, while cargoes of 2,500 tons are frequently put on board in eight hours.

The shipbuilding trade had been completely revolutionised while all these varied improvements were in process of execution, wood vessels having altogether disappeared from the yards, of which there are now seventeen in the port, and five marine engine factories. The year 1863 may be described as the opening of the age of iron on the Wear, 17,724 tons of iron shipping having been launched during the twelvemonth. After that date the declension of wood shipping proceeded apace; and the progress of the trade from that time will be seen at a glance by the subjoined record of the number of ships built, with their aggregate and average tonnage, in the years named, the construction of wood ships having closed by about the year 1878:—

Year.	No. of Ships.	Gross Tons.	Average Tons.
1863	171	70,040	410
1864	153	71,987	470
1865	172	73,134	425
1866	145	62,719	432
1867	128	52,249	401
1868	131	70,302	$509\frac{1}{2}$
1869	122	72,420	$585\frac{1}{3}$
1870	103	70,084	$686\frac{1}{2}$
1871	97	81,903	$844\frac{1}{3}$
1872	122	134,825	$1,080\frac{1}{4}$
1873	95	99,371	1,046
1874	88	88,022	$1,000\frac{1}{4}$
1875	91	79,904	$878\frac{1}{19}$
1876	60	54,041	$900\frac{2}{3}$
1877	75	87,578	$1,167\frac{2}{5}$
1878	89	112,602	$1,265\frac{1}{5}$
1879	60	87,432	$1,457\frac{1}{5}$
1880	71	108,626	$1,529\frac{8}{10}$
1881	79	130,862	$1,656\frac{1}{2}$
1882	109	183,350	1,682
1883	120	207,254	1,727

The steady growth of their revenue, and the manifest desirability of keeping the port abreast of the times, induced the Commissioners, on the completion of the lock, to turn their attention more closely than they had done before to an unusually important project for improving the entrance to the river; and as the result of oft-renewed deliberations, it was resolved, in the early summer of 1883, to proceed with the contemplated work. The Wear has never claimed to be a harbour of refuge, but the undertaking in question will, undoubtedly, warrant it aspiring to such a distinction. The plan having received the sanction of the Board of Trade, operations were commenced at Roker, on the north side of the river last summer. The great feature of the scheme is the erection of two piers, each of which is to be formed of concrete. They will extend to a distance of 2,700 ft., where there will be a navigable depth of fully 35 ft.; and the estimated cost of the entire undertaking is £300,000. The extension of the coal trade that has followed each of the great events in the history of the port of Sunderland will be seen at a glance from the subjoined figures, which ought to be prefaced by a note of the shipments in 1836, when they amounted to 1,155,414 tons:—

Year.	Tons Shipped.
1840 (North Dock opened)	1,318,497
1850 (South Docks opened)	1,718,427
1856 (Sea Outlet opened)	2,204,898
1859 (River and Docks amalgamated)	2,606,513
1883 (Greatly improved Port and neighbouring coal-field developed)	3,958.564

During the year 1883, 7,310 vessels, registering 2,490,562 tons, cleared from the port. This was a decrease, as compared with the year 1882, of 208 vessels, but an increase of tonnage to the extent of 155,297 register tons. The increase of the coasting trade in 1883 was 2·7 per cent.; and the European trade increased 18·4 per cent. The average tonnage of vessels increased by 9·7 per cent.; and the increase of vessels over 500 tons was 16·8 per cent. The general export trade of the Wear has for its principal articles lime, glass bottles, and creosoted sleepers. Its imports are chiefly timber and grain; and in 1883 the quantity of the former was 107,001 loads, and 406,327 dozen of pit props. Of grain, the quantity imported was 173,672 quarters.

The expansion of the borough of Sunderland has kept pace with the advancement of the port. In 1851, the population, in round numbers, was 63,000; in 1884, it is close upon 120,000, within the Parliamentary boundary. Sunderland has often been termed the most American town in England; and in many respects this is an accurate description of a place on whose spirits the vicissitudes of commercial life exercise only the most bracing of influences.

The new Manor Quay Works of Messrs. J. L. Thompson & Sons, Sunderland, are fast approaching completion. With these new facilities a ship launched by this firm will be towed up the Wear a few yards, where she will be fitted up in all her departments and made ready for sea. Hitherto Messrs. Thomson have been obliged to take their launched ships into the North Dock for masts, engines, and other fixtures; and the new quay will effect a substantial saving in time, trouble, and money. These new works are on the river's shore, between those of Messrs. Dickinson and the Corporation Quay, and enjoy a frontage of 550 feet, with a width of 350 feet, reaching back to Huddlestone-street. A new block of offices has been built, and the works throughout have been fitted up with all the best modern appliances, including cranes, steam hammers, condensing engines, &c. This enterprising firm is also contemplating the construction of graving docks of about 450 feet in length. Depression in shipping has not dampened the enterprise and hope of Messrs. J. L. Thompson & Sons; and they intend to be ready when the present cloud lifts, and orders begin to flow. This spirit is creditable to the Wear, and has given it its high position among the shipbuilding rivers of the United Kingdom.

THE TAFF: CARDIFF.

The Taff is not an industrial river in the same sense as the Mersey and the Tyne, but it occupies a position somewhat identical with that of the Tawe. It is a fast flowing stream, and, indeed, its currents are too rapid to permit of navigation on any other than a very limited scale. Generally speaking it is shallow, but in times of rain it swells considerably, and rolls down with the appearance and force of a flood into the Bristol Channel. On these occasions it passes under Cardiff Bridge with great impetuosity, bearing upon its troubled surface trees and various *débris* which it has gathered in the hill districts. And when it sometimes meets the flowing tide, the accumulation of surging waters is very great.

For many years the Cardiff district has been protected from the inroads of these wild waters by embankments. Last year, however, a very high tide coming up the river found out a weak point in the banks at Grangetown, and the consequence was that that locality was flooded disastrously. There was no loss of life, but much deplorable inconvenience was occasioned to poor persons. Bread was immediately sent round by the Mayor in boats for the relief of the inhabitants, and a public subscription to enable them to meet their losses was set on foot. It should not be understood, however, that the Taff is always fierce and unruly. In its course from the Brecon Beacons many pleasant spots can be found, where the river flows serenely through beautiful landscapes. It broadens at Llandaff, where, for boating purposes, a capital weir has been formed. It passes east of the old cathedral, and then finds its way to Cardiff through a tract of picturesque and well-wooded land, the Sophia Gardens being the boundary on one side and the Castle grounds of the Marquis of Bute on the other. Looking at the river as it flows beyond the Cardiff Bridge, the spectator sees a broadening stream hurrying on, apparently in the direction of the Penarth Headland, which stands out boldly at a distance of two or three miles. The Taff finally flows into the Bristol Channel, a mile or two from this point of view, and near the outlet of the Ely River at Penarth.

Llandaff Cathedral has had a remarkable history. Its secluded site near the Taff is exceedingly venerable, but the structure itself, now restored, has undergone great vicissitudes. It is said that a church was founded in the ancient city when Christianity was first introduced into this country, and the original see was endowed in the sixth century. The founders were SS. Dubricius and Teilo. In 1107 the cathedral, formerly of small dimensions, was extended by Bishop Urban, and in later years other additions were made. After the Reformation the building was allowed to fall into a state of decay; it was put to various purposes, and within the old walls an Italian temple (afterwards removed) was erected in 1732. Great efforts were made some years ago to effect a restoration of the ancient edifice, and this was at length accomplished at considerable cost. In 1851 a choral service was celebrated here, after a lapse of more than a century and a half. The south-west tower and spire rise to a height of 200 feet, and add to the imposing effect of the western façade, which is in the Early Pointed style. Many of the old monumental effigies of knights, bishops, and ladies are preserved within the ancient fane, but in most cases they bear marks of their long exposure in the roofless ruins. Early in the sixteenth century a proposition was made to remove the see to Cardiff.

Cardiff Castle, the western grounds of which skirt the Taff, embraces many features of historical and architectural interest. It is being constantly added to by its owner, the Marquis of Bute, and occupies a very prominent position in the town. As to the story of the cruelty which is said to have been practised upon Robert, Duke of Normandy, in the twelfth century, the following reference by the Marquis of Bute in a paper read before the Royal Archæological Institute will not be without interest. His lordship said: "In the year 1108, Henry I., having taken prisoner his eldest brother, Robert, Duke of Normandy, imprisoned him in

Cardiff Castle, where he was confined for twenty-six years until his death in 1134. As he is said to have been at Devizes in 1128, when his son was killed, it is possible that he was occasionally allowed to change his abode. The authentic records concerning his imprisonment are very few and scanty, and it may be hoped that the gross cruelties, such as putting out his eyes, with which it is said to have been accompanied, are without actual foundation. Such stories, however, were rife at the time, and in the year 1119, when Pope Calixtus met Henry I. at Gisors, he remonstrated with the King upon his treatment of his brother, Henry replied that 'as for his brother, he had not caused him to be bound in fetters like a captive enemy, but treating him like a royal pilgrim worn out with long sufferings, had placed him in a Royal castle, and supplied his table and wardrobe with all kinds of luxuries and delicacies in great abundance.'" It is related that during the Civil War the library of Llandaff Cathedral, which included very rare MSS., was removed to Cardiff Castle "for security." It was, however, burnt by the partisans of Cromwell "with a great heap of prayer-books." It is highly edifying to learn also that "the Cavaliers of the country and the wives of several sequestered clergymen were invited one cold winter's day to warm themselves by the fire which was then made of the books there burnt."

The Sophia Gardens were so named after the late Marchioness of Bute, in accordance with whose desire they were opened to the public.

They are beautifully laid out, and comprise various ornamental attractions. Adjoining is the Sophia Gardens Field, which was thrown open to the public by the present Marquis. The Cardiff Arms Park, which is preserved by the same nobleman for the use of local cricket and other clubs, and which has often been the scene of very interesting gatherings, is on the eastern bank of the Taff, and lies nearer to the centre of the town.

On both sides of the Taff, for many miles before it reaches its outlet at Cardiff, there are large iron-works and collieries, and "Cardiff coal"—now known favourably all over the world—is extracted from the adjacent hills and valleys by many thousands of workmen. The coal districts of the neighbourhood are teeming with life.

The Taff may be considered the main artery of the local river system. From various adjoining valleys mountain streams flow into it. The railway system seems to follow the natural condition of things, branch lines coming out of these valleys and joining the Taff main railway. As the Rhondda and other streams are tributaries of the River Taff, so are many of the local valley lines feeders of the Taff Vale Railway. Everything tends Cardiff-wards, and owing to a powerful combination, in which nature herself would appear to have played no inconsiderable part, the little antiquated town of sixty or seventy years ago has to-day become, near the mouth of the Taff, the metropolis of South Wales, and the seat of a University College.

Let us note, however, that before the railway era the Taff relatively occupied a more important status as a commercial river. The trade of that time was of course small, but, proportionately, the river was more generally utilised. Two hundred years ago, Cardiff was described as being "two miles from the sea." Until recent years the Taff washed the old quay wall which occupied part of the site of Westgate-street, and small craft came up for coal cargoes, or, perchance, to discharge. We may imagine the Taff to have been the original means of developing Cardiff as a coal port. It was due, probably, to the position of the river that, ages ago, the first castle was erected; in ancient times the castle became the nucleus of a town establishment, and the quay on the Taff led the way for a more extended commerce, in connection with which docks and railways now play so prominent a part. The old town walls are now indicated only by scanty remains, and the quay walls have quite disappeared, although a small street still commemorates by name the ancient approach to the "Quay."

In days of old the Taff followed a sinuous course from Cardiff Bridge in the direction of Westgate-street and the Great Western Railway-station, but it has here been diverted into a straightened channel, much to the advantage of the surrounding land. The Docks which have brought the name of Cardiff into such repute in the shipping world, will be found lying near the coast of the Bristol Channel. The town, too, which may be said to have been formerly grouped round the old church of St. John—to which, by the bye, a fine embattled tower is attached—has outgrown its ancient limits in all directions; on most sides of the Docks streets have been established, and every week the Borough more and more approaches general consolidation. The main thoroughfare from the centre of the town to the Docks is Bute-road. A few years ago the distinction between "Town" and "Docks" was greater than it is now. The change is due to increased facilities of locomotion and to building operations, which have had the effect of making a more complete junction between these two localities. What is traditionally styled the "Town" is not what it was a hundred, or even ten years ago. Great improvements have taken place in all respects; streets have been widened, old premises have been pulled down, and many noble buildings erected. St. Mary-street, Crockherbtown, and the approach from Canton, compare favourably with the main streets of many ports and cities.

In speaking of the Taff in its industrial aspect, we can, perhaps, best exemplify the trade of the locality by noting briefly what has been done and what is being done at Cardiff, as it is to this place, situated on the plains intervening between the mountains and the sea, that the products of the Taff and adjacent valleys largely come. Go to Cardiff Docks, and you will see the evidences of the vast enterprise of the Dock promoters and shipowners; you will see the fruits of the labours

LOW WATER PIER.   PENARTH HEAD.

of an army of underground workers; and you will perceive, with interest, the devices which have been adopted to rapidly transmit the coal for shipment, and to put it on shipboard with expedition.

It has not been our purpose to give an imaginative description of the founding of Cardiff or of its Castle, nor can we stay to consider the value of legends which attribute certain strange adventures to King Arthur in the neighbourhood. All these things are of interest, but our object is rather to point out some of the main features in the commercial history of the town. In order to do this we have no need to go back more than a century. It was in 1798 that the Glamorganshire Canal, connecting Merthyr and Cardiff, was completed. The older method of bringing coal and iron to the latter place on the backs of mules was thus superseded by water communication, and the sea end of the canal was ultimately enlarged, so as to afford more accommodation to the class of vessels that once frequented the port. The canal, in its course from Merthyr to the sea, makes a descent, through locks, of about 600 feet. The work promoted by the Crawshays may, therefore, be regarded as one that involved much enterprise and engineering skill, and it is deserving of full recognition on this account, although it has now been surpassed by more modern means of transit. What its future may be is not quite certain. Only recently the undertaking was acquired by the owner of the present Docks, the Marquis of Bute. The iron trade, now somewhat depressed, provided much traffic for the canal, and the increasing outputs both of iron and coal at the great works in the Merthyr district demanded further accommodation. It was then that the late Marquis of Bute, the chief local land owner, came forward, and built on the Cardiff foreshore, at a cost of about £350,000, the West Bute Dock. This undertaking, which was completed in 1839, appears to have given a great impetus more particularly to foreign shipments, although the increased trade did not immediately take place. It now only ranks as one of the smaller local docks. Its leading dimensions are as follows: Basin, 300 ft. long, width 200 ft.; entrance to basin, 45 ft. wide; lock, 152 ft. long, 36 ft. wide; dock (18 acres), 4,000 ft. long, 200 ft. wide. The quayage is 8,800 ft. in length. The depth of water on the sill at ordinary spring tides is 28 ft. 9 in., and at neap tides of 18 ft. 8 in. There are here 13 coal staiths, 3 ballast cranes, and 4 lifting cranes. The graving dock connected with the West Dock is 235 ft. long and 12 ft. deep. Total water area, 19½ acres.

Captain W. H. Smyth, R.N., who took a prominent part in the establishment of these dock works, stated in his "Nautical Observations" on the locality, that—"It was originally intended that the sea gates, or entrance from the Bristol Channel into the Bute Ship Canal, should have been placed at the Eastern Hollows, and that the entire length of the canal should be protected on each side by stone quay walls, with towing paths

ENTRANCE TO THE BUTE DOCKS.

along which vessels were to be drawn to the wet dock, at the commencement of which another pair of gates were to be placed. The estimate for these works, which were designed by Mr. James Green, of Exeter, was £70,000; but when contracts were sought to be let, although no real engineering difficulties existed, no contractors could be found to tender for a given sum, in consequence of the unforeseen difficulties which might arise in the operation, carried on in tidal water. Under these circumstances, Mr. (afterwards Sir William) Cubitt was called in, and at his suggestion the original ship canal was abandoned, and in lieu thereof an open tidal cut or entrance channel was made through the mud from the Eastern Hollows to the shore, to be kept open by sluices from or near the dock gates. Vessels are now consequently towed by steam tugs, or sail up this entrance channel, instead of being tracked by land along towing paths as originally intended. The wet dock or basin was constructed pretty nearly on the original plan, but with the addition of a sea basin with a lock between it and the dock, which became necessary on the abandonment of the ship canal with its sea gates. Previous to the dock itself being commenced, a channel or feeder was cut from a point in the Taff some two miles above the mouth of that stream, with the object of supplying the projected dock with a constant supply of fresh water. This heavy and expensive piece of work was rendered necessary by the fact that the tidal water of the Bristol Channel is unsuited for use in a dock, owing to the large quantity of mud it holds in suspension, and the heavy deposit resulting from it when in a state of quietude. The actual cost of the work was £350,000; viz., £220,000 in hard cash, and the remainder in limestone and timber, obtained from Lord Bute's estates. On the 9th of October, 1839, the new dock was opened amidst general and enthusiastic manifestations of joy on the part of the inhabitants."

The Taff Vale Railway was opened in 1841, and the South Wales Railway, now part of the Great Western system, was also established. Owing to the expansion of trade, the dock accommodation again became insufficient, and in 1851—three years after the death of the late Marquis of Bute—the trustees of the Bute estate commenced the building of a second and larger dock, viz., the East Bute Dock. The basin was opened in 1855, and the whole of the undertaking was completed in 1859. At about the same period the Rhymney Railway, which connects Rhymney and Cardiff, was constructed by a company, and a still greater development of trade was inaugurated. The East dock added 44 acres to the port accommodation for shipping, and it afforded facilities for vessels of larger draught than any which had before frequented the older dock. The dimensions of this work are: Sea lock, 220 ft. long, 55 ft. wide; basin ($2\frac{1}{4}$ acres), 380 ft. by 250 ft.; inner lock, 200 ft. by 49 ft.; dock, 4,300 ft. by 300 ft. and 500 ft. (*i.e.*, 1,000 ft. by

300 ft. and 3,300 ft. by 500 ft.). Quayage, 9,360 ft. Depth of water on sill at ordinary spring tides, 31 ft. 8 in.; and at neap tides, 21 ft. 8 in. The coal staiths connected with this dock number 20. The engineers were originally Sir John Rennie and Mr. W. S. Clark, but the plans were subsequently modified for extensions by Mr. Walker, in conjunction with Mr. Clark. It may here be stated that the demand for Cardiff coal continued to increase so enormously that a company was formed to supplement the dock accommodation, with a dock at Penarth. This dock, when completed, had an area of 17 acres. It passed into the hands of the Taff Vale Railway Company in 1865, and it has now been extended by an additional acreage of $5\frac{1}{2}$. In 1874 another Bute dock, commonly called the Roath Basin, because it will, in fact, be the basin of a new dock of $33\frac{1}{2}$ acres now in course of construction, was completed. It gave an additional water space of $11\frac{1}{2}$ acres. This dock, or basin, has a depth of water on the sill of 35 ft. $8\frac{1}{2}$ in. at spring tides, and of 25 ft. $8\frac{1}{2}$ in. at neap tides. It is constantly filled with large ocean-going steamers. The new dock, which is being constructed at this moment, will be about 2,400 ft. long by 600 ft. wide. It will be approached from the Roath basin by a lock 600 ft. long and 80 ft. wide; the depth of water over the sills will be 30 ft. at ordinary spring tides, and 26 ft. at ordinary neap tides. The contractors are Messrs. Nelson & Co., Carlisle. The first portion of the dock is to be completed in

March, 1885, and the whole of the work a year after. The manager of the Bute Docks is Mr. W. T. Lewis, and the engineer, Mr. J. M'Connochie; dockmaster, Mr. J. Fraser. An energetic attempt is being made by these gentlemen to provide adequate means for dealing with the ever-growing trade of the port. New coal tips, movable and otherwise, have been added wherever thought desirable, and the work of loading vessels with " black diamonds," iron, and other commodities, seems to go on without intermission, day and night.

The Taff Vale Railway is perhaps the most important local mineral line. During the first half-year of 1841 the receipts on the first section of 16 miles then open were £2,902 for passengers and £706 for goods. The Dinas branch was opened in the same year, and shares were sold at a discount. The first dividend was 28s. per cent., in 1841. Various branch railways were incorporated, and in 1883 the capital amounted to £2,830,000 : the receipts were £769,246, and the average dividend was 17 per cent.! In the same year the Company conveyed over their lines 9,421,803 tons of minerals and goods, of which they shipped 2,274,000 tons at Penarth.

The Rhymney Railway, which is also a great feeder for Cardiff, communicates with Rhymney and Nantybwch. It proceeds through the historic valley wherein the ruins of Caerphilly Castle stand, and is the means of conveying to the docks many thousands of tons of minerals every week. The dividends, at one time very small, now average 10 per cent. Mr. John Boyle, the original chairman of the directors, still presides over the destinies of this railway. It may also be observed that for some years he managed the Bute Docks. Mr. W. T. Lewis has, in fact, succeeded him in that respect.

The borough of Cardiff was in 1875 extended, but the growth and influx of population during the present century, in consequence of the rapid advances of local trade, will be generally indicated by the following table:—

Date.	Houses.	Population.
1801	327	1,018
1811	491	2,457
1821	671	3,521
1831	1,296	6,187
1841	1,832	10,077
1851	2,621	18,351
1861	5,161	32,954
1871	8,156	59,494
1881	12,137	85,378
1884	est. 16,000	100,000

In the course of evidence in opposition to the Barry Dock and Railway Bill before the House of Commons' Committee in June, it was stated by the manager of the Bute Docks that, including the prospective expenditure of half a million on the new dock, the total outlay on the dock works was £3,160,000. He intimated also that the Marquis of Bute was rapidly improving the entrance. The channel was being dredged by a powerful machine, which had removed 300,000 tons during the six months it had been in operation. As to the capacity of the Cardiff and Penarth

Docks, present and prospective, the conclusion he had arrived at after the experience of the month prior was that they would be able to ship annually 15,179,229 tons of coal, and provide for an import trade of 2,276,186 tons. He had not the slightest doubt that with movable tips, proper railway accommodation, and additional storage sidings, they would be able to do even more than that. In order to make ample provision for the import timber trade, Lord Bute had acquired practically the whole of the Glamorganshire Canal property.

The coal resources of South Wales appear to be inexhaustible. The demand at Cardiff and other local ports continues to increase, and yet the extended output at the collieries is well maintained. The President of the South Wales Institute of Engineers (Mr. James Colquhoun, F.G.S.) recently made an interesting reference to the progress of local trade, and he quoted the folowing figures as to the produce of coal in South Wales:

	1882.	1883.
Glamorganshire	16,393,253	17,708,940
Breconshire	143,753	164,438
Carmarthenshire	486,796	664,102
Monmouthshire	5,721,961	6,345,503
Pembrokeshire	71,615	92,650
Total	22,817,378	24,975,633

The output of the United Kingdom in 1883 had risen to 156,499,977 tons. Mr. Colquhoun expressed his surprise that in a district so rich in minerals, and with such immense facilities for the production of iron and steel, shipbuilding was not in a more flourishing condition on the coast. Chepstow, he said, had been the most important shipbuilding place, and from 1879 to that date had built 12,796 total gross registered tonnage. That, although showing some advance, pointed to the fact that it would be interesting to discover a reason why the industry had not received greater attention from the enterprising people who were largely concerned in the prosperity of South Wales. He thought there would be no difficulty in obtaining a supply of skilled men in the shipbuilding profession.

Cardiff is now the first coal-exporting port in the world. The progress she has made in order to attain this position is most striking. In 1844 the registered tonnage of vessels, inwards and outwards, was 184,405; in 1845 it had risen to 298,576, and in 1846 to 327,637. In 1844 the shipments of coal amounted to 256,332 tons; iron 8,497 tons; in 1845 353,890 tons of coal were shipped, and 70,085 tons of iron, and in 1846 415,115 tons of coal and 66,171 tons of iron. Last year (1883) the quantity of coal shipped at this port was 6,761,455 tons! The shipments of iron amounted during the same period to 108,510 tons, coke 25,069 tons, patent fuel 166,823 tons, and the amount of coal sent coastwise was 1,038,596 tons. In the aggregate as well as in the foreign tonnage of coal shipments Cardiff has passed Newcastle. Great advance has also been made in the number of locally-owned vessels. In 1840 there were 64 vessels registered here, with a tonnage of 6,057;

in 1878 there were 204 vessels, with a tonnage of 70,911; and in 1883, 313 vessels, with a tonnage of 159,977.

The following is a statement of vessels that have entered Cardiff during the last few years.

	Sailing Vessels.	Tons.	Steam Vessels.	Tons.
1880	2,375	885,347	1,837	1,171,254
1881	2,096	824,001	1,712	1,183,774
1882	1,899	770,208	1,866	1,381,543
1883	1,656	615,103	2,106	1,737,040

VESSELS CLEARED.

	Sailing Vessels.	Tons.	Steam Vessels.	Tons.
1880	3,379	1,408,524	2,983	2,054,681
1881	2,948	1,344,301	3,000	2,301,153
1882	2,587	1,213,877	3,342	2,686,183
1883	2,429	1,181,374	3,719	3,134,475

These figures at once demonstrate the increased capacity of the steamships which frequent the port.

Coal and coke, foreign and coastwise, shipped during the last ten years reached the tonnages below specified:—

Year.	Foreign.		Coastwise.	
	Coal.	Coke.	Coal.	Coke.
1874	2,924,638	7,099	837,384	894
1875	2,800,510	2,868	74,913	595
1876	3,508,755	5,160	865,214	843
1877	3,658,003	16,128	808,410	1,599
1878	4,100,221	14,174	814,871	479
1879	4,305,793	18,737	826,044	1,209
1880	4,997,450	25,268	864,899	1,127
1881	5,496,442	17,999	933,505	858
1882	5,799,919	28,850	951,197	764
1883	6,761,455	25,069	1,038,596	690

The chief imports are iron ore, pitwood, bricks, corn, flour, &c. There are capacious warehouses for storage purposes, and pre-eminent among the proprietors of flour mills and grain warehouses is the firm of Messrs. Spiller & Co.

The establishment of a Harbour Trust at Cardiff is a subject which has been mooted on various occasions, but nothing has yet been done in the matter. The docks are regulated by the Bute officials, and, owing to the enormous development of shipments, it has been suggested that a representative control would be most suitable for the port. In the course of a recent correspondence between the solicitor of the Marquis of Bute and the solicitors to the promoters of the proposed Barry Dock, it was intimated, in fact, that the Marquis of Bute would not be averse to the establishment of a Harbour Trust on certain equitable terms, provided that the Barry Dock scheme was abandoned; but the latter condition was not agreed to. The local pilotage is regulated by a representative Board, and the shipowners of the port have established an influential Chamber of Commerce and Shipowners' Association.

Cardiff and Penarth are largely frequented by seamen, as it will be understood when it is mentioned that during last year the number of men engaged at both places was 46,340. Mission rooms are provided for them in various parts of the locality, and near the Cardiff Pier Head is an excellent Sailors' Home, which was founded by the late Marchioness of Bute. "Poor Jack" is fairly well cared for. Great attention is bestowed upon him by the local officials of the Mercantile Marine and Board of Trade. These two departments, together with the docks post-office, are located in a large new building at the docks. The Board of Trade officials are: Inspector, Mr. W. H. Neate; Engineers' Surveyors, Mr. Foxdale, Mr. R. Mayor, and Mr. Butterworth; Shipwright Surveyor, Mr. T. H. Slogett; Mercantile Marine Chief Superintendent of the district, Mr. W. Turner; Assistant Superintendent, Mr. C. Hughes. The collector of Customs at this port is Mr. G. M. Douglas.

Speaking of Cardiff generally, it may be said that it abounds in important mercantile and other institutions. The town, as a whole, is well looked after by the municipal authorities, and no expense is spared in order to remove eye-sores and to improve the streets. Enterprise is the order of the day. An extensive new waterwork system is about to be inaugurated, and although bickerings sometimes arise between various sections, the general good is usually sought to be advanced, and we may hope that the day when Cardiff is to be "dismembered" (*vide* the words of the sitting Member, Sir E. J. Reed) is a long way off. In connection with the port, the names of the late and the present Marquis of Bute cannot fail to be remembered. Both father and son have spent a great deal of money on these docks, and they deserve to be appreciated for what they have done. At the same time, it must cheerfully be granted that the late Lord Bute was backed up in his enterprises by a host of colliery owners, railway promoters, and other capitalists. There are yet branches of trade in which Cardiff may develop. Dry docks have been constructed on a liberal scale; others are projected; shipbuilding is now being fostered, and several vessels have lately been built at the port. It is in exports that Cardiff chiefly excels, but imports have increased. A considerable American trade has been cultivated, and there are signs of an earnest desire to place the port on the most permanent commercial basis.

THE AVON: BRISTOL.

The Avon, the Gloucestershire Avon, as it is sometimes called, to distinguish it from its sister river by Stratford, is charming in parts for its lovely scenery, and fascinating throughout for its wealth of traditions and associations. Its narrow gorge was in the far past the doorway through which the Norsemen obtained entrance to a series of fertile valleys so rich in plunder as well to repay for the long and dangerous voyage around the South of England; and centuries later its waters, for the rich prizes which they bore, were eagerly watched from the Severn, sometimes by Irish freebooters, and sometimes by outlaws from Lundy Isle, who "were always doeing much mischief by piracie." The Welsh, too, took a hand, but they were apparently moved more by desire of monopoly than plunder, for "they stole the dregs and floats from the Avon in order to compel the hiring of the Welsh trows to carry goods, and the giving the Welshmen what they pleased to ask." The incoming tide of the river in 1069 bore the fleet of the three sons of Harold, who made what was almost the last effort to expel the Norman invader; and long after its outflowing waters carried numerous expeditions to Ireland to take possession of the liberal gift of that country made by Pope Adrian to the Second Henry. Still farther on in time, privateering became the favourite relaxation of the dwellers on its banks, and when nought was stirring at home, they were wont to start on a cruise for a "Frenchman" or a "Spaniard." Many a rich prize they took, and many a great fortune owed its foundation to the well-filled hold of an enemy's merchantman. Not always, indeed, did they go abroad to attack the foreigner. If his provision-laden craft came to their port in a time of scarcity, Woe be to him! for he must sell at their price, not his. Especially was he in danger if his cargo consisted of butter, for the people seem to have held a firm determination to pay no more than $2\frac{1}{2}$d. a pound for that useful commodity. When it rose above that figure all the convenient "Kinterkins" were seized *vi et armis*. The frequent result of these proceedings was a pitched battle, in one of which, history tells us, so much blood was shed as to "ensanguine the waters," which, on several other occasions, by the way, were reddened in a much more innocent manner when Turkish Corsairs were captured in mimic fight by Christian vessels for the delectation of royal visitors to Bath and Bristol.

The story of the Avon is the story of Bristol, for though the river from its source in the Lower Cotswolds of Gloucestershire to its point of junction with the Severn has a winding course of seventy-two miles, it is navigable for ocean vessels no farther than this city, seven miles from its mouth; and so narrow and tortuous is its channel for even this distance, that only undaunted energy in her citizens could have kept Bristol through all of England's history up to the last century the next after London in maritime affairs. As early as the twelfth century her port was said to be full of ships from Ireland, Norway, and the Mediterranean, and her vessels were penetrating to every accessible part of Europe. From this time on, there was no trading town where Bristol vessels where not sometimes seen, not excepting such outlying and far-off places as Archangel, the Canaries, and even Thule in Iceland; but not *Ultima* Thule for long, for her indomitable mariners soon passed beyond, and were the first, under the leadership of the Cabots, to cast anchor by the mainland of the new continent. As time went on, and new discoveries were made, and new openings found for commerce, the passion for adventurous trade so permeated her citizens that "there was scarcely a shopkeeper who had not a venture on board some ship bound for Virginia or the Antilles." Such a spirit was sure to result in great activity and enterprise, and the traffic on the Avon grew apace, until in the latter part of the last century it reached its highest relative development. In 1764, for instance, a representative year of this period, 2,353 ships entered the port, and the

CLIFTON SUSPENSION BRIDGE.

customs duties collected were £195,000, against £70,000 at Liverpool. The principal trade of Bristol was now with the West Indies, with America, and with Africa; and being connected by various waterways with Birmingham and the North, she could send out their manufactures as well as her own, bringing back in her vessels rich freights of sugar, rum, mahogany, tobacco, rice, tar, deer-skins, timber, fur, logwood, indigo, ivory, palm-oil, and gold-dust; all redolent of the romance of commerce, now, alas! so entirely gone. A less adventurous, but by no means unimportant traffic was also maintained with various European ports, especially with those on the Baltic and the Mediterranean, and with Hamburg and parts of Norway. All these outlets not proving sufficient for her superabundant energies, she tried a fling at the whales, but this not turning out sufficiently lucrative for ideas enlarged by Colonial and African trade, was abandoned.

And now Bristol began to feel the need of better port accommodation. The shipping, at this period, "used to lie securely on a soft bed of mud" when the tide was out, a state of things manifestly impossible to continue. Various comprehensive plans were considered for providing a system of floating docks commensurate with the trade, and after deliberation so long continued as to bring the date into the present century, the bold expedient was adopted of providing a new course for some three miles of the tidal Avon, and of locking in and dockizing the old channel, which ran through almost the heart of the city. Upon the completion of this great work in 1809, Bristol was enabled to claim great advantage for her port. It now had 84 acres of floating harbour, most conveniently situated and liberally supplied with all known conveniences for handling cargo; its lock gates were seven miles one chain from a great estuary, the Severn, which was accessible from the Bristol Channel and the sea at all tides and times; its river, the Avon, for that seven miles one chain had sufficient depth for the then average draught of vessels; and the King-road, the meeting-point of the two waters, was a safe and commodious roadstead, with a good holding ground. But these signal advantages were neutralised in part by the indifference of the citizens to half a century of apathetic management and excessive charges. The completion of the Docks marks a period in Bristol annals, and the people seemed disposed to rest on their laurels. The old maritime enterprise was gone, and from this time on, the history of the Port is a history of delay, and doubt, and indecision. For the first time in her existence Bristol yielded up the control of the waterfront, and the new docks were constructed and managed by a private company, which, as the future proved only too conclusively, was most unfortunately constituted. Its directing body numbered 27, chosen in equal numbers by the shareholders, the Corporation, and the Society of Merchant Venturers, the latter a survival of the companies of mediæval times, and which should only have continued to exist, if at all, as an almoner of charities. The Corporation being in these years thoroughly unrepresentative, and composed of men who belonged to an era almost past; and the Merchant Venturers being even less alive to the needs of the hour, it is obvious that Bristol at the beginning of a time when every energy was needed to keep her in the front rank, put in charge of her port the very elements least likely to possess the necessary qualities.

During the time of private dock management, which ended only in 1848, the foreign import trade of the port was gradually increasing, but only increasing about three-fourths as fast as the trade of the rest of the United Kingdom. The average annual income of the docks for the first decade of their existence, ending 1825, was £18,500; for the second £24,300; for the third, £22,000; and for the fourth, ending 1845, £29,500.

The unsatisfactory commercial progress of these years may be accounted for in several ways. The manumission, about 1830, of the West Indian slaves, an Act that will stand for ever as a monument of England's justice, was a fatal blow at one of the greatest of the industries of the city on the Avon. The planters who lived there locked up their compensation grants in public securities; the imports of sugar fell, and the refineries one by one were compelled to cease operations, though other causes besides cessation of slavery helped them to their ruin. The African trade ceased to be as lucrative as formerly, and was no longer pursued with the same energy and to the same extent. The building of railways connecting South Wales and the extreme West of England with London diverted considerable of its domestic commerce from Bristol, and it ceased to be in more than name the capital of the West. And while the old trades that had made the city were dying, no effort was made to attract new; conservative and unenterprising elements, as we have seen, were in control; and new lines of traffic were being laid down, indeed were already fixed, with Liverpool as their terminus, but they passed the Bristol Channel unnoticed and unsought, with their ships barred out by excessive port charges, the main reason, after all, for the slow advance of the city. How important a factor in retarding the growth of the commerce of the Avon these almost prohibitive rates were may be seen by a glance at this table, which shows the proportionate local taxation on the trade of several ports in the year 1832, after, it should be noted, several considerable reductions had already been made by the dock company.

	*			†			‡			§		
	£	s.	d.	£	s.	d.	£	s.	d.	£	s.	d.
Bristol	0	2	6½	1	0	0	1	0	0	1	0	0
Liverpool	0	1	8½	0	9	11	0	11	5	0	6	1½
London	0	1	2¼	0	8	11	0	10	4	0	3	4
Hull	0	1	7	0	6	9½	0	7	3	0	2	5
Gloucester	—			0	6	0	0	6	2	0	1	9

* Mean rate payable on vessels per ton.
† Mean rate payable on vessels and goods taken together.
‡ Average mean rate payable on one year's import of twenty-three principal articles.
§ Average mean rate payable on seven articles most heavily taxed in Bristol.

And these rates were maintained at that period

in the history of the world when every effort should have been made to attract commerce. The age of steamships was beginning, the immense trade with the United States was developing. The gates of Bristol were shut when the very walls should have been levelled.

And yet, in 1837, occurred an event that should have marked the beginning of a new era. The *Great Western*, the first steamer to cross the Atlantic under conditions proving its practicability, was launched into the floating harbour from the shipyards of William Patterson. She started for New York on the eighth day of April, 1838, arriving there after a voyage of fifteen days ten hours' duration; and her return trip occupied fourteen days. Such a brave beginning deserved surely a good ending, and it was reasonably to be expected that she would be the pioneer of a regular line of steamers that would bring with them fame and fortune to Bristol, and that would make of her port the last European milestone in the great highway connecting New York with London and the Continent. But the immediate result of the success of the *Great Western* was a line, not from the Avon, but from the Mersey, and she herself was soon transferred to other places, taking with her more than half of the direct export trade of Bristol; and all this was done despite certain advantages possessed by the old home port over that of Liverpool. It was in more direct line between New York and London; it could be reached by a shorter course, thereby saving time and coal. This latter it could provide cheaper, a most important consideration. It enabled the steamers to avoid the dangers of the Irish Sea and St. George's Channel; and, lastly, it was more accessible, barring the seven miles of Avon navigation (now eliminated by a dock at its mouth). On the other hand, the port of Liverpool had the signal advantage of close proximity to a manufacturing district that consumed largely the imports, and at the same time provided a return cargo. It was already the terminus of fixed lines of commerce, made by the packets, and it had become a radiating centre for inland roads and waterways leading in every direction. Its citizens appreciated the importance of low duties and charges on shipping, and, besides, kept a keen look-out for every means of advancing themselves. Before the people of Bristol had done congratulating themselves on the success of the *Great Western*, Mr. Cunard had four steamers running at regular intervals to New York, and thus the Avon lost its chance.

The exactions of the Bristol port authorities were not viewed with indifference by all, and persistent attempts were made to arouse public sentiment to the pressing need for immediate action; but it was not until 1845 that there came a unanimous demand for a radical change. In consequence of this demand an Act was procured three years later " enabling the Municipal Corporation to resume their ancient rights as owners and conservators of the river and harbour by taking upon themselves the responsibilities of the Dock Company, amounting to between £500,000 and £600,000, which thus became a charge upon the Municipality ; " and the ratepayers also consented to be taxed fourpence in the pound, in order that the dues on ships and goods might be lowered. Acting under the provisions of this Bill, the Town Council at once made sweeping changes, and general reductions of at least 50 per cent. in respect of ships, and 20 per cent. in respect of goods. The inevitable and satisfactory result of the altered conditions was a striking and immediate increase in the number of ships entering the port. The first decade of municipal control showed an advance of 66 per cent. over the last corresponding period of the Company's management; whereas a comparison made between the two last decades of the private control shows an increase of only 33 per cent., or exactly one-half.

But the people had no sooner got rid of the incubus of the Dock Company than they found themselves confronting the beginnings of a new difficulty. Ships began to be built larger and larger, and the Avon remained the same. What was possible with care for a vessel of a thousand tons became difficult indeed to one of 1,500, and impossible to one of 2,000. What was to be done? became the burning question, and everybody had an answer, and every answer was different. After long discussion, however, extending over many years, the people became almost unanimous as to the necessity of a dock at the mouth of the Avon, directly accessible from the magnificent roadstead at Kingroad. Eminent engineers, several of whom were consulted by the Corporation, concurred in this opinion, which was also endorsed by the engineer of the Bristol Docks, a high authority; but the Town Council, moved by fear of encouraging what might grow into a rival, and by fear of depreciation of city property, did nothing. At length, weary of waiting for the Municipality to act, a private company took hold of the matter, and after obtaining authority from Parliament, immediately began (in 1864) the construction of the much-needed docks.

While they were building, other evidences of progress and activity were visible. A second and smaller dock was started at the mouth of the river. The Great Western Steamship Line, started in 1870, had added materially to its fleet, and was now carrying passengers and cargo at short and regular intervals to New York. Its steamers did not pretend to compete in size and appointments with the Liverpool liners, but that they were all that was necessary to a safe and comfortable Transatlantic voyage the writer of this can testify from personal experience. The Bristol City line of steamers, exclusively for cargo, was inaugurated during this period. Both these Companies still maintain their fleets, and though participating in the prevailing depression, make their trips regularly. The coasting trade at this time also received a considerable impetus, and steamers regularly plied to many of the Irish and English ports, and to Glasgow, in Scotland, and also to many of the Continental commercial cities. These various channels of export were, and still are, utilised to carry the manufactures of Bristol; for, though the banks of the Avon have no one predominating industry, yet all branches of trade are represented, and the yearly aggregate of products of all kinds is no mean figure.

The new dock was completed in 1877, and its opening in February of that year was hailed by all Bristol as the beginning of a period when the Avon was to have "its fair share of ocean steam trade," which was certain to be attracted by the facilities offered by the new enterprise, for the dimensions of the now completed dock were such as to admit all but the largest steamers; its length was 1,400 feet, with an entrance lock one-third as long, and it had a depth of water on its sill of 27 ft. at the lowest neap tide of the year. It was accessible at all times and tides by means of the safe and easily-navigable Bristol Channel, whose mouth was most favourably situated for the Atlantic trade. The Town Council shared the prevailing opinion that these advantages would bring larger vessels, and they held that "while the new docks would probably be a keen competitor with the Bristol Docks for every branch of trade," yet that the two would "work in harmony and flourish together," and to carry out this, perhaps, optimistic idea, and to enable the home docks to "contend on fair terms with an efficient and well-situated rival, they proceeded to a considerable expenditure to improve the navigation of the Avon. They did not wish nor intend, however, to do more than to effectually open the river to sailing vessels of 1,200 tons and steamers of 800 tons register. The larger vessels they left to the new docks; and as they had had none of these before, they hoped that the new undertaking would build up its own trade, which would be an entirely new one, and leave them undisturbed in their old connection with the "smaller fry of the deep."

It soon became apparent that no fresh commerce was attracted to the dock at the mouth of the Avon, and that it was becoming—indeed, had already become—a most energetic and successful competitor for the trade of Bristol. While the foreign tonnage entering the port, which now must be considered to include the two docks, was actually 3,000 tons less in 1878 than in 1876; of this decreased amount no less than 159,000 tons were diverted to the dock at Avonmouth, so that in the second year of its existence the private Company secured nearly 31 per cent. of Bristol foreign commerce, besides making something of an inroad into its coasting trade. The income of the City Docks averaged £73,000 for the five years ending with 1877, and was £71,000 for the year 1876; but in 1878 the revenue fell off to £59,000, which was actually £10,000 less than the average annual expense had been for the five years preceding. And the competition about this time was rendered even more severe by the opening of a second and smaller dock at Portishead, near the mouth of the

THE AVON: BRISTOL.

Avon. The following table of entries shows the division of traffic in later years, and will also indicate the extent of the commerce of the Port :—

1881.	From Foreign.		Irish & Coastwise.		TOTAL.	
	Vessels.	Tons.	Vessels.	Tons.	Vessels.	Tons.
Bristol	721	278,771	7,021	587,342	7,742	866,113
Avonmouth	138	150,450	1,700	94,488	1,838	244,938
Portishead ...	63	55,855	—	—	63	55,855
	922	485,076	8,721	681,830	9,643	1,166,906
1882.						
Bristol	755	323,278	6,674	597,250	7,429	920,528
Avonmouth	148	164,134	1,411	74,250	1,559	238,384
Portishead ...	56	60,124	—	—	56	60,124
	959	547,536	8,085	671,500	9,044	1,219,036
1883.						
Bristol	812	376,921	6,408	590,575	7,220	967,496
Avonmouth	148	174,522	1,143	59,212	1,291	233,734
Portishead ...	44	46,744	—	—	44	46,744
	1,004	598,187	7,551	649,787	8,555	1,247,974

The income of the City Docks for these three years was £40,125, £41,100, and £46,875 respectively. When we compare these figures with the income prior to the year 1878 we see at once how great reductions have been made to meet the competition at the mouth of the river, for here is a falling-off of some £24,000 per annum, notwithstanding a large increase of tonnage.

That such ruinous competition must not continue was the general opinion as soon as the figures for the first year were out, and attempts were made by the town authorities to inaugurate a plan by which all interests could work together in harmony; but no such arrangement could be maintained, as the private docks, having been opened at a time of general and world-wide depression, were forced to give every concession to attract vessels. The conflict became more and more severe, and it was seen that there was but one course open to the city, and that was to buy the docks; but even this was a choice of evils, for it was proven that even as sole owner the Municipality would be obliged to meet an annual loss, there not being trade enough at this depressed period for so large an area of docks; but this loss would be about half what the city was subjected to under the existing circumstances. Besides, when the inevitable reaction came in commercial interests, the city would be in a position, if it controlled the entire shipping accommodation of the port, to take the fullest possible advantage of the increased activity. So it was wisely decided to purchase the docks, provided they could be got on equitable terms; and negotiations, having this end in view, were entered into with the companies. After considerable delay and much discussion, an agreement was arrived at by which their properties are to be transferred to the city on the 1st of September next upon payment of a sum closely approximating £800,000, and provided the agreement is sanctioned by Parliament.

While the progress of the port of Bristol has

been since 1848 in proportion with the advance of the rest of the Kingdom, it has been held, and justly held, that its geographical position with regard to the United States, its proximity to great coal-fields, its nearness to London, the accessibility of the Bristol Channel from the ocean at all tides, and the considerable extent of country for which the city is a distributing centre, entitle the port to a rate of progress greater than the average and more nearly commensurate with that of Liverpool; and it is hoped that this acquisition of docks may, when the clouds of adversity hanging over the commerce of the world are dissolved by the bright sun of prosperity, be the beginning of a series of improvements conceived on a grand scale, and including the dockizing of the entire Avon, thus exchanging for a tortuous and narrow channel a magnificent dock extending for ten miles, and capable of holding in its shelter all the navies of the world.

SOUTHAMPTON.

The name of Southampton is derived from "Anton," the ancient name of the River Test, whose estuary forms the upper part of Southampton Water. In the Doomsday Book the "Town" is spelt "Hantun," the prefix South probably arising from its relative position to Northam, a hamlet in the same borough, on the banks of the Itchen. Though we have no proof that Southampton was a town in the time of the Romans, yet undoubtedly it is a place of great antiquity, and the rise of the town may be assumed to date from the decay of the Roman station, Clausentum, at Bitterne, on the River Itchen.

The earliest mention we can trace of the record of Southampton is to be found in the Saxon Chronicle, wherein we read that this town was attacked by the Danes in 873, and that after fierce conflicts they were repulsed and obliged to return to their ships. It is interesting to note that at Southampton, Canute, the wise and pious Danish monarch, resided, and it was here that he reproved his flattering courtiers. We cannot do better than quote here a description of Southampton, as found in the "Encyclopædia Britannica" (1860):—

"Southampton is situated on the south coast of Hampshire (Lat. 50·55, Long. 1·32), at the junction of the small river Itchen with a straight arm of the sea, which runs inland from the Solent. This inland sea, called the Southampton Water, extends for four miles above the town to the village of Redbridge, and for seven miles below it to the promontory of Calshot Castle, a small fort nearly opposite Cowes, in the Isle of Wight, which commands the entrance. The width of this arm varies from one and a half to two miles, and being skirted on the north bank by the wooded heights about Netley Abbey, it forms a beautiful sea-approach to Southampton. Being, from its position, completely land-locked, it is exempt from the swell of the open sea, from whichever direction the wind may blow; and possessing at the same time a straight channel, with considerable depth of water, and good holding ground, it is not surprising that Southampton Water should be regarded as one of the safest and most commodious harbours on our coast."

In the following pages we propose to trace the rise and progress of Southampton from prior to the opening of the docks, when it was a fashionable resort and watering-place, down to the present time, and to show by figures and facts how this natural commercial port has come to be of such importance to the trade of the country, and to have taken its stand as one of the most important commercial ports of the United Kingdom. Beyond doubt, one of the chief causes which has given to Southampton so prominent a position in the annals of commerce, is its well-known safety as a port. As stated above—

    (*a*) The entrance to Southampton is a straight arm of the sea.

    (*b*) The port is completely land-locked, and is, therefore, exempt from the swell of the sea, in whichever direction the wind may blow.

(*c*) There is a considerable depth of water.

(*d*) There is good holding-ground.

Naturally, therefore, Southampton is in the happy possession of everything needful to constitute it a *safe* port, the *sine quâ non* to a successful port. We can say, unhesitatingly, that there is no port in the United Kingdom possessing so excellent an approach as that afforded naturally by the Southampton Water.

But Nature, not being satisfied with having given Southampton all these excellences, has further bestowed on that fortunate port a peculiar advantage with reference to the tides, viz., that instead of the usual high water, there is a *second high water* about two hours after the first. This peculiarity—found in no other port—is accounted for thus: the Isle of Wight being situated across the entrance to Southampton Water, a portion of the great tidal wave, in its progress up the Channel, becomes separated from the main body, and, flowing up the Needles passage into the Solent, reaches Southampton, and causes the first tide about the same time that the main body arrives at Dunnose Point. This tide beginning to ebb, is stopped and driven back again by the main stream from Spithead, and this causes the second tide, about two hours later, and six inches higher than the first tide. Low water is about three and a half hours after the second flood tide.

To ships using the port this is obviously of great advantage, the water remaining nearly stationary for two hours, thus allowing vessels to come out of the graving docks without risk, and others to enter without losing a tide. And when we have stated that the largest ships can arrive at and leave the harbour at all times of the tide, we cannot think of any other facility which could be desired for the welfare of a port.

As long ago as the year 1834, when evidence was being heard as to the desirability of constructing a railway from London to Southampton, much valuable information was given bearing upon the safe position of Southampton as a port.

Captain George Elliott, R.N., spoke of the anchorage as being very extensive and very secure, and the port as being "extremely accessible." That gentleman went further, and asserted that "Southampton was the only eligible situation for a commercial port between Plymouth and the Thames."

In 1859 the *Great Eastern*, drawing 27 ft. of water, was anchored in Southampton Water for several months, without obstructing the navigation. This is an instance of the room there is for approach to the port.

Captain Cornelius Cator, R.N., "considered the neighbourhood of Southampton to be the best anchorage on the southern coast of England," and that "if Southampton had all the proper facilities of a large mercantile port, an expedition might be fitted out there with the greatest possible advantage." Many other gentlemen of the Royal Navy, and numerous other professions, gave similar testimony—one and all believed Southampton to be possessed of more advantages than other ports of the United Kingdom.

As to the fitting out of an expedition as suggested by Captain Cator, R.N., our readers will remember the expedition to Egypt in August, 1882, and that at that time Southampton was unanimously selected as the chief port for embarkation. The writer of these pages happened by chance to be passing through Southampton the first week in August, on a pleasure trip to the Isle of Wight, and was unexpectedly able to see the conduct of the expedition for a day. During the first ten days of the month there were despatched from Southampton to Egypt eleven large steamships, their aggregate tonnage being 37,352 tons. In one day five ships were despatched, their united lengths being one-third of a mile. These conveyed, besides stores and war materials, about 1,200 men and 850 horses, all of which embarked on the day of their arrival at Southampton.

The eleven transports took out in all 175 officers, 3,264 non-commissioned officers and men, and 2,002 horses, three batteries of artillery, besides sundry equipments.

Her Majesty the Queen, T.R.H. the Prince and Princess of Wales, and other members of the Royal Family, came over from Osborne to Southampton to inspect the expedition, and were highly gratified at all the arrangements for the same, which had been conducted by the dock officials.

The Southampton Docks, which are owned by the Southampton Dock Company, were commenced in 1838, and were opened for business in 1844. There are also at Southampton quays which are under the jurisdiction of the Southampton Harbour Board.

It will be here appropriate to give a description of the facilities which are afforded for shipping at Southampton.

There is a town quay, with an extensive quayage space, with convenient and commodious warehouse accommodation, and cranage power. Goods are run alongside vessels by the railway.

There are also piers for the arrival and departure of passenger steamers, and at these piers is conducted the extensive traffic with the Isle of Wight. At these quays and piers there is ample water at all times of the tide for this trade.

The estate of the Dock Company covers 208 acres, and there is at present a tidal basin of sixteen acres, with an entrance 150 ft. wide, and a depth of nearly 31 ft. at high water spring tides, and 27 ft. at high water neap tides.

Adjoining the basin is a close dock of 10 acres, with a depth over the sill of 29 ft. h. w. s., and 25 ft. at neaps. The width at the entrance is 56 ft.

It is proposed to extend the docks by the construction of another tidal dock, with a minimum depth of water of 26 ft. at low water spring tides, and plans are prepared for a dock 37 acres in extent in connection with the extension quay already constructed. The total length of the present quays exceeds 7,500 ft. apart from the extension quay, 1,820 ft. in length, with 20 ft. of water at low tide, which forms the eastern arm of the intended new dock.

The dry docks are capable of taking vessels of 8,000 tons. They are four in number, and there are three sets of shears, worked by steam power, for lifting up to 100 tons.

The following are the dimensions of the dry docks:—

	Length. Feet.	Width. Feet.	Water over blocks. Feet.
No. 1	400	66	21
,, 2	250	51	15
,, 3	500	80	25
,, 4	450	56	25

There is a complete system of railways throughout the dock property, ten miles in length, extending to all the quays, and into and alongside each warehouse—and connected with the main line of railway—so that trucks pass direct between the docks and every railway system of the United Kingdom. The warehouse accommodation is full and convenient, and every modern improvement for the satisfactory working of a large export and import trade is to be found in use at these docks.

We will now proceed to consider the increase which has been found to have taken place in the trade at the docks and town quays respectively, before looking generally at the geographical position and trade of the whole port.

The Docks.

The capital of the Southampton Docks Company is £1,214,575. The dividends on the ordinary stock were for many years up to 1881 4 per cent. per annum, whilst for several years it was 5 per cent. On the preference stocks, which are nearly half the entire capital, the average dividend exceeds 5 per cent. per annum.

We have before stated the docks were opened in 1844. Hereunder is given the revenue of this Company since 1844:—

Year.	Revenue.	Year.	Revenue.
1844	£4,018 7 5	1864	£58,358 6 5
1845	8,977 11 0	1865	62,449 14 8
1846	13,203 1 5	1866	66,011 7 0
1847	17,333 14 7	1867	68,132 17 2
1848	19,534 8 7	1868	65,636 15 7
1849	20,543 16 6	1869	68,033 5 7
1850	20,613 18 6	1870	74,479 13 3
1851	26,391 1 11	1871	85,827 3 2
1852	30,302 0 6	1872	90,717 18 6
1853	39,705 15 10	1873	111,218 15 0
1854	43,501 12 0	1874	102,366 11 7
1855	52,442 3 10	1875	103,424 11 4
1856	54,180 2 9	1876	106,135 12 5
1857	53,066 5 8	1877	112,222 14 7
1858	48,800 1 0	1878	113,921 6 9
1859	53,850 9 11	1879	117,551 8 4
1860	54,558 5 0	1880	119,954 4 11
1861	55,341 10 11	1881	109,316 1 1
1862	58,120 13 3	1882	108,447 17 4
1863	57,738 17 2	1883	110,592 8 10

Thus showing a remarkable and continued increase in the revenue. Again, the tonnage arriving at the docks tells the same tale, showing the present tonnage to be over 2,150,000 tons per annum, as against 600,000 tons in 1863. And it must be remembered that these figures of revenue and tonnage have to be considered together with the fact that in 1874 the Peninsular and Oriental Steam Navigation Company removed their fleet to London, which meant a large annual loss to the docks.

The following are the various Acts of Parliament by which this Company is constituted:—

6 Will. IV. May 19, 1836. "An Act for making and maintaining a dock or docks at Southampton."
1 & 2 Vict. July 4, 1838. "An Act for extending the time for making a dock or docks at Southampton."
6 & 7 Vict. July 4, 1843. Raising further money, &c.
8 & 9 Vict. June 31, 1845. Dry docks, &c.
34 & 35 Vict. July 13, 1871. Consolidation of previous Acts.
37 Vict. May 21, 1874. Additional capital.
38 Vict. May 13, 1875. Amendment.
39 & 40 Vict. July 13, 1876. Graving dock.

The Southampton Dock Company have Parliamentary powers to extend and enlarge the docks, and to raise the necessary capital, also to own warehouses within the port of London for the safe custody of goods, and to own steam tugs for towing within the port and any part of the British Channel.

By the Docks Act (1871) all the docks and premises of the Company are deemed and held to be within and part of the port of Southampton, and the rights and privileges which belong to the port extend to the docks and premises of the Company.

THE HARBOUR BOARD.

In the same way the income of the Harbour Board has increased in twenty years from £7,329 8s. to over £11,000 per annum.

THE PORT.

But it is when we come to consider the statistics as found in the various published records, that we find the most remarkable increase in the trade of the port.

Below is given a statement showing the registered tonnage of ships which have arrived at Southampton and other ports of England from foreign countries and British possessions in 1862, 1872, and 1882 :—

	1862. Tons.	1872. Tons.	*	1882. Tons.	†
London	3,347,080	4.326,236	$29\frac{1}{4}$	6,130,027	$83\frac{1}{2}$
Liverpool	2,617,164	4,073,779	$55\frac{1}{2}$	5,165,211	$97\frac{1}{3}$
Hull	707,465	1.329,658	88	1,623,435	$129\frac{1}{2}$
Bristol	267,883	388,283	45	502,088	$87\frac{1}{7}$
Sunderland	480.662	717,503	$48\frac{1}{4}$	703,288	$54\frac{1}{4}$
Southampton	362,583	744,414	$105\frac{1}{3}$	908,834	150

* Percentage of increase of 1872 over 1862.
† Percentage of increase of 1882 over 1862.

Here we have compared Southampton with five of the principal ports of England, and we find that in the first ten years of our comparison the average increase of tonnage at the five ports was 53 per cent., whilst at Southampton it was $105\frac{1}{3}$ per cent., and that in no individual case did the increase at any of the other ports reach 90 per cent. Further, in twenty years, Southampton had grown by 150 per cent., whilst the average increase at the other five ports had been only 90 per cent.! And this is the foreign trade—and does not take into consideration the trade with the Channel Isles, the increase of which has been remarkable, of which we shall speak further. In the same way, when we turn to the value of exports at the following principal ports for the same years—1862, 1872, and 1882—Southampton increased its exports in ten years from 1862 by 164¾ per cent., as against an average of 104 per cent. at the other ports; and in twenty years by 129¾ per cent., as against the average of 108 per cent.

Value of Exports at the following Principal Ports of England in 1862, 1872, and 1882.

	London. £	Liverpool. £	Bristol. £	Hull. £	Sunderland. £	Southampton. £
1862	31,523,812	50,297,135	298,260	11,916,375	480,912	3,379,503
1872	53,222,779	100,066,410	565,849	23,034,662	1,306,134	8,946,570
Percentage of increase of 1872 over 1862.	68½	99	89¾	93½	171½	164¾
1882.	58,585,803	91,247,543	1,442,642	19,671,989	614,153	7,763,882
Percentage of increase of 1882 over 1862.	85¾	81½	383½	65	27¾	129¾

The principal imports at Southampton are animals (many cows and oxen), cocoa, corn, coffee, cotton, drugs, dyes and dyeing stuffs, fruit, hides, provisions, seeds, skins, tea, cigars, tobacco, wool.

Taking the record of some of these imports individually, it seems almost wonderful with what steadiness and regularity the trade at Southampton in each one has grown. To give one or two instances:—

In 1872 there were imported into London

1,511,113 cwts. of Coffee; Liverpool, 119,379 cwts.; Southampton, 3,721 cwts. (a new trade then). Ten years later, in 1881, we find the imports at London have decreased by 515,418 cwts., and at Liverpool by 14,464 cwts., whilst at Southampton the importation of this article had *increased* to the marvellous total of 127,292 cwts., and in the past year it has grown to 410,000 cwts.

In the same way with Wool, although the increase at London from 1872 to 1882 had been very considerable: 1872, 217,210,533 lbs.; 1882, 388,956,558 lbs.; Liverpool having fallen off to the extent of 17 millions of pounds, the wool imported at Southampton was in 1882 upwards of 30 millions of pounds, as against 11 millions in 1872.

And so, did space permit, we might go *seriatim* through the above list, and we should find in each case the same story of an increase in trade so marvellous as to be almost incredible.

When we refer to the records of vessels arriving from various ports abroad, we find again the same surprising growth of trade with Southampton. Let us take a few instances. In the first place, there arrived at Southampton from Russia, bringing grain and timber, in—

Year.	Vessels.	Tons.
1863	11	2,566
1873	29	6,772
1883	91	32,741

From Sweden and Norway, in—

1863	2	255
1883	55	14,901

From Holland, in—

Year.	Vessels	Tons.
1863	3	293
1883	117	129,898

From France, in—

Year.	Vessels	Tons.
1863	309	42,735
1883	978	288,247

From Spain and Portugal, in—

Year.	Vessels	Tons.
1863	21	12,046
1883	31	17,881

But, perhaps, the most wonderful increase of trade has been that with the Channel Islands, which has grown from an inward tonnage of 49,809 tons in 1862, to 138,084 tons in 1882, and to 276,640 tons in 1884.

As a fact, the tonnage at Southampton in 1883 from the Channel Islands alone was equal to three times the total tonnage arriving at Newhaven, and nearly 30,000 tons more than the total tonnage arriving at Weymouth. Southampton is undoubtedly *the* port for the Channel Islands, as it may be said with truth that more than one-half of the entire trade between the Channel Islands and England passes through Southampton.

Below is given a statement showing the total tonnage which arrived at the port of Southampton at various years since 1874:—

Year.	Tonnage Inwards.	Tonnage Outwards.
1875	1,696,246	1,697,935
1880	2,017,118	2,012,382
1881	2,089,874	2,088,066
1882	2,028,661	2,029,142
1883	2,206,567	2,219,858

Showing an increase in ten years of upwards of half a million tons.

At the present time the following important Steamship companies employ Southampton as their port:—

Name of Company.	No of Ships.	Aggregate Tonnage.
Royal Mail Steam Packet Company	26	64,476
Union Steam Ship Company	17	45,531
North German Lloyd	44	108,320
Brazil and River Plate Company	50	85,861
Nederland Steam Ship Company	12	33,960
Rotterdamsche Lloyd	8	17,071
British and Irish Steam Packet Co.	5	2,562
City of Cork Steam Packet Company	13	13,550
Clyde Shipping Company	24	10,509
Cork Steam Ship Company	13	13,694
London & South Western Railway Co.	18	9,129
Southampton and Isle of Wight Co.	12	1,079
Liverpool Company	3	1,689

Besides a large number of other steamers and large sailing vessels.

Southampton as an export port is particularly well situated, and the fact of its being a rising and important port was fully recognised by Parliament in 1882, when a new railway was authorised to be worked by the Great Western Railway Company, called the "Didcot, Newbury, and Southampton Railway," which will put Southampton in direct communication with the Midland counties. In 1883 another railway, the "Pewsey, Salisbury, and Southampton Railway" was authorised, to bring this port into direct communication with Bristol, and the West of England generally.

As a coaling port, Southampton will certainly before many years occupy an important position.

Placed as it is within 170 miles of the Aberdare coal fields, coal can be carried through from the pit to the docks in 10 hours, so that with the existing and contemplated arrangements of the Dock Company the advantages to be derived by shippers using this port for coaling will soon be felt. When the Severn Tunnel is opened, Southampton looks, and very naturally, to a large increase in the coal trade, which will undoubtedly occur, as the distance will be shortened 36 miles.

The great competitor of Southampton will be, of course, the new dock at Tilbury, on the Thames; but even when this is completed Southampton will, so far as distance from the centres of manufacture is concerned, be still in a very favourable position.

The export rates for goods are in all cases the same to Southampton as to London, and goods sent off from most towns at night are on board ship at Southampton the following morning, so that the few miles extra in distance are no consideration.

With regard to the charges levied at the port, these are very reasonable; for instance, at Barrow, Bristol, Fleetwood, Hull, Liverpool, and the principal ports, the charge per ton on a steamer from the Baltic is 10d. or 1s., whilst at Southampton it is 9d. per ton. In the same way, foreign vessels, as from Australia, America, &c., pay at most ports 1s., or even 1s. 4d. per ton, whilst the charge at Southampton is only 9d.

The dues on goods are equally favourable, and

as to the despatch which can be obtained at the docks, the following is an instance: In March, 1883, the steamer *Werra* (5,109 tons) arrived at Southampton and went into dry dock to replace propeller at noon on Saturday, undocked on Sunday, took in her English cargo and 1,137 tons of bunker coal, and proceeded to sea at 11 a.m. on Monday, having occupied only forty-seven hours, and the greater part of these being at night and on the Sunday. The engineering work in this instance was executed by Messrs. Oswald Mordaunt & Co., whose shipbuilding works are on the east bank of the Itchen, facing the docks. This firm has large and convenient works, and has executed within the past few years some very important work. 110 steamers, with a gross tonnage of 149,184 tons, and representing 17,295-horse power, together with 99 sailing vessels, of 132,369 tons, have left Messrs. Oswald & Mordaunt's yard since 1876. Some of the steamers have been over 4,000 tons, the largest, the *Bitterne*, being 4,800 tons. Facilities for quick execution of repairs to the largest vessels, and every facility in connection with shipbuilding, is to be seen at this busy establishment. This firm despatched seventy boats for the Nile Expedition.

In a future issue we shall give some further interesting facts with reference to this port, but now we must not omit a reference to a most important matter in which Southampton claims to have a voice—we refer to the mail service to America. Voluminous statistics have been prepared, and kindly placed at our disposal, and by these we learn that so much as seventeen and in some cases twenty hours would be saved, or rather gained, if the mails to America were to be sent *viâ* Southampton. This is a matter of great moment, and is one deserving full consideration, which we shall assuredly give it.

There is a regular weekly Express Service by North German Lloyd Company from Southampton to New York. The constant increase in the number of cabin passengers by this route indicates the high character and speed of this fine fleet of steamers, and the facilities of embarking and landing at Southampton are becoming more widely known and appreciated. The five newest vessels of this line—the *Ems, Eider, Werra, Fulda,* and *Elbe,* made 43 voyages during the year 1884. The fastest runs made, so far, from port to port (about 3,100 nautical miles) are: *Eider,* 7 days 17 hours; *Werra,* 7 days 19 hours: *Ems,* 7 days 19 hours; *Fulda,* 7 days 21 hours; *Elbe,* 8 days 7 hours. And the averages for the past year are: *Eider,* 8 days 3 hours; *Werra,* 8 days 8 hours; *Ems,* 8 days 3 hours; *Fulda,* 8 days 9 hours; *Elbe,* 8 days 17 hours.

In the present Session there has been deposited a Bill in which power is sought by the Corporation of Southampton to make arrangements with the Dock Company, which, if concluded, will begin a new era in the commerce of Southampton as regards its accommodation for shipping.

THE HARTLEPOOLS.

In the North of England ports and towns have been built up on the two foundations of coal and iron: the primary cause of the prosperity of the Tyne is coal—that of the Tees is iron. And the modern history of the two Hartlepools is traceable to the export of coal. The old municipal borough of Hartlepool dates back for many generations, the first charter of incorporation having been granted by King John in the year 1200. It was, as quoted by Mr. Belk, the present Recorder of the borough, "to the men of Hartlepool, that they be free burgesses, and that they have the same liberties and laws in our town of Hartlepool as our burgesses of Newcastle-upon-Tyne have in our town of Newcastle." In later years it had its ships and its haven, but at the beginning of this century it had sunk out of the range of ports; in the year 1808, the inner harbour was "enclosed for agricultural purposes," and only restored after a trial some years later to its earlier use. When the railway system had taken root in Durham the facilities of the little place were recognised, and largely through the influence of Mr. Christopher

Tennant, of Stockton, a Bill was passed in 1832 "for establishing a harbour and docks at Hartlepool and for constructing a railway;" whilst a further Act for borrowing the funds to improve the pier and port of Hartlepool was passed. Its corporation, meantime, had dwindled, and the number of Aldermen became too few to legally act, and in 1833 the ancient corporation fell into abeyance. Meantime its docks were in progress, with the line to the coal field to the north; and with the opening of the "Hartlepool Dock and Harbour" on July 9, 1835, dates the modern history of the older town—the younger, as we shall see, being still nearer our own times. In passing, it may be said that a new charter of incorporation was granted in 1841, and that the old borough has been recently extended. The port itself advanced as the coal field of Durham was developed, and as railway facilities were afforded; and in the year 1837 a movement was made which had an important conclusion—that of the formation of a company to make a railway from the old and unfortunate Clarence Railway to Hartlepool, which was north-east of the terminus of that line. In the prospectus of the railway it is stated that coals were shipped at Hartlepool—about 20,000 tons monthly; that it was "the best and first fishing station on the East Coast of England;" and that for the new line there were good prospects. A company was formed—the Stockton and Hartlepool Railway—which made the line without Parliamentary powers,

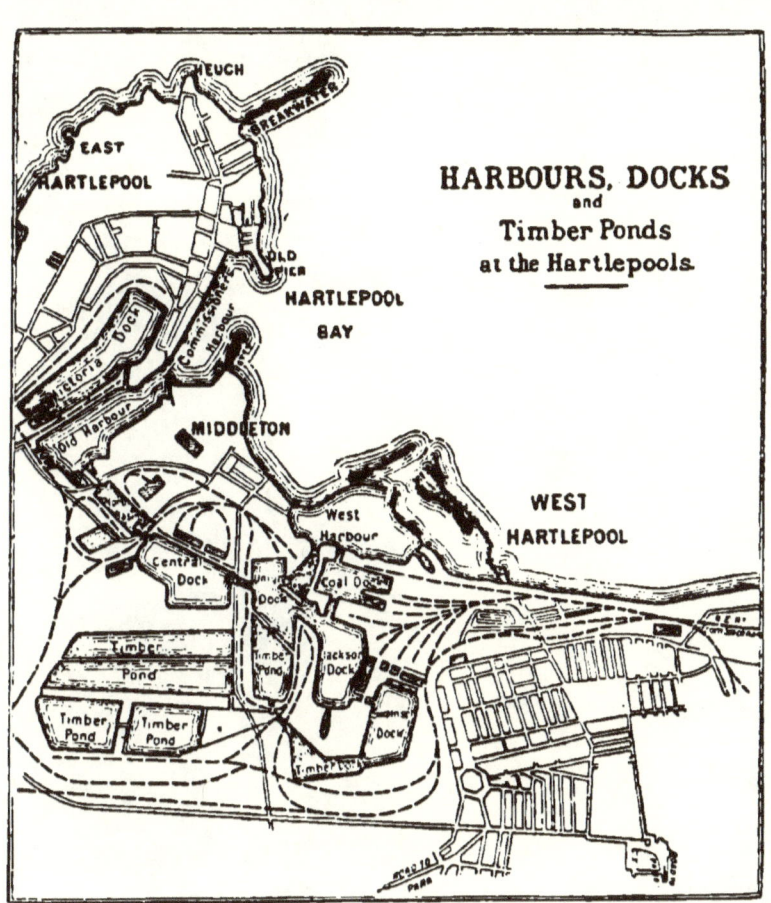

by private contract purchases of land. When it was nearly finished they approached the older "Hartlepool Dock and Railway Company" to make arrangements to use their dock, but disagreement as to terms followed; and thence arose a new dock system to the west, and a little later there sprung up the newer and the larger town of West Hartlepool. In 1841, the new line was opened; in 1844 the Bill for constructing the west harbour and dock was passed, and in the following year Hartlepool was created a separate port. Finally, the separation of the new dock system from the older one was effected by the opening in 1847 of the west harbour and docks.

There are few ports that could show for twenty years such growth as West Hartlepool. In 1852, a second dock—the Jackson Dock—of fourteen acres was opened, the outer harbour was increased from thirteen to forty-five acres; a third dock, the Swainson, followed; and when the Harbour and Railway Report was made in 1860, West Hartlepool "consisted of a harbour of forty-five acres, three deep-water wet docks of 32 acres, two large graving docks and shipbuilding yards, fifteen acres of floating-timber ponds, eight acres of bonded-timber yards, warehouses," upwards of seven acres, with twenty-one miles of railway laid down, the total area occupied by the works being about 230 acres. Concurrently a trade had been developed at the port, both in shipment and receipt, steamship lines to the Continent had been established, and a large town had been built, largely by the energy of Mr. Ralph W. Jackson, managing director of the company that acquired the Clarence and the Stockton and Hartlepool, as well as the docks. It is not needful that the successive steps in the growth of the town or the port should be named, nor the mistake recounted that led twenty years ago to a check in the growth, and finally to the sale of the whole of the docks, railways, and warehouses to the North-Eastern Railway, of whose system the Hartlepools form one of the most important links. In forty years the population of the old borough of Hartlepool has risen from 5,236 to 13,000, and the township where West Hartlepool now is had in 1841 some 380 inhabitants, and now has nearly 34,000. These brief and pregnant figures include the story of the building up of a great community, dependent upon trades of vast moment. Prior to turning to these, it may be said that the one work that the North-Eastern Railway has effected at the port was the formation of two additional docks, which, with basins, united the systems formed by the two rival companies of the past, and thus made the docks seven in number, which, with the harbour, timber ponds, and locks, gave a total area of water space of 177 acres. With the wood-yards and general storage ground they make 350 acres in all devoted to the reception of vessels and storage of cargoes. The fine new docks merit a more lengthened description, as follows:—

The latest addition to the dock and warehouse

accommodation of the port, stretching in one continuous line from the lock or tidal basin at West Hartlepool to the north-western end of the harbour at Hartlepool, and joining the docks of the two towns into one system, was commenced in 1872, and water was admitted in March, 1880. These docks were constructed under the superintendence of Mr. Charles Harrison, for the North-Eastern Railway Company, by Mr. Walter Scott, contractor. The new docks consist of an enlargement of the

Tidal Basin, West Hartlepool	$2\frac{1}{2}$ acres.
Union Dock, adjoining same	$10\frac{1}{2}$,,
Central Dock	$15\frac{1}{2}$,,
Tidal Lock, Hartlepool end	3 ,,
Entrances, &c.	$2\frac{1}{2}$,,
Total acreage of New Docks	34

This brings up the area of docks and timber ponds altogether to the grand total of $176\frac{1}{2}$ acres.

The length of the new Docks in a straight line from the entrance at the Hartlepool end to that at West Hartlepool is 1,000 yards. The total length of new quay walls, including the entrances, is 8,050 feet, of which about 5,200 feet will be available for shipping purposes. The longest quay wall is 960 feet in length. The total amount of excavation that has been required is 1,295,000 cubic yards, and the quantity of clay puddle placed behind the quay walls is 36,810 cubic yards. The total cost of the stone and brick work on the new Docks has been £380,200. The Gas and Water

Companies' pipes are carried under the caisson entrance in a watertight brick culvert. All the new entrances are 60 feet wide, and that leading from the Hartlepool harbour is 215 feet in length, and has two pairs of gates 132 feet apart. The sills at this entrance are 30 feet below the coping, have 26 feet depth of water on ordinary spring tides, and will admit vessels drawing 25 feet of water. The sills at the two entrances from the tidal basin at the West Hartlepool end are 27 feet below the coping, having 22 feet depth of water, and will admit vessels drawing 21 feet. The entrances at this end are the same depth as the old entrances to the West Hartlepool Docks. The depth of water in the

Tidal Basin is	22 feet.
New Dock, adjoining same	26 ,,
Large New Dock	26 ,,
Tidal Lock, Hartlepool end	27½ ,,

There are six pairs of new iron gates, all worked by hydraulic machinery, each pair weighing 87 tons, and each gate being divided vertically into three watertight compartments. The total cost of these gates was £18,000.

There are twelve culverts for locking purposes at the entrance from Hartlepool Harbour to the lock, and twelve also at the entrance from this lock to the large dock. These culverts are 138 feet long, 5 feet 6 inches in diameter, and lie at a depth of 15 feet below high water-mark. There are also four culverts at the West Hartlepool end, from the tidal basin to the West Harbour. These are 21 feet wide at the tidal basin, and are narrowed to 12 feet wide at the harbour. All the culverts are regulated by brass-faced cast iron sluices, which are controlled by hydraulic machinery.

SWING BRIDGES.—Over the entrance from Hartlepool Harbour to the lock, and also over that from the lock to the large dock, there are large iron swing bridges, 208 feet long and 40 feet wide, composed of two outside and one central girder. The bridges are pivoted in the centre, and divided so as to comprise railway, road, and foot-bridges in one. The ironwork in each of these bridges weighs about 730 tons, and their cost was about £12,000 each. There is also a swing bridge, for road traffic only, over the entrance between the Central and Union Docks. All these bridges are worked by hydraulic machinery, and the total cost of the three was £29,000.

HYDRAULIC MACHINERY.—All the bridges, gates, sluices, pumps, and cranes are worked by hydraulic machinery supplied by Sir W. Armstrong & Co. The engine-house is situated near the Union dock, and contains two pairs of horizontal high-pressure direct-acting steam pumping engines, which pump the water into the accumulators. The pumps take the water first at that end opposite to the pump rod, and on the return stroke compress it into the other end, which is of smaller capacity, owing to the space occupied by the pump-rod. On the next stroke being made the water is further compressed into the accumulators. There are two accumulators, consisting of huge plated cylinders loaded with rubble, and having a cylindrical opening through the centre to admit the accumulator barrels. In these barrels the accumulator rods work, whose upper ends are firmly attached to crossheads fixed to the upper ends of the accumulators. The engines pump the water into the lower ends of the barrels and underneath the rods, so that as the quantity increases and the rods rise they carry up with them the weighted accumulators, the travel available being about 14 or 15 feet. From the pipes between the pumping engines and the accumulators the supply pipes branch off to the various bridges, gates, &c., at each of which a set of hydraulic engines is fixed. The exhausted water returns by pipes to the tank in the engine-house.

The new warehouse on the east side of the new docks is six stories in height, the first being 18 feet high, and the rest 9 feet. Its length is 307 feet and breadth 107 feet. Each floor is supported by seventy cast iron columns, standing in five rows, about twenty feet apart each way. These columns are $16\frac{1}{2}$ inches diameter at the base, and 9 inches diameter at the top of the building. The floors are carried on wrought iron girders, stretching from column to column both longitudinally and transversely. The roof is in two spans. An iron balcony runs the whole length of the warehouse on the side facing the dock. The traffic is worked by two lines lengthwise and three across the building, and six turn-tables. The cost of the warehouse above ground was about £34,000, and the cost of the cellars for it, including that of the hydraulic engine-house combined, was £15,500.

And here the port authority may fittingly be referred to. In 1845, when the harbour and docks had restored the trade to the port, it was created a separate port; and the revenue, which had been in 1836 £305 only, rose to £2,021 in 1843; to £2,841 in 1850; and to £5,286 in 1866,—the present revenue being between £8,000 and £9,000 yearly for the Port and Harbour Commissioners. No statistics are available to show the receipts of the owners of the docks, the North-Eastern Railway Company. The Pier and Port Commissioners —appointed by the Board of Trade, the two local governing authorities (Hartlepool Corporation and the West Hartlepool Improvement Commissioners), the merchants and the North-Eastern Railway Company—have had for some years in course of elongation the breakwater which stretches seaward from the headland of Hartlepool, a work of importance in extent, in cost, and in the effect it has had in tranquillising the sea at the entrance to the older port channel. On this work from £3,000 to £4,000 are yearly expended, and it now slowly approaches completion. Dredging is largely carried on in the port: the tonnage raised varying in recent years from 123,000 tons to 324,000 tons, and the cost fluctuating from slightly over 2d. per ton to 4d. The Chairman of the Port and Harbour Commission is and has for some years been Mr. W. J. Young, J.P., the Managing

Owner of the West Hartlepool Steam Navigation Company.

Coal, as we have said, was the first of the trades, and it may be of interest to give some of the earliest of the figures that show the shipment of coal and to contrast them with the present quantity. Prior to the year 1844 the shipments were included with those of Stockton, but since that time the figures are procurable, and they may be given as under:—

COASTWISE AND FOREIGN SHIPMENT OF COAL FROM PORT OF HARTLEPOOL.

Year.	Tons.
1845	884,000
1847	889,000
1850	1,562,000
1859	2,130,000
1869	1,453,000
1883	1,213,000
1884	1,263,000

The declension in the coal export is due largely to the fact that South Durham has found in the manufacture of coke a more profitable use for part of her coal than to export; but in addition to this and to the increased home use, it is probable that more coal is now sent from the Durham coal field to the Tyne and the Wear, which must be looked upon as the natural outlets for the coal-field of the north of England, because of their contiguity, the distance of other ports, and for similar reasons.

The story of the growth in its early years of the export of general goods from West Hartlepool is one which has been often told; but for the last decade the figures have shown little fluctuation. A table showing the growth and the present position is as follows :—

MERCHANDISE GOODS EXPORTED FOREIGN.

Year.	Value.
1853	£23,846
1854	276,499
1855	782,739
1856	1,537,764
1857	1,767,160
1858	2,469,313
1859	4,214,783
1860	5,386,177
1861	5,926,909
1862	5,464,244
1863	2,353,289
1864	2,161,660
1865	3,837,097
1866	2,949,664
1867	2,382,417
1868	3,696,286
1869	1,412,009
1870	1,714,413
1871	2,323,558
1872	2,271,492
1873	2,188,309
1881	1,145,394
1882	1,417,959
1883	1,060,727
1884	1,156,962

And now we may give figures as to a trade which has grown, and is still growing, at West Hartlepool—the timber trade. The following is a statement of the imports of timber for a considerable period, and which Messrs. Wade, Sons & Co. very largely contribute :—

Year.	Loads.	Year.	Loads.
1852	531	1865	155,869
1853	1,234	1866	187,533
1854	4,536	1867	161,232
1855	8,982	1868	202,713
1856	15,389	1869	231,139
1857	14,297	1870	243,843
1858	33,456	1871	270,900
1859	57,661	1872	271,533
1860	74,297	1873	300,205
1861	57,250	1874	344,095
1862	85,724	1875	322,462
1863	121,625	1876	418,947
1864	136,005	1883	327,925

In addition, grain to the extent of about 300,000 quarters, and live stock to about 28,000 yearly, form part of the imports. Coming next to one of the manufactures, we find that in shipbuilding the port launched in 1883, 67,000 tons, and is fourth in the ranks of the shipbuilding ports of the Kingdom, as the following statement will show:—

	Tonnage of Vessels Built.	
	1883.	1884.
Clyde	372,000	299,000
Tyne	219,000	124,000
Wear	214,000	99,000
West Hartlepool	67,000	31,000

The chief of the shipbuilding yards of the port—that of Messrs. W. Gray & Co.—has on more than one occasion stood second on the list of the shipbuilding yards of the Kingdom. The exact tonnage of the port for the year 1883 was made up by the contributions of three shipbuilding firms, as under:—

	Tons.	H.P.
Messrs. W. Gray & Co.	37,597	3,550
,, Edward Withy & Co.	21,193	1,800
,, Irvine & Co.	8,269	780
	67,059	6,130

Not the least interesting of the factories of the Hartlepools is that of the firm of which Mr. T. Richardson, the member for the borough, is the head. Messrs. Richardson inherit a well-known fame as marine engineers, and alike in extent of the production and in quality their establishment at Middleton has long been noted. At present, dulness characterises the marine engineering trade, but it has not been so fully felt at Middleton, the "triple expansion engines" of the firm having been recently and successfully introduced. That dulness has not prevented, either, the erection, and within the last few weeks the completion, of the new central marine engine works. The three graving docks at West Hartlepool, respectively 308 ft., 333 ft., and 365 ft. in the length of floor, are being supplemented by another and a larger one, 550 ft. long, on which, up to June last, £25,921 had been spent by the North-Eastern Railway Company, and on which a considerable sum remains to be spent before completion.

There are three sets of rolling mills at West Hartlepool; and the Seaton Carew Iron Company owns there three blast furnaces, two of which are in blast. About twenty years ago a modest venture was made by the firm of George Pyman & Co., in steam shipping at West Hartlepool, and for a score of years there has been a development under the principle of associated ownership of the trade of steamship owning at work at that town, which has had few parallels in the history of the steamship. It is impossible to give with exactness the number of the vessels owned, but the following list is substantially correct:—

WEST HARTLEPOOL STEAMSHIP OWNING FIRMS.

Firm	No. of Steamers	Firm	No. of Steamers
R. Ropner & Co.	19	J. H. Murrell & Co.	4
Herskind & Woods	15	C. Nielsen & Son	4
Wm. Gray	12	Hardy, Wilson & Co.	6
George Pyman & Co.	13	Gladstone & Cornforth	4
West Hartlepool Steam Navigation Company	11	Callender, White & Hunter	3
T. Appleby & Co.	9	George Steel & Co.	4
C. Furness	9	Murrell & Yeoman	2
Groves, Maclean & Co.	8	G. T. Pearson & Co.	2
Hudson Shipping Co.	8	English & Co.	2
E. Cory & Co.	8	Ebdy, Blacklin & Co.	2
George Horsley	7	M. Rickinson & Co.	2
Middleton & Co.	6	G. B. Harland & Co.	2
R. Irvine & Co.	7	Sivewright, Bacon & Co.	1
C. S. Todd & Co.	5	John Wood & Co.	6
J. Merryweather & Co.	5	Lilly & Wilson	2
O. Trechman	5	Brewis, Smith & Co.	1
J. Lohden & Co.	5	Leask, Clark & Co.	1

We also give the gross tonnage of their boats:—

Firm	Tons	Firm	Tons
R. Ropner & Co.	31,099	J. H. Murrell & Co.	8,999
Herskind & Woods	23,118	C. Nielson & Co.	5,546
Wm. Gray & Co.	15,388	Hardy, Wilson & Co.	6,978
George Pyman & Co.	12,018	Gladstone & Cornforth	5,410
The West Hartlepool Steam Navigation Co.	11,609	Callender, White & Hunter	4,505
T. Appleby & Co.	11,893	George Steel & Co.	4,043
Christopher Furness	21,836	Murrell & Yeoman	2,678
Groves, McLean & Co.	10,295	G. T. Pearson & Co.	3,527
Hudson Steamship Co. (Limited)	12,731	English & Co.	2,746
E. Cory & Co.	6,198	Ebdy, Blacklin & Co.	1,718
George Horsley & Co.	9,179	G. B. Harland & Co.	1,477
Middleton & Co.	8,854	Sivewright, Bacon & Co.	1,773
R. Irvine & Co.	8,498	John Wood & Co.	3,526
C. S. Todd & Co.	7,345	Leask, Clark & Co.	1,245
J. Merryweather & Co.	8,556	John Coverdale & Son	6,309
Otto Trechmann	5,776		269,488

In addition to others privately held, so that it is computed that 200 steamers, of a tonnage of 260,000, are registered as owned at the port.

This vast creation of industry was largely due, as we have stated, to Mr. Ralph Ward-Jackson. A year ago, in the words of a little local work, a memorial public park, procured by subscription, was opened, which "will serve to keep the name of Ralph Ward-Jackson green in the memories of successive generations of Hartlepool folk, but after all it may be truly said that the marvellous creation of West Hartlepool itself is the best memorial." The situation near to the Durham coal field gives it fuel cargoes; its splendid docks and timber storage-ponds and yards make it the chief of the Northern timber-importing places; and cement, earthenware, and iron give it enlarging exports. But the port needs associated effort more; and, above all, it needs conclusion of the internecine warfare between the two towns—the older and the younger. Since the abdication of Mr. Jackson there has been less of that earnest effort that led to the forcing of the port; its recent growth has been almost against neglect, and because capitalists like Mr. William Gray saw its facilities, and utilised them. With coal six miles from the port, with iron close at hand, with the forests across the Baltic ready to send their growth, and with abundant facilities for manufacture, there should be a great future for the two Hartlepools. United in one great borough as they might be, and as they will be literally by houses soon, old local jealousies ought to pass away, and the bounds of the Parliamentary borough should be also those of the municipal one of the future. As yet only the first stage of growth of West Hartlepool has been passed. There were not 400 dwellers in its large township forty years ago, where there are now over 30,000; and in that period the older town has also grown in numbers. That outgrowth was first due to the development of the export and import trades, fostered by Mr. Jackson from its commencement, and for a score of years. The railway and docks he formed passed from the broken financial waters to the North-Eastern Railway's hands, and the score of years that have nearly passed since then have seen a vast addition, first to the manufactures of the town, in the iron and timber trades, and next to the steam fleets owned at the port, whilst, guided by Mr. John Bland, their local manager, and Mr. R. Murray, their local engineer, the Company has recently done great things in that addition to the dock accommodation, and is still doing, in the enlargement of its graving dock system. In the next era the increase of the manufactures may be that which is needed. Already, in the large timber-working establishments, such as those of Messrs. Thomas Walker & Co., Robert Lauder, Harrison & Singleton, J. & T. T. Brown, and others; in the rolling-mills at both sides of the bay; in the lard refineries of Messrs. Thomas Furness & Co; the creosoting works of Burt, Boulton & Haywood; the wagon works of what may now be called the Parent

Railway Company; the blast furnaces already named; the timber yards, on a scale of magnitude unequalled on the North-East Coast; together with the marine-engine works—in these there are large trading and manufacturing capacities, but if the growth of the port is to continue, these must be enlarged and added to. There is a growing rivalry in the ports on the North-East Coast—a rivalry especially in the desire to enlarge the exports, but none of those have the special feature of the Hartlepools—a magnificent dock system on the seashore, and an area around these docks which is practically unlimited for purposes of storage and of manufacture. We may fairly hope that in the next two decades this will be to some extent taken advantage of; and this, with the growth of the mercantile fleets of the port, should give to it a great impetus in the future. In the present, the dulness that is general in the shipbuilding and shipping ports marks the Hartlepools: trade is depressed, and manufactures and exports seem to shrink, but as past eras of depression have only tested the strength of the place, it is tolerably certain that out of that dulness will spring the impulse of the future. It needs the aid of the owners of the docks, of the Conservators of the port, and of the busy, pushing men at that port, and, with united effort, it will still increase, in extent and in trade, in the early future.

THE HUMBER—HULL.

Of the three Humber ports, Hull, Grimsby, and Goole, we propose to deal first with Hull—" the third port of the kingdom," as the inhabitants of this ancient city will have it known.

At the time of the Norman Conquest, and about the year 1068, there were two small villages on the northern coast of the Humber. These were known as Myton and Wyke respectively, and even in those old days Wyke was a port of considerable magnitude. What may have been the special facilities which this village afforded we are unable to say, but certain it is that much importance was attached to it. Very little is known of these two villages in their early days, except that about the year 1260 they were merged into one town.

In 1298, Edward I., on returning from the Battle of Dunbar, happened to reach this town, and he was at once struck with the advantages it offered as a commercial port. At this time the place was ecclesiastical property. Edward, with great foresight and shrewdness, saw that a fine port could be constructed here, and accordingly he purchased the town and immediately proceeded to fortify it. He created the town a

A BIT OF HULL.

manor, bestowed upon it the name of "King's Town upon Hull," and gave special inducements to people to adopt it as a place of residence. A Royal Charter was granted in 1299, constituting "King's Town upon Hull" a free borough. In a few years great works had been completed in the harbour, and the progress towards an important town, which has hardly ever flagged, was initiated. A ferry for communication with Barton (on the opposite side of the river) was started in 1316. With all the early successes of this commercial town is associated the name of the De la Poles, a firm of most successful merchants. The head of this house was created Earl of Suffolk in 1385.

In the year 1359, when a fleet was being organised, during the war with France, Hull sent sixteen ships and 466 seamen. As a comparison, to show how important this town had now become, for this same purpose Newcastle found seventeen ships with 314 men, whilst the total sent by London was only twenty-two ships with 590 men.

During the reign of Richard II., Hull Castle was erected. Henry VI. granted additional charters to the town, and constituted it a corporate town. During the "Wars of the Roses" Hull was most loyal to the cause of Lancaster, and much support—financial and physical—was given to this cause. A great check to the rapid development of the town was threatened in the years 1400 to 1600, by reason of frequent and disastrous visits of the plague, together with serious floods which occurred in 1527 and 1549.

In 1536, during the insurrection, Hull was seized by the insurgents, but was soon freed, and the principal ringleaders were executed. Again, in 1537, the town was possessed, but after a month the inhabitants recovered possession, and severely punished the insurgent ringleaders. Henry VIII. visited Hull in 1540, and was much pleased with the town. By the direction of this monarch the fortifications were strengthened, a new castle was erected, and instructions were given to cut a canal from Newland to Hull, "in order to provide more fresh water."

On account of its importance as a port and dépot for military arms and stores, Hull was much coveted by both parties during the Parliamentary War. In 1642, Sir John Hotham, then Governor, refused to admit Charles I. into the town, and during the years 1643-4 Hull sustained two long sieges, and held out bravely against the violent attacks of the Royalists. When we proceed to consider the town of Hull as a port, we find that by an Act passed in the reign of Queen Elizabeth, in the year 1559, legal quays were established at all the ports in England, *the port of Hull only excepted*. Again, in 1674, a second Act was passed dealing with the question of legal quays, *and again the same singular exception* was made.

Previous to the formation of the Dock Company at Kingston-upon-Hull, in 1773, much robbery occurred, and illegal practices were so frequent, that in the year 1746 the Customs Commissioners reported that, if their work was to be carried on properly, it was imperative that legal quays should be established. For twenty-six years this question was allowed to stand in abeyance; the Corporation of Hull would not move in the matter, the town would do nothing, the Trinity House also refused to act, and it was not until the Commissioners of Customs threatened, in 1772, that if some steps were not at once taken to comply with their request they would establish a dock and quay at some other place on the River Humber, that the necessary steps were taken. In 1773 the Dock Company at Kingston-upon-Hull was established. The capital was to be £80,000, in 160 shares of £500 each. This, however, was modified by the issue of 120 shares at £250 each, and a total capital of £30,000. The Corporation took ten shares, the Trinity House ten, and the inhabitants eighty-one. The first Dock Act was passed in 1774, and the foundation of the Queen's Dock was laid on October 19, 1775, by the mayor. The first ship entered the dock in 1778, and business was commenced at the quays in 1779. In 1777 the total tonnage using Hull was about 100,000; last year (1884) it was 2,385,585.

In the year 1803 it was found that more accommodation was required. Accordingly a new dock—the "Humber Dock"—was commenced in 1807, and opened in 1809.

We give herewith a statement showing the various docks which have been constructed by the Dock Company, together with the area of the same, the date of construction, and cost of each.

Statement showing the Docks which have been constructed by the Dock Company at Kingston-upon-Hull.

Name of Dock.	Date of Opening.	Cost. £	Area, Acres.	Depth of water on sill O. S. T. ft. in.
Queen's	1779	83,355	9¾	20 8
Humber	1809	233,086	7¼	26 8
Princes	1829	165,033	6	20 8
Railway	1846	123,023	2¾	26 8
Victoria	1850	431,922	20	27 6
Albert	1869	1,009,746	24½	28 5
William Wright	1880	214,501	5¾	28 5
St. Andrews	1883	414,708	10½	28 5
Timber Ponds, Nos. 1 and 2	—		14	
No. 2 Extension	1883		25¾	

There are two large graving docks, of the following dimensions respectively:—

	No. 1. Feet.	No. 2. Feet.
Length from gates to head	501	420
Length on blocks	460	400
Width at top	85	100
Width of entrance	50	35
Depth of water on the sill at spring tides	21	18
Do. at neap tides	16	13

The total water area of the Dock Company is about 140 acres, whilst the total estate of the Company covers upwards of 400 acres.

The warehouse accommodation is most extensive; there is space for the storage of about 350,000 quarters of grain alone.

Every modern appliance is to be found throughout the docks and warehouses.

The growth of the importance of Hull as a port has been phenomenal. A glance at the number and tonnage of vessels using this port shows a steadiness and rapidity of growing importance not to be met with in the record of any other port.

The following figures show the total tonnage which entered at and cleared from the port of Hull in various years since 1853, and by these we see that in thirty years the inward tonnage has increased by more than one and a half million tons.

	Entered.		Cleared.	
	No.	Tons.	No.	Tons.
1853	2,290	384,838	1,481	235,494
1863	2,959	723,901	2,238	591,301
1873	4,817	1,499,924	4,705	1,470,272
1874	4,907	1,623,383	4,732	1,486,724
1875	4,631	1,615,956	4,355	1,454,642
1876	4,802	1,746,591	4,543	1,324,034
1877	4,854	1,764,825	4,460	1,519,772
1878	4,996	1,750,977	4,802	1,788,214
1879	4,217	1,637,509	4,144	1,644,398
1880	4,784	1,841,868	4,671	1,836,004
1881	4,322	1,738,554	4,246	1,748,584
1882	4,725	1,925,032	4,638	1,915,436
1883	4,642	2,055.091	4,421	1,981,994
1884	4,604	1,904,203	4,481	1,887,402

The revenue of the Dock Company tells the same tale of continued increase of trade, as will be seen by the figures given herewith:—

Revenue of the Dock Company at Kingston-upon-Hull in each of the above years.

1853	£ 65,262
1863	83,192
1873	176,716
1874	183,079
1875	193.029
1876	215,721
1877	229,510
1878	226,187
1879	199,775
1880	209,437
1881	206,780
1882	226.750
1883	254,616
1884	232,850

When we look at the various trades which, combined, have so greatly swelled the commerce of the port of Hull, we find that the following countries have been the largest contributors, viz., Norway, Sweden, Russia, Germany, Denmark, Holland, Belgium, France, Portugal, Spain, the Mediterranean, the Black Sea, India, Australasia, North and South America. The trade of Hull may be truly said to be with the whole world.

There is a regular service weekly, and in some cases bi-weekly, between Hull and every principal port of the world.

As a comparison of the importance of Hull we give herewith the total tonnage which arrived at London, Liverpool, and Hull in 1883:—

Port.	Tons entered in 1883.
London	11,440,707
Liverpool	8,194,129
Hull	2,055,091

In twenty years—*i.e.*, from 1862 to 1882—there was an increase in the tonnage arriving at London of 83 per cent.; at Liverpool of 97 per cent.; whilst at Hull it increased by 130 per cent.

Looking generally at the principal imports of Hull, we find that the following quantities were entered at Hull in 1883, viz.:—

Wheat	qrs.	1,357,850
Barley	,,	547,608
Oats	,,	318,634
Beans	,,	126,166
Peas	,,	53,259
Maize	,,	326,802
Tares	,,	10,486
Linseed	,,	899,450
Rapeseed	,,	200,403

Cottonseed	tons	112,309
Cloverseed	,,	25,939
Flax	,,	3,772
Hemp	,,	11,000
Timber	loads	94,229
Deals	,,	373,985
Bacon	cwts.	319,376
Lard	,,	60,640
Butter	,,	272,175
Cheese	,,	33,825
Eggs	cases	11,977
Sugar	cwts.	258,791

Added to these there is also a very large annual importation of manufactured goods, iron manufactures, cotton yarn, raw cotton, petroleum, resin, turpentine, hides, vegetables, fruit; and the live stock imports form a large portion of the trade of Hull. In 1884 there were imported 14,036 horned cattle, 60,996 sheep, 1,114 pigs, and 252 horses.

There is a very large miscellaneous trade conducted between Hull and Germany, Denmark, Holland, and Belgium. With Germany, both directly and indirectly, Hull does a larger trade than with any other country. Holland is said to have sent the first ship which ever sailed into Hull, and as years have passed the trade with this country has steadily increased. Upwards of 161,000 tons of shipping came to Hull from Holland last year. The trade has been with Belgium for more than 500 years. About 76,000 tons came from this country last year. From Portugal, too, a large quantity of wine is brought annually to Hull, while Spain sends large quantities of fruit. A large import trade comes also from the Black Sea. From India, 67,000 tons of shipping arrived last year. The grain trade with the Pacific has risen to great importance recently, and from Brazil, Demerara, and the River Plate large importations of linseed, wheat, &c., have developed a very important trade.

Upwards of 100 vessels came to Hull from the United States in 1884, representing about 130,000 tons.

More than two hundred years ago the people of Hull sent ships to America, and from Hull the Washington family is said to have emigrated.

With regard to the export trade of Hull, we subjoin a statement, showing the nature and quantity of the principal articles exported last year, and this may be taken as a fair specimen of the general export trade of the port :—

Article.		Quantity.
Machinery (agricultural)	packages	36,602
,, (general)	,,	145,195
Manufactured goods	,,	45,134
Hardware	,,	43,329
Linseed oil	cwts	254,280
Cotton oil	,,	194,740
Iron, &c.	—	—
Chemicals	—	—
Cotton, plain	yards	50,832,300
,, printed	,,	31,961,800
,, yarn	lbs.	72,814,500
,, thread	,,	2,254,430
Lace, gauze, net, and crape	£	162,915
Cottons, unrated	,,	62,055
Linen, declared in length	yards	2,170,300
Linen, declared in value	£	48,679
Linen thread and yarn	lbs.	2,157,220
Woollens, broad and narrow flannels	£	686,249
Worsteds, of all kinds	,,	389,362
Woollen and worsted yarn	lbs.	18,506,200

The coal exports at Hull are large: 639,066 tons were shipped in 1884. The following summary shows the shipments of coal from Hull in in five years:—

	Tons.
1879	460,832
1880	570,071
1881	636,556
1882	645,686
1883	643,672

As a shipbuilding port Hull also holds an important position. The following important firms are large contributors in this respect:— Messrs. Earles, Messrs. Head & Riley, and Messrs. J. Bremner & Co.

The following is a brief summary of the iron ships built at Hull in 1884:—

IRON SHIPBUILDING IN HULL IN 1884.

Messrs. Earles launched the following vessels:—

	Tons.	H.P.	Owner.
Chandos	1,896	154	H. Briggs & Co.
Finland	1,954	152	D. Wilson, Esq.
Dynamo	529	110	T. Wilson & Co.
Mosquito	62	45	Do.
Electro	544	112	Do.
Martello	3,709	400	Do.
Albatross	244	68	Grimsby Ice Co.
Pelican	244	68	Do.
Gannet	244	68	Do.
Cormorant	244	68	Do.
Enterprise	206	88	W. Burdett-Coutts.
Caisson	300	—	Lucas & Aird.
Light Ship	129	—	Hull Trinity House.

Messrs. Head & Riley launched four barges, with a carrying capacity of 180 tons each, for Messrs. Wilson; the steamship *Trent*, 101 tons gross, 35-h.p., for the Gainsborough Steam Packet Company; and two barges, of 180 tons each, for the Hull Dock Company.

A new dock, called the Alexandra, belonging to the Hull, Barnsley, and West Riding Junction Railway and Dock Company, was opened in Hull on July 16, 1885. This dock is in no way connected with the system of the old Dock Company.

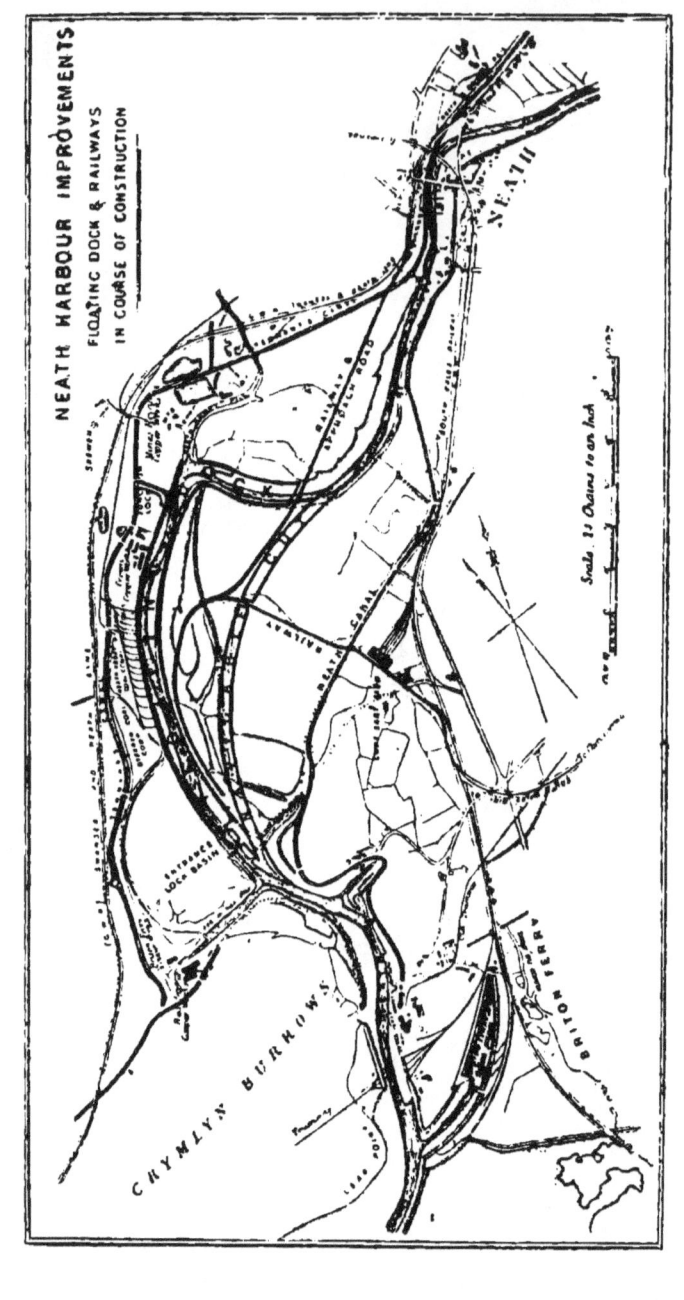

NEATH, PORT TALBOT, & CAERMARTHEN.

THE keen competition now existing between the ports of the Bristol Channel, notably in regard to Cardiff, Swansea, and Newport, seems to have awakened in the smaller ports of Neath, Llanelly, and Port Talbot a corresponding spirit of enterprise, and have attracted to them a considerable amount of public interest. To merchants and manufacturers, colliery proprietors, shipowners, and shippers, the growth and progress of these smaller ports is no less important than that of their larger neighbours, who, by the massing of capital in their midst and the energy and foresight of their traders, have obtained the prominent positions they hold among the harbours of Great Britain.

Of the three ports of Neath, Port Talbot, and Caermarthen, of which we purpose to treat in this article, Neath holds the foremost place, both by virtue of its position and the new docking accommodation which is in process of construction. Caermarthen, as a port, ranks considerably lower than either Neath or Port Talbot, having no docking conveniences, and being neither an important centre of manufacture nor coal-working, save to a very limited extent. At a time, however, when Port Talbot was undreamed of, and Neath a small fishing village of a few hundred inhabitants, Caermarthen, or Caermyrddin, was an important fortified town, and played a prominent part in the civil wars of the Cymri.

NEATH.

The town of Neath is situated $2\frac{1}{2}$ miles from the mouth of the River Neath, on the east bank, and $8\frac{1}{2}$ miles N.E. by E. from Swansea. Including the outlying districts of Briton Ferry and Skewen, the population is estimated to exceed 20,000. The population of the municipal borough in 1881 was 10,409. About $1\frac{1}{2}$ miles from the town stand the picturesque ruins of Neath Abbey, but the romantic effect they have on the landscape is much marred by the proximity of railway lines and other unsightly evidences of our modern civilisation. It was founded early in the twelfth century. The borough received its first charter from Edward II.

The first historical mention of Neath which we have been able to find is in the Margam Chronicle, which states that one Llewellyn, Prince of Aberfraw and Lord of Snowdon, in the year 1231 A.D., being enraged exceedingly by the conduct of the people, who were killing and ravaging in the south-east part of the country at their own sweet will, determined to make a descent on them, and, accordingly, having collected an army, he marched forthwith into Gwent, and subjugated all the lords of South Wales—subsequently taking the town of Neath; and that one Morgan Cam, in revenge, destroyed the place and exterminated the inhabitants—so that if the Margam Chronicle is to be believed (and what shall we believe if not a chronicle?) Neath had to make a new start altogether, there being no town and no inhabitants.

During the civil wars of the Marches it was on several occasions the scene of bloodshed and affrays between the petty princes of Wales, which our space does not allow us to dilate on. It occupies the site of the old Roman Nidum. Some vestiges of the Julia Strata still remain, and also traces of a cross-road leading to Baunium, now Caer Banna, near Brecon. Part of the walls of the old castle and a gateway flanked with two towers are still standing. The parish church has an ancient embattled tower, square in form, and which is supposed to have been at one time connected with the castle.

Apart from historical reminiscences, Neath has no other points of interest than are possessed by the majority of quiet country towns of its size. To the tourist it is known as the place from which a start is to be made to the far-famed Vale of Neath and the justly celebrated Falls of the swiftly-flowing, pebble-bedded river, which are surpassed in beauty and boldness by few in the British Isles.

In 1849 we find the town described as " being

well paved and lighted, and having many good houses. There are the remains of an ancient castle, to which the church is supposed to have belonged. The town has a good trade, and the river is navigable for small vessels, but barges are generally used. It is a tributary borough to the Swansea parliamentary district. Population of the municipal borough and parish 4,970."

Whatever may have been the condition of Neath in 1849, certain it is that it is neither particularly well-lighted or well-paved at present; though we know of no town of its size and population that has a larger number of fine, well-built stone villas than Neath. The quarries of the district abound in stone of a high class for building purposes, and, with raw material so cheap and accessible, it is strange that the streets and pavements are not better cared for.

The principal industries of the district, apart from coal-raising (which is, of course, the most important), are the manufacture of Dinas firebricks from the celebrated clay of that name, which furnishes material for one of the highest-class bricks in the trade, and the production of iron and tinplates. Among the persons engaged in the manufacture of the latter articles we may mention Messrs. Leach, Flower & Co., of the Melyn Iron and Tinplate Works, who, apart from the rolling and finishing of tinplates in the ordinary way, have an extensive factory for the decoration of the plates by a patent process, which has resulted in a complete and successful revolution in this branch of the trade. The plates so decorated are used for the making of small match-boxes, sweetmeat and biscuit tins, and like uses, and are embellished in various colours.

The Dinas fire-bricks are of the very best material for use in the erection of steel furnaces and cupolas, and are exported in large quantities to America and elsewhere for this purpose. The principal firms in the Vale of Neath engaged in brick-making are the Vale of Neath Dinas Brick Company and J. B. Jenkins & Co.

Amongst the shippers of coal from the port are the Dynevor Coal Company, Evans & Bevan, and Nixon & Co., of Nixon's Collieries.

The chief imports are copper and iron ore, corn, flour, and timber. There is water communication with Abernant and Swansea by means of canals.

At the entrance to the River Neath, from the South Pier Head of Briton Ferry Docks, an embankment, or slag breakwater, projects about half a mile, 2 ft. above high water, ordinary spring tides. The passage to the Briton Ferry Basin (Great Western Railway Company's) lies close along this embankment, and throughout there will not be found less water at an ordinary spring tide than 25 ft., and at neap 17 ft. The River Neath is navigable for small vessels up to the town.

The limits of the port extend from Aberdulais Weir, along high-water mark each side to certain depressed points on the sand hills, each side of the entrance in Swansea Bay; an imaginary line across the bay from these points fixes the limits seawards—as per Sec. 6, Neath Harbour Act of 1874. The Neath Harbour Commissioners receive tolls, according to their powers, from all vessels within these limits, no distinction being made between Briton Ferry or any other part so far as the Commissioners are concerned. Briton Ferry Dock, now the property of the Great Western Railway Company, was opened in 1862, and was the first floating accommodation provided in the port.

Whatever progress, politically, the inhabitants of the port have made in the last twenty years, the progress in dock accommodation has been decidedly conservative, and it was not until 1880 that the Commissioners received powers from Parliament for the issue of £370,000 Five per Cent. First Mortgage Debentures, for the purpose of paying off all outstanding bonds issued since 1843, and, further, to defray the cost of the new works necessary to meet the rapidly-increasing requirements of the harbour. The new dock, which is only partially completed, will have a floating area of 64 acres, and will be $1\frac{1}{2}$ miles long, having warehouse frontages on either side and also important frontages to face a new navigable channel which has been constructed by diverting the River Neath. The dock itself consists of a portion of the river to be converted so as to enable ships to lie afloat in the harbour, instead of, as hitherto, lying aground at low water.

Neath Harbour possesses most complete connections with the great railway systems of England, having junctions with seven railways and two canals, viz. :—The Great Western (South Wales) Railway; the Great Western, Swansea and Neath section; the Great Western, Vale of Neath section; the Neath and Brecon Railway; the South Wales Mineral Railway; the Midland (through the Neath and Brecon Railway); and the London and North-Western (through the Vale of Neath Railway). The canals in connection are the Neath and Tennant.

When "we say that upwards of fifty collieries and works of every description abut immediately upon the Neath and Brecon and Vale of Neath Railways, nearly the whole of the output from which, on account of there being no floating accommodation, at present passes the intended floating harbour to other ports, at a considerably extra cost to the exporters, it will be seen how beneficial the completion of the new dock and works will be both to the harbour and the trade of the district generally." The powers by which the Commissioners act for the consolidation of the debts, &c., of the port are derived from the Neath Harbour Special Acts of Parliament of 1843, 1874, 1878, and 1880.

The following we extract from the list of total receipts of the harbour dues, to show the progress of the port :—

Year ending March 31.	Total Receipts.
	£ s. d.
1846	1,043 11 9
1861	2,106 13 1

Year ending March 31.	Total Receipts.		
	£	s.	d.
1871	2,823	19	7
1876	3,497	9	2
1881	3,354	1	4
1884	3,627	7	8

which show a steady, though somewhat sluggish, rate of increase, which, when the new floating harbour is completed, must increase at a ratio many times the above figures. In the year ending March 31, 1885, the revenue, from a variety of temporary causes, was slightly under that of 1884.

The progress was most marked in four years ending March 31, 1882, as will be seen by the following table :—

Year ending March 31.	Number of Vessels.	Tonnage of Vessels.	Tonnage of Cargoes Entered and Cleared.
1878-79	1,529	165,935	326,429
1879-80	1,556	178,611	352,175
1880-81	1,836	209,522	410,868
1881-82	1,899	228,671	447,406

The tonnage of cargoes in the year ending March 31, 1884, was upwards of 490,000 tons, but in 1885 fell to 400,000 tons—a decrease attributable to the reduction of docking accommodation incidental to the construction of the new works.

There is no port in the Bristol Channel that should have a brighter future before it than Neath, if advantage be taken of its natural position. The partial conversion of the river into a dock, when complete, will give it facilities for the shipping of minerals equal, if not superior, to any port in the West, and it is to be hoped that ere long this work, which by the original contract was to have been finished in 1883, but has been delayed by financial difficulties, will be swiftly carried through to a successful issue, and Neath take that position as a port to which, on account of its physical superiority and as a centre of a large colliery and iron district, it is entitled.

PORT TALBOT, OR ABERAVON.

The town of Port Talbot is situated on the Avon, about two miles from the sea, amidst a very thickly-populated district, rapidly increasing both in population and importance. To the stranger the town appears to consist of one singularly long street, with a number of irregular straggling lanes leading out of it—an arrangement which is quaintly picturesque. Historically it has very few points of interest. Near it are the ruins of Margam Abbey, and the magnificent mansion of Mr. C. R. M. Talbot, "the father of the House of Commons."

The trade of Port Talbot consists principally in the smelting of copper ores, iron and tinplate working, and coal-raising.

The Margam Tinplate Company, of Taibach, have six tinplate mills in operation, and have recently added furnaces for the production of steel by the Siemens-Martin process. The brand of tinplates manufactured by this company stands very high in the market, and in old days the works were considered to have the finest charcoal forge in the trade for the turning out of bar iron of the best charcoal quality. There are a number of other tinplate works in the district.

The works in the Cwmavon Valley, which were at one time among the largest working factories in South Wales, have of late years experienced various changes of ownership. From the hands of the Governor and Company of Copper Miners in England, they passed into those of Mr. James Shaw, and have recently, we understand, been taken over from the liquidators of the affairs of the latter gentleman by Messrs. Leach, Flower & Co., of Neath.

From the Mumbles Head Lighthouse, Port Talbot is E.S.E. distant about six miles, and from Swansea S.E. by S. about five. There is but one dock, which has a dredged area of 30 acres, in which are four wharves :—

    (1) The Port Talbot Company's public wharf, at which from 17 ft. to 18 ft. of water is available for vessels loading and discharging there.

    (2) The Cwmavon Wharf, having a depth at one end of 16 ft., shoaling to 13 ft. at the other end—a distance of 1,000 ft.

    (3) Messrs. Viviant's wharf, at which there is 15 ft. of water.

    (4) Messrs. Byass's wharf, which has 14 ft. abreast of it.

Besides the above 30 acres, there are 120 acres which might easily be rendered available for shipping purposes by dredging.

Important improvements to the harbour have been executed in the last two years, embracing, firstly, an additional lock of 150 ft., which, taken together with the old one, gives the advantage of one long lock of 290 ft. Secondly, a projection of the breakwater 370 yards beyond the old extent, which has been found to have the effect of making the entrance, that used to be considered dangerous at times, as safe and convenient as that of any port in Swansea Bay. And, thirdly, a line of wharfage connected by a branch railway with the Great Western Railway has been constructed, and the float considerably deepened by dredging.

A section of the Rhondda and Swansea Bay Railway has just been opened to Port Talbot, and when this line is completed the harbour will have direct communication with the collieries of the Rhondda, which must result in an immensely increased trade for the port. Even at the present time iron ores can be easily landed and forwarded to the ironworks at Merthyr, Aberdare, Cwmavon, Pyle, Llynvi, and other works of the district. The harbour is upwards of a mile in length, with an average depth of 16 to 18 ft. of water at all times, and is entered by a lock 44 ft. wide by (as above mentioned) 290 ft. long. The name of Aberavon Harbour was changed to Port Talbot, July 4, 1836, 6 Wm. IV. c. 98.

The principal imports are iron ore, copper ore, and timber. The exports are coal, iron, tinplates, and copper.

Below we give a table showing total receipts of harbour dues on registered tonnage of ships for 1876, and during the last five years; also number of vessels entering the port, and total register tonnages of same, for same dates :—

Year ending April 30.	Number of Vessels entering Port.	Registered tonnage.	Total receipts of Port dues. £ s. d.
1876	450	36,151	675 8 10
1881	811	82,133	1,308 7 10
1882	789	82,907	1,270 19 10
1883	716	87,663	1,403 12 11
1884	691	91,032	1,501 10 0
1885	695	92,897	1,538 11 7

The following is an estimate of imports and exports for last five years :—

Year.	Imports.	Exports.
1881	106,000	107,000
1882	106,100	108,300
1883	113,000	115,100
1884	118,200	119,000
1885	120,100	122,000

Comparing the receipts of 1884 with those of Neath Harbour for same date, we have £3,627 7s. 8d., and Port Talbot £1,501 10s.—showing trade of Neath to be considerably over double that of the latter port. But with its advantages of position, its nearness to the sea, and the fact of its being the centre of an industrial district of growing magnitude, and that it will be before long in direct connection with that vast coalfield, the Rhondda Valley, it takes no gift of prophecy to foretell with surety that the Port Talbot of the future will be as far advanced from the Port Talbot of the present, as that is from the little fishing village of Aberavon of seventy years ago.

CAERMARTHEN.

The town of Caermarthen stands on the right bank of the Towy, about nine miles from the sea. The river, which bends south to empty itself into Caermarthen Bay, rises in the heart of the lower regions below Plynlimmon, divides Caermarthenshire from Brecknockshire, and then conforms its course to the Precelly Mountains, receiving the various rivulets from their south sides, the greatest being the Cothy, and runs into the bay through a great rent in the newer rocks.

The name Caermarthen is variously determined:—(a) Caer-fyrddin, from the Welsh sage who flourished at Caermarthen in the fifth century, and was named Merlin Ambrosius, or Myrddin Emrys. (b) From the Celtic Caer, and "dun," signifying a "hill fortress." Thus Latin, "Maridunum." (c) Old Welsh chronicles assign derivation to "Caer fyrdd ddyn," the citadel of 10,000, from "myrdd," a myriad, and "dyn" a man.

The castle is said to occupy the site of a Roman station founded as early as A.D. 70.

It was for some time the residence of the lords of South Wales, and in the wars between the Anglo-Saxons and the Normans the castle of Caermarthen frequently changed hands, and suffered much in the sieges. In the time of Charles I. the castle was garrisoned by the Royalists, and captured from them by the Parliamentary forces, and shortly afterwards dismantled and allowed to fall into decay. General Sir Thomas Picton and

Lord Nott were natives of Caermarthen, and a monument to the former stands on an eminence adjacent to the town. The situation of the town is very beautiful, but the streets are irregular and steep, and many very narrow. It has a few fine old-fashioned edifices, the principal one being the Guildhall.

The population of the county of the town of Caermarthen (for Caermarthen is a county as well as a town) was in 1851, 10,524, and in 1881, 10,514, showing a decrease of 10.

On the Towy, a wide, tidal stream, celebrated for salmon, and sewin, and trout, the old-fashioned coracles are still used for fishing. In the bay, about six miles from the mouth of the river, lies a sand shoal called "Burry Bar," on either side of which is a district rich in coal and minerals.

There is no floating dock accommodation at Caermarthen. A large quay extends along the bank of the river, and vessels of 300 tons can float to quay to load and discharge their cargoes. Four small steamers trade to Bristol and Liverpool from the town—the *Cambrian* and *Neath Abbey* to Bristol, the *Ibis* and *Lady Kate* to Liverpool.

Woollen-weaving, matting, tanning, and rope-making form the staple trade, and Messrs. T. Lester & Co. have a small tinworks in the vicinity. The exports are principally timber, bark, marble, slates, lead ore, bricks, grain, butter, and eggs.

Of the future of Caermarthen it is difficult to speak with any degree of certainty. It is not, as is the case with Neath and Port Talbot, a centre of a large and increasing manufacturing district, nor has it in its neighbourhood the resources necessary to attract capital and enterprise. Though it is not likely to retrogress, there appears to be no immediate prospect of any increase in the trade of the place, and it will probably remain, as at present, a quiet, respectable, country town, with about as much business energy and foresight as was possessed by that very unimaginative article the poet Shelley's "pint-pot."

THE LIFFEY.

From the earliest existing records we learn that in the remote ages Ireland was governed by numerous petty princes and chieftains, who were constantly striving among themselves for the mastery. As a natural consequence the power of each prince or chieftain extended over a very limited area, and the population of the country was very thinly scattered. There were thus very few important centres in these old days, but Dublin appears to have been in ancient times one of the most flourishing towns.

Dublin is first mentioned by the historian Ptolemy in the second century of the Christian era as one of the chief places in Ireland. It was at that time known as "Eblana," from a corruption of which word, or from "Duiblinn," "the black or dark water," the present name of the city has been derived. Another ancient name which was applied to Dublin was "Bally-ath-Cliath-Duiblinne," or "the town of the ford of hurdles on the Blackwater," a title given, it is supposed, in consequence of the people having access to the river by means of hurdles laid on its marshy borders before it was embanked. It was also called Direlin by the early Danish settlers, and until quite recently it was known by the Welsh as " Dinas Dulin." In the year 140, it is stated by various Irish historians, Dublin was selected as the eastern boundary of a line of demarcation drawn westwards across the island to Galway, for the purpose of putting an end to a war between two rival monarchs, Con-Caed-Cathach, King of Ireland, and Mogha Magad, King of Munster.

In 291 the inhabitants of Leinster were defeated in a great battle fought at Dublin by Fiacha Sravtine, then monarch of Ireland. In the year 836 the Danes, or Easterlings, as they were called, entered the River Liffey in a fleet of sixty ships, and for the first time the inhabitants of Dublin submitted to the rule of a foreign power. These Danes appear to have been a very warlike people, and for many years subsequent to the close of the fifth century they maintained, with varying success, their supremacy in Dublin and the surrounding districts. One of their monarchs, Tor-Magund, or Turgiscus, who had reigned despotically for upwards of forty years over a very large portion of Ireland, was, in 845, killed by Malachy, a native king, and the Danes were driven out of Dublin by the Irish inhabitants of Meath and Leinster, who plundered the city. The Danes, however, soon re-established themselves, and in 853 their power was greatly increased by the arrival of a large number of Danes and Norwegians, who entered Ireland under Aulaffe. For many subsequent years the history of Dublin presents a record of internal strife among those who sought to be rulers. When the party who were in power felt strong enough at home they made frequent wars against the inhabitants of South Wales, but these expeditions were generally unsuccessful. In 964, Edgar, King of England, subdued Wales, the Isle of Man, and part of Ireland, Dublin being specially named.

In 980 a great battle was fought at Taragh, in which the Danes were severely defeated. They suffered another signal loss at Clontarf in 1014, and from this date their power in Dublin steadily declined. They made one final effort for mastery in 1165, when they entered the Liffey in a fleet of seventy ships; but the invasion was unsuccessful, and after this date the Danes disappear from history as a power in Dublin. The city now became closely connected with the kingdom of England, and in 1172 Henry II. held his court in Dublin. Richard II. was sumptuously entertained in Dublin by the Provost of the city, and under the following monarchs Dublin is in many instances mentioned as having entertained Royalty.

In 1649 Cromwell, with 13,000 troops, entered the Liffey as Commander-in-chief under the Parliament. In 1689, when James II. landed in Ireland to assert his right to the British throne, he held a Parliament in Dublin. In the year 1800 the Act of Union between Great Britain and Ireland was passed in both Parliaments, and on January

1, 1801, the Imperial standard of the United Kingdom was hoisted on Dublin Castle.

As a port, Dublin has always held a strong position. In the olden days for the ships which used to enter the Liffey with warlike crowds there was no need for landing-stages; and in those days the constant warfare which was being carried on precluded any commercial transactions. After the expulsion of the Danes, however, and when quiet times succeeded the turbulent years, the inhabitants of Dublin began to consider the question of commerce. The first quays on the Liffey at Dublin seem to have been constructed just prior to the reign of King John, as that monarch in 1209 confirmed a charter of the citizens as to the possession of their buildings upon the river (*edificia supra aquam*), and he further granted permission for the erection of other buildings on the banks of the Liffey. In many local documents of the thirteenth century there are to be found various references to buildings on the bank (*super ripam*). For many years ships bound to Dublin used to unload portions of their cargo at Dalkey to enable them to proceed to the city, where they discharged the balance of their goods at the "crane." This "crane," or building, was for a long time used at the Dublin Custom House, and was destroyed in 1596 by a great explosion of gunpowder, which also caused serious loss of life.

Several slips or landing places are alluded to in the sixteenth and seventeenth centuries. We read that Sir William Skeffington, lord-deputy, landed in 1544 "at the slip near the bridge of Dublin." In 1575 an order was made by the Corporation of Dublin for the removal of certain "stayres" on the Liffey, which were to be "plucked down, forasmuch as they were builded without the lycens of the city." At this time the "depth of the Liffie was four foot demy," and in another part "six foot." In 1559 the city had granted all or most of the "slippes" to one Thomas Simon Fitz Michell. In 1643 Catherine Daffe, a widow, was tenant to the city "of all the slips, which she was bound to make up, repair, and keep from time to time stiff and staunch with good stone and lime," in return for which she received fourpence for every boat, gabbart, and bark using the quays. In the latter part of the reign of James I. the Government erected a new Custom House, crane, and wharf, "as well for his Majesty's service as the convenient loading, landing, putting aboard and on shore all and every such wares, merchandise, and commodities whatsoever as should at any time thereafter be exported or imported into and forth of the Port of Dublin, or any number thereof."

In consequence of a petition, dated 1697, which stated that "The river Anna Liffey which passes through this city (Dublin) is become so shallow and choaked up in every part that it is become in a manner useless for trade, which is occasioned by the great quantities of gravel and sand brought by the fresh-water floods, and ashes and dirt that from time to time has been thrown in by the inhabitants," a Bill was prepared to constitute a Corporation "for preserving and improving the Port of Dublin." This Act, however, was not finally passed until the reign of George III., when by an enactment (26 Geo. III.) a body, commonly known as the Ballast Board, was incorporated and vested with the care, management, and superintendence of the whole of the river and the walls bounding it. The jurisdiction of this Board was subsequently extended by several successive Acts, and the management of the port and harbour of Kingstown was also vested in this Corporation; but in 1836 an Act was passed which placed Kingstown under the government of the Board of Works.

About the time of the Revolution the woollen trade flourished in Dublin, and the production of this article was widely known and reputed for its excellence. The cheap rate at which labour could be obtained induced many capitalists to embark in this business, and extensive factories were started in the town.

In 1700 William III. was prevailed upon to give his assent to legislation which almost crushed the Irish trade. All exportation, save to England, was peremptorily forbidden, and the woollen manufacture then fell into decay.

In 1715 the manufacture of linen was very extensively pursued, and the cotton trade was soon after introduced. Silk manufacture was begun by the Huguenots, who had settled in Dublin in large numbers after the revocation of the Edict of Nantes. The old jealousy, however, soon became again apparent, and in the reign of George I. and George III. Acts were passed which brought ruin to these industries.

The commerce of the port had, however, increased so considerably towards the close of the last century, that the accommodation offered on the river for shipping was found to be quite inadequate, and about this time the Irish Parliament granted £15,000 for constructing docks on both sides of the Liffey.

The Floating and Graving Docks communicating with the Grand Canal on the south side, including a basin covering forty statute acres, and a quay and store frontage of 7,500 feet, were opened in 1796; and St. George's, the latest of the Custom House Docks, in 1821. A Parliamentary Report issued in 1805, says:—

"One of the great obstacles to the present trade of the city of Dublin is that there being a bank of sand stretched across the mouth of the River Liffey (which bank it would be impossible, or even if possible useless to attempt to remove, because another bar would immediately form itself) it compels the trade to be carried on in small vessels of 150 to 200 tons in general, instead of those large vessels used at London, Bristol, and Liverpool, to the very great increase of expense to the trade, and at times causing great difficulty of getting vessels to charter fit for the harbour in order to carry on the trade."

The extensive harbour at Dublin is now under the control of a body called the Dublin Port and Docks Board, the history of which constitution may be given as follows:—

In the year 1786 (26 George III., cap. 19) the Irish Parliament passed an Act "For promoting

The Bank of Ireland. (*Formerly the Irish Parliament.*)

the trade of Dublin by rendering its port and harbour more commodious," and repealing all previous Acts affecting the Government of the Harbour of Dublin. This Act constituted certain persons named therein as a corporate body, by the name of "The Corporation for Preserving and Improving the Port of Dublin," and as such to have perpetual succession.

In the year 1810 an Act (50 George III., chap. 95) was passed by the Imperial Parliament, transferring to the aforesaid Corporation the erection, repairing, and maintaining lighthouses round the coasts of Ireland. This power was continued and re-enacted with certain reservations by the Merchant Shipping Act, 17 and 18 Vict., cap. 104.

In the year 1867 an Act was passed to alter the constitution of the Corporation for Preserving and Improving the Port of Dublin, and for other purposes connected with that body, and giving it the name of "The Dublin Port and Docks Board;" and with respect to the future care and management, &c., of the Irish lighthouses, a distinct body corporate was created by the name of "The Commissioners of Irish Lights," whose constitution was to remain under the Act of 26 Geo. III., cap. 19, and as if the Act of 1867 had not been passed.

The Port and Docks Board has effected very considerable improvements in the harbour during the last twenty years.

The quay walls along the River Liffey were originally built at a very shallow depth, and about twenty years ago the foreshore in front of most of these quays was exposed at low water for many feet outside their bases, and vessels used to lie aground during the greater portion of each tide.

Timber jetties 2,646 feet in length have been built outside some of the old quay walls along both sides of the river, so as to permit the various berths to be deepened considerably.

At the south side of the river the shallow quays have been replaced by 2,793 lineal feet of deep-water quays, and on the north side the old shallow quays have been replaced by 2,317 lineal feet of deep-water quays. The North Quay has also been extended eastwards for a distance of 2,142 feet. The river or harbour channel has been improved by constant dredging, and the depth of water has been considerably increased.

Dublin Harbour now covers 205 acres, the entrance to the harbours, between the North Bull and Poolbeg lighthouses, being 1,000 feet wide. The area of the harbour has not been extended from that of twenty years ago, but it has altogether been considerably deepened, so that a much larger space is now available for shipping. About 2,600 feet of new quays have been added, the depth of water now allowing vessels drawing 22 feet to lie alongside at low water.

There are four Docks at Dublin, viz.:—

    Custom House (George's) Dock.
        ,,   Inner   ,,
        ,,   Old   ,,
    Ringsend Dock.
    Spencer Dock.

There are also four Dry Docks, of the following dimensions :—

	Length.	Breadth.	Depth of Water.
Dry Dock No. 1	280	35	$12\frac{1}{4}$
,, 2	165	35	$12\frac{1}{4}$
,, 3	80	22	$12\frac{3}{4}$

together with a graving dock 412 feet long by 70 feet wide, with a depth of 16 feet, and two patent slips.

There is very extensive accommodation for building and repairing vessels, also hydraulic machinery for all purposes.

There is a very extensive trade at Dublin, the tonnage entering in 1884 being 1,773,505 tons.

Two great lines of inland communication commence in Dublin City. These are: The Grand Canal originally commenced in 1755 by the Corporation for promoting inland navigation in Ireland, for which a subscription was opened in 1772, the subscribers being incorporated under the title of "The Company of Undertakers of the Grand Canal," who, by the completion of this work connected Dublin both with the Shannon and the Barrow. The entire cost was £844,216, besides £122,148 expended on docks; of this amount one-third was defrayed by Parliament.

The other, the "Royal Canal," was incorporated by a charter of George III. in 1789, and afterwards aided by a grant of additional powers from the Legislature. This canal extends for 92 miles, and cost £776,213, which was wholly defrayed by public expenditure.

The Port has been steadily increasing its trade,

as may be seen from the following statement of tonnage entering the Port of Dublin at every tenth year, viz :—

Year.	Tonnage Entered.
1794	320,183
1804	378,659
1814	366,799
1824	386,328
1834	513,974
1844	610,092
1854	927,133
1864	1,143,137
1874	1,563,847
1884	1,773,505

The income of the Port and Docks Board arising from tonnage and quay wall dues on shipping, which was less than £7,000 in 1789, now amounts to about £60,000 per annum.

The cross-Channel trade forms a very important item in the commerce of Dublin. The first steamboat entered Dublin Bay from across the Channel in 1816, and in 1824 steamers were generally used for the transmission of merchandise.

The principal import trade of the Liffey consists of sugar, ice, grain, phosphate rock, timber, manure, and general merchandise, whilst a large Export Trade is carried on, consisting of cattle, grain, manure, whisky, beer and porter, linen, and general merchandise.

A very important work in connection with the commerce of the Liffey was recently completed, viz., the Alexandra Basin, which has been constructed by the Dublin Port and Docks Board, and one of many improvements in connection with this

Port, now being carried out by this enterprising Board. The naming of this basin by H.R.H. the Princess of Wales, in April, 1885, was the occasion for one of the most patriotic exhibitions of loyalty made by the people of Ireland during the visit of their Royal Highnesses the Prince and Princess of Wales to that country.

The spirit which has been displayed by the Port and Docks Board in the various improvements they have effected, and on which they are still engaged, to provide adequate accommodation for the increasing trade of the Port, deserves every success.

THE USK.

The Usk, with its neighbouring rivers the Wye and the Monnow, flow through some of the most lovely scenery in England. The district is in parts undulating, rising here and there into bold bluffs, and diversified by wide knolls and deep, shaded dells. The scenery is greatly set off by a background of misty mountains on the north and west, by numerous primitive churches half concealed by clustering ivy or the shade of aged yews, and by the picturesque ruins of feudal strongholds and grand ecclesiastical structures. Of the three streams, the Usk is the only one which can be considered industrial. It enters Monmouthshire about three miles west of Abergavenny, flows near that town, and through the middle of the county, passes the towns of Usk and Caerleon, where it becomes tidal, and finally flows into the Severn.

On the right bank of the Usk, and about four miles from the mouth of that river, stands the important, prosperous town of Newport. It was at one time part of the city of Caerleon, but its excellent geographical position, which made it the natural outlet for the produce of the extensive s

NEWPORT.

collieries and iron and tin works of the neighbourhood, soon placed it in a position independent of the historic city. Newport was called by Giraldus *Novus Burgus*, or New Town, to distinguish it from Caerleon. It was afterwards called *Castell Newydd*, or New Castle, because the Earl of Gloucester, a natural son of Henry I., erected there a castle for the defence of his possessions. The castle descended from him through several noble families till, on the execution of Edward Duke of Buckingham, it was seized, together with the lordship, by Henry VIII. Its present owner is the Duke of Beaufort. Some of the towers and part of the walls of the castle still stand between the bridges which cross the Usk.

The great prosperity of Newport may be attributed almost entirely to its proximity to the rich coalfields and mineral treasures of Monmouthshire and South Wales. In the county of Monmouth alone there are twelve beds of coal, which vary in thickness from three to nine feet. The area of the coalfield is estimated at about 90,000 acres; the seams which can be profitably worked averaging a thickness of fifty feet. Ironstone occurs both in beds and in large detached masses, and yields from 18 to 55 per cent. of iron. The ore is the common clay called ironstone.

Large works for the manufacture of iron are situated in the neighbourhood of Pontypool, where iron was probably first made in this country. A family named Grant were the first ironmakers in the district. About the year 1565 they were succeeded by Mr. Richard Hanbury, of London, who held a third part of the immense tract of mineral property in the neighbourhood at a rental of 3s. 4d. a year, the whole of it having been let by the owner, the Earl of Abergavenny, for 9s. 4d. per annum! Mr. Hanbury made great additions to the works, and they were still further extended by his grandson, Mr. Capel Hanbury, who was esteemed the first ironmaster of his age. At that time—the reign of Elizabeth—the ore was smelted with charcoal; and in order to prevent the destruction of timber a statute was passed prohibiting the erection of ironworks except in certain districts, and of these Monmouthshire was one. Yet in 1740, nearly a century and a half afterwards, when coal was first successfully employed in iron smelting, Monmouthshire contained only two iron furnaces, capable of producing 900 tons annually; while the invention of the steam-engine in 1788 only led to the building of a third furnace, by which the "make" was increased to 2,100 tons. In 1790, however, three new furnaces were erected at Blaenavon, and others at Blaendare and Ebbw Vale.

The Nantyglo works were commenced five years later. At first they were not successful, and at last work there was discontinued altogether. Under the management of the Bailey family, however, the industry thrived, and the works are now ranked amongst the greatest of the kind in the United Kingdom. A great impulse was given to the Monmouthshire iron trade by the success of

Blaenavon, and very soon numerous furnaces sprang up along the valleys that run towards Merthyr Tydfil. In 1803 the Beaufort, Ebbw Vale, Clydach, and Varteg works began operations. They were followed by the Tredegar in 1805; the Coalbrooke Dale in 1821, the Blaina in 1824, the Pentewan in 1825, the Abersychan in 1827, the Bute in 1828, the Golynos (afterwards united with Pentewan) in 1837, and the Victoria works in 1838. In addition to these there are numerous other works more or less extensive. The South Wales iron works commence at Clydach, about four miles from Abergavenny, and extend in an unbroken line to Merthyr, a distance of twenty miles. The Monmouthshire coal and iron trade is greatly facilitated by a succession of valleys with a gradual inclination towards Newport, where the produce is shipped for exportation.

There are also several important manufactories in the immediate neighbourhood of Newport, the most important of which are the Dos nail works of Messrs. J. J. Cordes & Co. Limited, the engineering establishments and iron foundries of T. Spittle, Limited, Messrs. C. Jordan & Sons, the Isca Foundry Company, and the Uskside and Engineering Company, Limited. Near the Great Western wharf Messrs. Morris and Griffin, of Wolverhampton, have erected large chemical works. They import phosphate rock from South Carolina, the West Indies, and Lisbon, and convert the same into manure. Messrs. Mordey, Carney & Co., Limited, and the Usk Shipbuilding Company,

Limited, carry on the work of shipbuilding and repairing. Works of a kindred character are the Newport (Mon.) Slipway, Dry Dock and Engineering Company, Limited, who, having acquired a valuable site, 23 acres in extent, with 1,766 feet of river frontage, have erected thereon a wharf and landing stage.

Important works for the manufacture of glass, bottles, &c., have been established in the neighbourhood within the past two months. Several of the most prominent local gentlemen are connected with the company, which has commenced operations under the most favourable circumstances.

As the trade of the town continued to grow, and the number of vessels entering and clearing from the port steadily went on increasing, floating dock accommodation became absolutely necessary. The Newport Docks were opened in 1842, and sixteen years later were enlarged. This accommodation proving inadequate to meet the requirements of a growing trade, it was further increased in 1875 by the opening of the Alexandra Docks. These docks are the property of the Alexandra (Newport and South Wales) Docks and Railway Company, who are also proprietors of the Newport Old Docks, of the Alexandra Graving Dock, and the Blaina Wharf, on the west side of the Usk. The dimensions of the Alexandra Dock are as follows: Length, 2,500 ft.; width, 500 ft.; length of lock, 350 ft.; width, 65 ft.; depth of water on cill, spring tides, 35 ft. 9 in.; neap tides, 25 ft. 9 in.

It covers an area of 28¾ acres. The Old Dock is 1,753 ft. in length, 300 ft. in width, while its lock has a length of 220 ft., a width of 61 ft., and depth on cill, spring tides, 31 ft.; neap tides, 20 ft. It has an area of 11½ acres. The Graving Dock is 532 ft. long, 74 ft. wide, and has an average depth of 20 ft. at the entrance. Since the opening of the Alexandra Dock, in 1875, there has been a steady increase in the trade of the port, especially among large steamers, which, for want of suitable dock accommodation, formerly kept away from Newport. The increase in the depth of water is 5 ft. more at the Alexandra Docks than was obtainable in the port before they were opened. Vessels of the largest size can now enter the lock of the Alexandra Dock at all tides; and some idea of the rapidity of the despatch may be formed when we say that ships of 2,400 tons capacity have been loaded and despatched in thirty-five hours. The docks are in direct railway communication with all the collieries in South Wales, including a direct line from the Rhondda Valley. The dock lines are connected with those of all the great railway companies of the country. Another new dock, the first sod of which was cut in the spring of 1883 by Sir George Elliot, Bart., M.P., is in course of construction by the Alexandra Dock Company.

In order not to be behind the docks in offering increased facilities to vessels visiting the port, several of the wharves have been rebuilt and fitted with modern machinery, especially the Nantyglo and Blaina, by the Dock Company, the old Blaina and Blaenavon by the Patent Nut and Bolt Company, and the Pontypool by the Ebbw Vale Company, where steamers of large tonnage can load and unload.

The following are the harbour dues on all vessels entering the port :—

Per reg ton.

With Cargo Coastwise, entering and leaving, each way ¼d.
" Foreign " " " ... ½d
Light or in Ballast, Coastwise or Foreign .... free
Vessels loading or discharging at River Wharfs............ 1d.

The Old Dock rates are as follows :—

ON VESSELS ENTERING AND DEPARTING WITH CARGOES

From Ports of U. K. and Ireland, and Channel Islands... 2d
From Ports in Europe, North Cape to Gibraltar .... 5d.
Vessels with Cargo and departing light or *vice versâ*, under 100 tons, 3d. ; to 150, 4d. ; and above 150 tons .... 5d.
From Ports east of North Cape and in Mediterranean... 7d.
Vessels with Cargo and departing light or *vice versâ*, under 100 tons, 5d. ; to 150 tons, 6d. ; above 150 tons .... 7d.
From any other Port or Place .... 9d.
Vessels entering and leaving in Ballast........................ 3d.
" " without breaking bulk or with the same Cargo, within three weeks............... 6d.
Vessels entering after having left with the same cargo ... 3d.
" from U. K. and leaving Foreign are rated as to Port of destination.
Vessels receiving or landing cargo at Co.'s Wharves outside docks .... 2d.

Vessels of less than 20 are rated as 20 tons.

RENT CHARGED ON VESSELS Entering

in ballast to load, not over 200 tons, after two weeks, under 400, three weeks, under 700, four weeks, 700 tons upwards, five weeks.

with cargo to load, not over 200 tons, after three weeks, under 400 tons, four weeks, under 700, five weeks, above 700 tons, six weeks.

For periods over the above, first week, ½d.; second, ¾d.; third, 1¼d.; and fourth and every other week, 1d. per reg. ton.

Vessels entering to lay up after discharged, as agreed.

POLICE AND WATCHING CHARGES.

On all vessels entering dock, per week or part, 1/-.
Special watchmen, per night, 3/6.
BALLAST, discharged and removed, 1/- per ton.
  „   supplied and shipped, 2/- „
when beyond 15 ft. of hatchway, 2d. „ extra.
      Working by night, 3d. „ „

CHARGES FOR LOADING—USE OF MACHINERY.

Coal, 2d. per ton. Weighing, ½d. per ton, if required.
  „ before 6 a.m. and after 7 p.m., 1d. per ton extra.
  „ shipped for stiffening ....per ton 4d.

ALEXANDRA DOCK RATES.

Dock rates, &c., on vessels, &c., same as the Old Dock.

Exception.—Vessels under 100 tons from or to the United Kingdom or Channel Islands, 1½d. per registered ton.

Use of hydraulic machinery and cranes ... 3d. per ton.
Use of weighing machine ... ... ½d. „
Use of shipping staiths for coal, culm, or coke 2d. „
Water supplied at 1/- per 100 gallons.

The Pilot Rates, which are not compulsory, are as follows:—

No 1. From Newport to River's Mouth.
  „ 2.   „   Holmes.
  „ 3.   „   Nash Point or Minehead.
  „ 4.   „   Ilfracombe or East of Combe.
  „ 5.   „   Lundy I. or W. of Ilfracombe.

	No. 1.	No. 2.	No. 3.	No. 4.	No. 5.
under 100 tons,	10/	15/6	22/6	32/6	45/
100 and under 200 „	15/	20/	35/	47/6	60/
200 „ 300 „	17/6	30/	45/	65/	80/
300 „ 400 „	22/6	35/	57/6	72/6	92/6
400 „ 500 „	25/	41/	61/	83/6	110/6
500 „ 600 „	26/	43/	65/6	90/6	118/
600 „ 700 „	28/	48/	73/	103/	133/
700 „ 800 „	29/	50/	75/	107/6	135/
800 „ 900 „	30/	52/	82/	117/	157/
900 „ 1000 „	32/	55/	85/	120/	160/

			No. 1.	No. 2.	No. 3.	No. 4.	No. 5.
1000 and	tons	1200 tons,	35/	60/	100/	140/	190/
1200	,,	1500 ,,	45/	70/	110/	160/	122/
1500	,,	1800 ,,	50/	80/	130/	185/	240/
1800 and upward	,,		60/	90/	145/	195/	260/

When requested, Pilots remain on board—10/6 per day.

Pilots moving vessels in docks or river, if one tide, if 100 tons, 5/; 300, 10/; 600, 12/6; 1000, 17/6; 1500, 20/; over 1500, 25/.

Collector's fee, if 100 tons, 6d; under 300, 1/; under 500, 1/6; under 800, 2/; over 800, 2/6.

TOWAGE RATES, TO OR FROM—

Watchhouse Reach	2d.	per reg. ton.
Bridgwater Reach	2½d.	,,
River Mouth	3d.	,,
Spit	3½d.	,,
Holmes	4d.	,,

If towed beyond the Holmes, under 600 tons, £5 per stage; above 600 tons register, 2d. per ton each stage in addition. The stages are the Nash, Ilfracombe, and Lundy.

SECOND TUG (HALF RATES).

Shifting towage in river, under 90 tons, 7/6; over 90 tons, 1d. per ton. Shifting towage to or from Dry Dock or Gridiron, 1½d. per ton.

The number of vessels registered as belonging to Newport in 1856 was 92, of an aggregate tonnage of 16,280. During the same year there entered the port:—Coasting trade, 1,544 sailing vessels of 86,246 tons and 468 steamers of 34,298 tons: colonial trade, 70 sailing vessels of 17,040 tons, and 1 steamer of 602 tons: foreign trade, 461 sailing vessels of 96,334 tons, and 2 steamers of 1,200 tons—in all 2,075 vessels of 199,620 tons, and 471 steamers of 36,000 tons. In the same year (1856) there cleared from the port:—Coasting trade, 6,777 sailing vessels of 414,002 tons, and 269 steamers of 17,259 tons: in the colonial trade,

151 sailing vessels of 39,019 tons: in the foreign trade, 898 sailing vessels of 183,440 tons, and 5 steamers of 2,828 tons—in all 7,826 sailing vessels of 636,461 tons, and 274 steamers of 20,087 tons. The register tonnage entered in 1878 was 578,608 tons; in 1880, 1,581,959 tons; and in 1884, 1,974,918. The steam tonnage cleared from Newport in 1876 was 314,776; in 1880, 893,149, being an increase of 184 per cent.; and in 1884, 1,408,616, or an increase of 345 per cent. in eight years. The following extract is taken from *The Times* of January 20, 1885:—

"The official statistics of trade for the year 1884 show most remarkable progress in regard to Newport. For years past Cardiff has taken the lead in the returns of both coal and iron, but since increased dock accommodation has been provided at Newport, and great improvements have been carried out in the river Usk, there has been a close race between the two ports in connection with all the leading staple trades. The shipments of coal from Newport to foreign countries in the year reached 1,721,512 tons, as against 1,581,463 tons in 1883, which is an increase of 9 per cent. Cardiff, on the other hand, secured an increase of barely 3 per cent. in the year, while Swansea showed a falling off of 4 per cent. In the shipments of coal coastwise the progress of Newport was still more significant, its total clearances having reached 1,031,540 tons, as against 977,495 tons in 1883, or an increase of 6 per cent. Cardiff, on the other hand, shipped 980,432 tons last year, as against 1,038,696 tons in 1883, being a decrease of 5 per cent. Swansea also showed a decrease of no less than 11 per cent. In iron and steel exports the figures for the three ports in the past year were as follows:—Newport, 108,572 tons; Cardiff, 83,199 tons; and Swansea, 4,979 tons. In the imports of iron ore and other produce Newport also takes the lead."

The following figures show at a glance the progress made by Newport in coal shipments, including bunkers, during the last five years:—

	Foreign.	Coastwise.	Total.
1881 ...	1,286,016	955,608	2,241,624
1882 ...	1,568,653	915,982	2,484,635
1883 ...	1,789,465	1,029,355	2,819,820
1884 ...	1,984,933	1,047,835	3,032,768
1885 ...	1,767,791	1,128,546	2,896,337*

* Exclusive of bunkers.

The quantity of tin-plates exported from Newport reached 29,699 boxes in 1880; in 1882 it was 107,770 boxes; and in 1884 it had risen to 250,333 boxes.

The iron exports were as follows:—

1881.	1882.	1883.	1884.	1885.
Tons.	Tons.	Tons.	Tons.	Tons.
172,495	174,828	187,584	108,554	169,844

For rails only, Newport stands first in the Kingdom.

The principal imports of Newport are iron ore, timber, pit props, railway sleepers, corn, potatoes, &c., while the exports comprise coal, iron, rails, machinery, tin plates, terne plates, &c.

Newport occupies a splendid position on the Bristol Channel. As a port for large vessels it offers great inducements, combining safety of approach, securing in entering and leaving at all tides, and quick despatch when discharging and loading. Shipbuilding, which formerly flourished in Newport, seems of late years to have languished; and when the wealth of the district is considered —the fine river, the splendid fore-shore, and the proximity of iron and coal, we cannot but feel regret that a river offering such exceptional advantages for the construction of iron vessels should be practically ignored by the shipbuilders of our country.

THE TEES.

To the story of the river Tees in the past poetry has lent its glamour, but in the present its attractions are utilitarian, especially in the lower reaches. Far away from the coast, on the bleak uplands, close to the sources of the Wear, the Tees rises—a river which is one of the "two pretty handmaids" that attended on the bride, Medway, on her marriage with the Thames, as Spenser records. The Tees is a river which is magnificent in its early course, churning over cataracts, dashing over High Force, sweeping round the fine old fortress town of Barnard Castle (Barnard standing, as in Leland's days, "stately on Tees"), passing Rokeby with its remembrances of Scott, and near to Winston and Darlington, sleepy Yarm, and thus with a rush to its thronged highway from Stockton to the sea; its banks being full of life and work, and the energy of two or three generations. It is a noble river; its history and associations well invite comment, but we have to do with it in its industrial aspect. Practically, the Tees, then, as we are to see it, is that part of the river from Stockton to the sea. And few of the rivers can boast of changes as great as that span of the Tees can in the last forty or fifty years. It is at these that we may thus first fittingly glance, for it is partly through them that Middlesbrough and Stockton, as we know them, became possibilities.

The River Tees.

The Tees runs a rather roundabout course from the mountain range eastwards to the German Ocean, and is for a large part of its one hundred miles the divider of Durham from Yorkshire. A little below Middlesbrough it expands into a wide estuary. It is within the century that the river has become practically a commercial one, though for a long period previously ships were built at Stockton and Yarm, and its shipping trade was "important" in the eyes of the people of the past. A scheme for the improvement of the course a little below Stockton dates back to 1769, but not until 1808 was the practical step taken of the incorporation of the Tees Navigation Company. It commenced the task of improving the river by making a "cut" through a narrow neck of land near Portrack, and the course of the river was shortened when, in 1810, that cut was opened. The effect was marked; the "rise of tide at Stockton Quay," says Mr. John Fowler, C.E., "which formerly was 8 feet, was increased to 10." The tonnage of the port of Stockton, "which in 1804 was 24,534 tons, had risen in 1812, only two years after the opening of the first cut, to 42,904 tons." Another impetus to the trade of the Tees was felt

THE CLEVELAND HILLS.

when, in 1825, the primal public railway, the Stockton and Darlington Railway, was opened. The growth of trade made better river facilities needful, and the Navigation Company carried out the plan of Mr. H. H. Price, and made a second "cut," 1,100 yards long, to cut off a bend of the river, which was effected and opened in the year 1830. Jetties to fix the sand-banks were next formed between Stockton and a little below where Middlesbrough was to be, and gradually the tonnage of the port increased (coal being the chief export), until the opening of West Hartlepool Docks, when a large part of the coal traffic was diverted to that place. The dues fell off, and with less revenue, the work of the Navigation Company grew less; the navigation itself and the bar grew worse; and, finally, when iron had been "found" near the river, and when its prospects were greatly improved, an Act was obtained for the creation of a public commission. The Tees Conservancy Commission began life with a debt of something like £80,000, and with a revenue of little more than £4,000, but gradually works have been carried out which have made the river what it now is. The Conservancy was composed of fifteen members, appointed—three by the Board of Trade, two by the ratepayers of Yarm, five by Stockton Council, and five by Middlesbrough Council. Aided by the Stockton and Darlington Railway Company, the Commission determined to carry out many needful works, and commenced by the dredging of a scarp at Cargo Fleet, which had much obstructed the navigation and through which a channel was cut. From that time a series of magnificent works have been executed. The new Conservancy has dredged on a scale of great magnitude, has constructed training walls, has reclaimed large quantities of land, and has constructed and is constructing great breakwaters. We may glance briefly at some of these works, and first at

The Breakwaters.

Twenty-four years ago it was decided to construct two breakwaters, on the north and south sides of the bay, plans being prepared by Mr. John Fowler, C.E., the engineer to the Conservancy then and now. After preparatory work, the foundation-stone was laid by Mr. Isaac Wilson, then the chairman of the Conservancy, on November 3, 1863. The breakwater is built of slag from the blast furnaces near—slag cast in solid square blocks, carried to the end of the breakwater, and there tipped, and thus over a score of years the breakwater advanced at an enormous cost. In 1863 there were 68,728 tons of slag deposited there, and the quantity rose until in 1869 it was 443,000 tons; and in the total up to 1874, the quantity deposited was 2,534,250 tons, at a cost of £98,949, after deducting sums allowed by the ironmasters. At this time Mr. A. M. Rendel, C.E., surveyed and reported on the works to the Conservancy, and remarked that "the slag deposits are doing their work satisfactorily. They have replaced the shifting Southgare sand by a solid immovable bank." And at the latest date for which we have official figures the cost of the breakwater was £211,328, a sum large in itself, but small when compared with the cost of similar works in other localities.

Dredging.

A very few figures will show how the Tees has been dredged, and that work the authority we have named, Mr. Rendel, pronounced the carrying out of a wise policy. A table will show better than any other method, the amount of dredging from the Tees in the years ending in October:—

Year.	Tons raised.	Year.	Tons raised.
1854	11,745	1870	560,205
1860	65,955	1874	848,673
1864	73,715	*1884	1,846,790

* At a cost of £26,434.

In addition to these works the Conservancy has constructed many miles of training walls, built of slag—twenty miles, indeed, in its first twenty years of life—that score of miles using about 1,248,000 tons of that popular Tees material. Competent authorities have pointed out the benefits that these works have conferred upon the river; Captain Calver, R.N., remarking that the increase in the depth of the navigable capacity of the river placed in strong light the wise character of the management of its Board, and "the practical value of its operations;" and Mr. Rendel summed up by saying that "the operations conducted on the Tees during" twenty years were, in his opinion, "amongst the most successful engineering works of the time." We need not quote other and later authorities, nor linger long amid the details and dry figures. The dredging, the wall-building, the breakwater construction, the defining of channels, the blasting of rocks, and the scooping of scarps have all had their value; and thus it is that whilst in 1853 the Commissioners had a revenue of £8,109, and in 1855 one of £4,807 only, it had risen in 1863 to £10,744, to £12,070 in 1865, to £18,214 in 1869, to £22,521 in 1874, and to £54,672 in 1884. And the debt of the Commission had necessarily risen—from £99,646 in 1853 to £204,233 in 1866, and to £768,993 in 1884. For this the Tees has magnificent works to show, and it can say that the "3 feet of water at Stockton at low water ordinary spring tides, and the $14\frac{1}{2}$ feet of water at high water," are replaced by "18 feet of water to Stockton and $25\frac{1}{2}$ feet to Middlesbrough at high water spring tides." Thousands of acres of land have been and are being reclaimed, and there has been an industrial development which has few parallels. We may glance at this in going down the river from

STOCKTON TO MIDDLESBROUGH.

Stockton thirty years ago had benefited from the two early railways it had helped to construct. It was cutting the sod of its first blast furnaces, and it had just commenced its iron shipbuilding yard. It was a town of about 11,000 inhabitants. These first furnaces are cold now, but two sets replace them in operation, and rolling mills are on the east and west of the town, whilst

THE PORT OF MIDDLESBROUGH.

four iron shipbuilding yards contribute to our merchant fleet. Stockton builds bridges, rolls lead as well as iron, manufactures pottery, bottles, glass and gasholders, and is one of the chief of the flour-producing towns of the North. Its engineering establishments are noted, its forges important, and its foundries large. But its growth has been in the thirty years unquestionably dwarfed by the town which is one of the marvels of Northern enterprise, and which Mr. Gladstone described, a score of years ago, as "the youngest-born of England's greatness." In 1831 there were in Middlesbrough 154 persons; in 1881 there were 55,281; and in that fact much of the story of the growth of the great town on the Tees is told. The world is familiar with the fact that in 1830 the "Middlesbrough Owners," headed by Mr. Joseph Pease, bought 500 acres of marshy land to make a town; a little port began to ship coals to manufacture pottery and to cast iron, and to it, in 1841, there came, attracted by Mr. Pease, Henry Bolckow and John Vaughan. As Mr. Joseph Cowen eloquently said at the Jubilee banquet, "Wherever the British flag flies, and to whatever corner of the world English enterprise has penetrated, the story of Middlesbrough is known. But with coal, and without iron, Middlesbrough would not have achieved its proud pre-eminence." It is iron, as that great North-country orator has said, which is "woven and interwoven, as no other article is, with the lusty life of the nation," and especially of Tees-side.

Iron on the Tees.

Bolckow & Vaughan had erected, as aids to their iron works at Middlesbrough, smelting plant at Witton Park, on the Wear, near Bishop Auckland, and, finding supplies of iron ore running short, they set about to search for the ironstone long known to be in Cleveland. They "opened" it, as the result of that search, at the output at Eston, and thence the course of the iron trade was changed. There were then in the North of England eleven smelting works, near the Tyne and the Wear almost exclusively. The discovery of John Vaughan drew the trade and the traders to the Tees. He and his partner built at Eston; Mr. Lowthian Bell at Port Clarence, Messrs. Gilkes & Wilson at Middlesbrough, and Mr. Samuelson near Eston, so that a continuous growth of furnaces on and near the Tees was known for two dozen years from the date of that "commercial discovery" of the Cleveland iron by John Vaughan twenty-five years ago. But it was not only the planting there of over 110 of these huge smelting works on and near the Tees; it was the development of the trade in its many branches, of allied industries, and of the formation of great firms which were powers in the land. Mr. Isaac Lowthian Bell has told the tale succinctly in one of his early addresses on that subject; he remarked: "In 1850 the first ton of Cleveland ironstone was worked, and the output in 1866 was $2\frac{3}{4}$ millions of tons of ironstone," but, treating even then of the foreign competition in the iron trade, he did not seem to contemplate a growth in the production such as has since been witnessed. Even at the risk of repetition, we will give the figures which show the production of pig-iron in the North-East of England (chiefly on and near Tees-side), since the year Mr. Bell wrote. For illustrative years the production was as follows:—

Year.	Tons.	Year.	Tons.
1863	1,233,418	1880	2,510,853
1872	1,968,972	1884	2,484,340
1875	2,047,763	1885	2,458,889
1879	1,781,443		

Thus, despite the increase of foreign competition, and although there was a very serious depression in the iron-trade last year, and there was a combination at work to lessen the production, the output of pig-iron in Cleveland was double what it was in 1868; and it may be fairly said that the growth of that immense trade in crude iron, within two dozen years after its commencement on Tees-side, is one of the wonders of the commercial age.

It is not needful to refer in detail to the varied industries which are clustered on the banks of the Tees. Nine years ago it was seen that the iron rail trade was declining, that on railways steel was superseding the older form of metal, and that it would be needful for Tees-side to turn its attention to the production of the newer form. And although it was unquestionably tardy in attempting to produce steel, yet the attempts of Mr. Lowthian Bell, and of Messrs. Gilchrist and Thomas, have acquired historic repute.

It should be mentioned that the process of making Bessemer steel from common iron ore, well known as the Thomas-Gilchrist process, was originated at Middlesbrough. This process effected a revolution in the iron and steel trades throughout the world, and to the discovery of the means of getting rid of the phosphorus from the pig iron when in a state of fusion may be attributed a great deal of the present prosperity of those trades. In the work of progressive improvements, Messrs. Bolckow, Vaughan & Company, Limited, the owners of the works founded by Messrs. Bolckow & Vaughan, occupied a foremost place. In 1876 they put down fine plant for steel-making at Eston. The firm owned large mines of rich hæmatite ore in Spain; this ore they brought over in their own ships, smelted it in their own furnaces, made it while molten into steel, and without having allowed it once to cool, delivered it in the form of steel rails, which were again shipped in the firm's own vessels to Germany, Italy, or India.

As the result of the success of Messrs. Gilchrist and Thomas, and of the development of the Bessemer process, pure and simple, Tees-side is one of the great steel-making regions in the kingdom. and Eston is certainly one of the most perfect and interesting types of steel works in the world. And, before leaving the aggregation of iron industries on Tees-side, it may be fairly said that, in attempts to utilise the blast furnace gases, in the definition of the most economic shapes and dimensions in smelting plant, and in the perfection of hot-blast stoves, the labours of Cleveland ironmasters—Bell, Gjers, and the Whitwells—have led the van.

We may, fittingly, here allude to the growth of shipbuilding on the river. At Stockton, there is an ancestry for the industry, its old wooden order, but iron shipbuilding dates back only to 1854, when the *Advance* was launched from the yard of the Iron Shipbuilding Company, South Stockton, on January 26. Soon after the yard passed into the hands of Messrs. Richardson, Duck & Co., by whom it has been long and successfully carried on. The second yard—that of M. Pearse & Co.—was begun on the northern side of the pier, and two others on a smaller scale have in the last two years been commenced. The first iron vessel launched at Middlesbrough was from the yard of Rake, Kimber & Co., on March 1, 1858; Messrs. Richardson & Co. opened there a yard about 1864, we believe, and this passing into the hands of Backhouse & Dixon, and then into those of R. Dixon & Co., its present owners, is far the largest of the Middlesbrough shipyards. Let us now show at a glance the progress of the shipping industry by contrasting certain figures—the launches from the Tees yards in 1866, in 1884, and in 1885.

	1866. Tons.		1884. Tons.		1885. Tons.
South Stockton	3,845	……	15,002	……	14,401
Stockton	5,460	……	8,267	……	11,711
Middlesbrough	4,741	……	7,067	……	8,226
	14,046		30,336		34,338

Whilst we have, of course, taken the figures for one of the most recent years, it is only fair to remember that that was a year of great depression for shipbuilding, and that the chief Middlesbrough yard was closed for many months. The producing capacity of the Tees must be held to be more than double that of the past year, but even that contracted production shows an enormous gain on the output of the former of the two years we have compared. And should the demand again give the needful stimulus, the tonnage launched in the future is capable of being considerably in excess of that of any year in the past.

The dock accommodation is being enlarged; it was made in 1842, was sold in 1852 to the Stockton and Darlington Railway, and enlarged to about eleven acres in 1872, whilst a further enlargement is now in progress. The imports are chiefly iron ore and timber; in the exports iron and steel in many forms play the chief part. Not much need be said of the shipping of the Tees, for it is comparatively limited amongst the ports, but both at Stockton and at Middlesbrough there are some fleets of vessels which are numerous if not of the largest sizes.

It is to be remembered that the Tees, as we see it, is the creation of fifty years. Three score years ago, there was a shallow, tortuous stream, with neither dock nor trade. Scarcely a house broke the solitude from Stockton to the sea, and nothing but the smoke from the infrequent farm chimney rose up into the ether. Now the sight in the

MIDDLESBROUGH RAILWAY STATION.

passage up or down the river by day is startling, by night is spectacular. The clang of the riveters in the shipyards, the roar of the blast furnaces, and the thud of the steam hammers at the rolling mills and the engineering works fill the ear. A long halo of light spreads over a large part of the scene from the Tees Bridge Iron Company's works at Stockton Bridge down to the huge steel works at Eston, and tongues and darts of flame rise up into it. Nearer this it is seen that fierce coruscations of light flame up and out from the furnaces; ever and anon, huge incandescent heaps are being hurried here and there in the rolling mills, and are taking shape beneath the rolls, whitening the faces of the workmen near; from little orifices pencilled streaks of painful light are visible; and now and again one of the huge steel converters sends forth "a hailing fount of fire" that rises high in the air, and casts a strange yellow gleam over the earth for miles. The home of Tubal Cain is here: this is the stream Scamander where Vulcan lives; iron is in and on the earth, in the atmosphere, on the streets, in statues, in bricks in the buildings, covering the steam pipes in the shape of slag wool, and is the material for the damming and the defining of the river. With its rise the fortunes of the town rise, and the upward movement in the price of "pig" figuratively affects the whole welfare of the town, just as through sliding scales it literally affects the wages of the workmen, the charges for carriage on the railways, and even the poor rates in the mining district.

With the price of pig iron, profits rise, palaces change owners, fields become furnaces, the puddler takes the place of the ploughman, and even the rate of marriage fluctuates!

It is as of old, "a good land" is this where the stones are iron, but it is best in the pluck, the sagacity, and the public spirit of its people. Coal failed the little port of Middlesbrough, and they turned the hills near them into gold; fashion, even in rails, changed, and they painfully altered the form of their manufacture to meet the change; and now new alterations are before them. It is not easy to assign full credit to all for their share in the work. In Stockton, the present member, Mr. Joseph Dodds, has been prominent, both on the land and on the river, and more than yeoman service has been done by Mr. Joseph Richardson and Mr. R. H. Appleton. Middlesbrough undoubtedly owes its existence to the late Mr. Joseph Pease, and that influential family have done much to build up and consolidate the town, and schools and other gifts show that they have largely and generously recognised the duties that wealth has. Unquestionably to the Vaughans, and the Bolckows, Middlesbrough owes much, and the two statues that are in the heart of the town are indications of appreciation. And amongst others, past and present, who have developed the industries of the iron town are Mr. Hugh Bell, Mr. Raylton Dixon, Mr. Wilson, Mr. Edgar Gilkes, Mr. Windsor Richards, Dr. Sadler, Mr. William Hanson, and the late Alderman John Dunning.

In the building up of the industries we have glanced at, there have been many others who have worked long and unselfishly, to name all of whom would be almost impossible. Suffice it to say that, fostered by the " Middlesbrough owners," the solid, broad-fronted, broad-brimmed Quakers "—described by Mr. Joseph Cowen—and supported by its stores of iron, Middlesbrough has grown and will grow, for its meridian is not yet. It has within it the element of further growth, in the iron near it, and in the salt which is proved in South Durham opposite it. It is on iron and salt that the future of the trade of the Tees rests chiefly, and there is still vast development before them, though it is probable that the iron may have to be brought a little longer distance. The Iron King rules the district; indications are everywhere seen of his power, and though he has been strong in the past, he will be still mightier in the future.

THE LAGAN.

Belfast, the second port in Ireland, was a place very little known until after the end of the sixteenth century. Holinshed, in a "Chronicle of the Chief Towns of Antrim and Down," written in 1586, makes mention of several places which have, even up to the present time, grown to be little more than fishing villages, but he does not allude in any way to Belfast, so we may very naturally assume that, prior to this date, the place was of very small importance. The origin of the name is Bel-feirste, which means "the town at the ford of the river's mouth." Undoubtedly, from its locality, and this derivation, Belfast was originally an obscure village at the ford which was, in very old times, a principal point of communication between the northern parts of Antrim and Down.

In 665 a battle was fought at Belfast, known as the battle of Fearsat (the Ford), and this is the first historical record of the place which is available. The next mention of the town is dated 1315, when it is recorded that the town of Belfast was destroyed by Edward Bruce. Passing on to 1476, we learn that in this year the castle of Belfast was taken and destroyed by O'Neil. Again, in 1503, during the reign of Henry VIII., Gerald, Earl of Kildare, in an expedition to Ulster, acquired possession of the castle. Prior to this date, what formed Belfast, that is to say, the castle and a small fishing village, which was described as the " Town and Fortress of Belfast" had been in the hands of the O'Neils. This family seems to have regained possession from the Earl of Kildare, for it is recorded that in 1552 Hugh O'Niel of Clandeboye promised allegiance to the reigning monarch, having at that time possession of " Carrickfergus, the town and fortress of Belfast, and all the surrounding lands."

In 1571 the town was granted to Sir Thomas Smith, a favourite of Elizabeth, but this grant reverted to the Crown in 1604, and was made over by James I. to Sir Arthur Chichester, who was in 1612 created Baron Chichester. The town at this time consisted of about 120 houses, mostly built of mud, with thatched roofs. It is generally supposed that the growth of Belfast as a port dates from about this period.

In 1613 a charter was granted by which Belfast was incorporated as a borough, under the style of "The Sovereign, Free Burgesses and Commonalty of Belfast." This body was empowered to erect and establish a "quay in some convenient place upon the bay or creek, where all native and foreign merchants might discharge and export their merchandise without any interference from any of the officers of the king at Carrickfergus, provided the same customs were paid as were payable at that place."

In 1632, Thomas Wentworth, Earl of Stafford, was appointed first Lord-Deputy of Ireland, and from this period the commercial prosperity of Belfast rapidly increased. Five years after, in 1637, a very important impulse to the trade was secured by the purchase by Lord Stafford, on behalf of the Crown, from the Corporation of Carrickfergus, of the privilege of receiving one-third of the duties payable on goods which were imported into that town, together with other important rights. As a consequence the trade of Carrickfergus was very soon transferred to Belfast.

In 1641 a rampart was built round the town; and in 1662 the town consisted of 150 houses within these walls, forming five streets. The surrounding district was a dense forest of gigantic oaks and sycamores, which yielded an excellent supply of timber.

In the "Municipal Corporation Reports of Ireland," it is stated that, in 1674, the Earl of Donegal exercised the rights of conservancy over the harbour, and that he granted to the sovereign of Belfast the office of water-bailiff, with all fees and perquisites belonging thereto, and that further, for the better encouragment of trade, he had thought fit that the office of water-bailiff should be vested in the sovereign for the time being, on condition of a yearly acknowledgment being made to his seneschal. A deputy water-bailiff was appointed, whose duty it was to mark out the channel of the river—and no doubt this official really received the various fees.

In 1686 the merchants of Belfast owned forty ships, with a total carrying capacity of 3,000 tons, and in this year the customs collected amounted to about £20,000.

Two years later (1688) a new charter for the government of the town was granted by James II. The provisions were practically the same as those in existence, and it further empowered the new Corporation to " mend the quays, and receive all such customs, petty dues, anchorages, wharfages, &c."

In the early years of the eighteenth century Belfast had acquired the reputation of a place of considerable trade, and was at this time looked upon as " a handsome, thriving, and well-peopled town, with many houses and shops." During the civil conflicts, which afflicted Ireland for many years, Belfast seems to have been practically undisturbed, and we learn that it was considered " the greatest town in the north of Ireland."

The first act for regulating the harbour of Belfast was passed by the Irish Parliament in 1729. This act recited " that the navigation of the port had been of late much more than heretofore obstructed, and the harbour and channel were becoming extremely shallow, to the prejudice of trade and of the revenue, occasioned by the irregular taking up and throwing out of ballast, and by the banks of the channel being broken from want of a proper supervision."

By this Act the Sovereign and Free Burgesses of Belfast were constituted the Conservators of the Harbour, with powers to issue bye-laws, to cleanse and amend the harbour, to levy dues, &c. Any surplus balance remaining was to be applied to the promotion of the manufacture of linen.

In 1777 the manufacture of cotton was introduced by Robert Joy, and in 1785 the trading community of Belfast obtained a legislative enactment, by which a new harbour corporation was constitued.

In 1763 the gross customs revenue of Belfast, including excise, amounted to £32,900, and in 1784 twenty-two years after, this had increased to £101,376, exclusive of excise. In this year there were 55 vessels belonging to the port, with a tonnage of 10,040 tons.

In 1763 the former Acts relating to the government of the harbour were repealed and a new governing body was incorporated, under the title of the "Ballast Board." With the passing of this Act in 1785 important improvements on the river were commenced and actively pursued.

In 1786, 772 vessels of 34,287 tons entered the harbour, these increased, in 1796, to 974 vessels of 63,976 tons, and in 1813 to 1,190 vessels of 97,670 tons, thus showing that with the important improvements which were in progress the size and number of ships rapidly increased.

Prior to 1821 vessels drawing more that 10 feet of water were unable to come up the Lagan on neap tides, and those drawing more than 14 feet could not come up on spring tides. They were therefore compelled to anchor in the Garmoyle Roads, about three miles below the town, where the greater portion of their cargo was discharged and brought up in lighters, at great expense. It was estimated that this mode of proceeding meant, apart from the cost of lighterage and probable loss by robbery, a loss to the merchants of about £50,000 annually.

Various engineers, including Mr. Rennie, were consulted about this time, and numerous reports and suggestions were prepared, none of which, however, were approved, and it was not until 1831 that a plan prepared by Mr. Walker received legislative sanction. At this time the accommodation for shipping consisted of quayage space of about 1,800 feet, of which length, however, only about 900 feet was adapted for vessels of any considerable size, three tidal docks, viz., the " Merchants " " Limekiln " and " Ritchie's "; but these were only capable of taking small boats and sloops, and also two graving docks with entrances of 29 and $34\frac{1}{2}$ feet respectively, which could accommodate vessels of from 300 to 600 tons. The depth of water opposite the quay was 5 feet at low water, the average depth in the channel being 8 feet.

The records of tonnage which has entered Belfast show that in 1837, when the various improvements on the harbour had begun to exercise a marked influence on the trade of the port, 2,724 vessels of 288,143 tons are recorded. This total steadily increased, and, to show with what continued steps the trade of the port has grown, we give a statement showing the tonnage which has entered in each year since 1728:—

Vessels Entered.

Year.	Number of Vessels.	Tons.
1728	370	9,180
1786	770	34,287
1805	840	64,585
1825	2,060	183,441
1835	2,950	290,769
1845	3,655	445,537
1855	5,211	768,505
1863	6,680	993,303
1864	6,929	1,020,037
1865	6,947	1,111,581
1866	7,442	1,366,788
1867	7,817	1,372,326
1868	7,156	1,201,306
1869	8,225	1,203,776
1870	8,303	1,225,566
1871	9,323	1,350,810
1872	8,230	1,309,251
1873	7,538	1,268,845
1874	7,012	1,305,016
1875	7,475	1,434,754
1876	7,150	1,497,585
1877	7,677	1,566,752
1878	7,793	1,605,897
1879	7,854	1,658,026
1880	7,965	1,616,908
1881	7,556	1,537,380
1882	7,429	1,459,651
1883	7,508	1,526,535
1884	7,821	1,570,062
1885	7,457	1,546,271*

* The increase in this year appears less than that of former years, owing, in a great extent, to the altered mode of measurement adopted by the Board of Trade.

Within the last twenty years works of great importance have been carried out on the Lagan. These may be briefly summarised as follows:—

THE DUFFERIN DOCK.—A floating dock, 630 ft. long by 225 ft. wide, with a water area of $3\frac{1}{4}$ acres, and a length of quayage of 1,645 ft. The average depth of water in this dock is 23 ft.

SPENCER DOCK.—A tidal dock, 600 ft. long by 500 ft. wide, with a water area of $7\frac{1}{4}$ acres, and having a quayage space of 1,900 lineal feet. The average depth of water in this dock is 16 ft. at ordinary low tide. It has an entrance 265 ft. long by 80 ft. wide. The Dufferin Dock opens from this dock, and on the river side an entrance basin is formed with an area of 5 acres, and 550 lineal feet of quayage.

Both the above docks were opened in 1872. In 1867 the ABERCORN BASIN was completed. This is a rectangular tidal basin having three sides. It is 725 ft. in length by 635 ft. in width, and has a water area of $10\frac{1}{2}$ acres, with a quayage space of 1,370 ft. The average depth of water in this basin is 11 ft. at low tide. Two timber jetties have lately been constructed in this basin, one 317 ft. in length and the other 350 ft. in length, and provide a line of quayage of 1,334 lineal feet, which is principally availed of by vessels either being repaired or new vessels being fitted out for sea. In 1867 was also completed the HAMILTON GRAVING DOCK. The dimensions of this dock are as follows: Length at top, 470 ft., at bottom, $451\frac{1}{2}$ ft. It is 84 ft. in width at coping, the bottom giving a width of 50 ft. The entrance to this dock is 60 ft. in width, and the depth of water on the sill is 7½ ft. below ordinary low tide.

All the old timber quays have been reconstructed since 1875, the Donegal Quay being carried out in concrete work faced with granite, and the water area available at these has been greatly increased, and additional depth has been obtained. Lines of rail have been laid, at the expense of the Harbour Commissioners, along the quays and docks connecting the shipping with the various railway systems which communicate with the interior; and modern mechanical appliances have been provided to facilitate the handling of goods and for the general convenience of the traffic of the port. Upwards of twenty years ago, in 1863, the area of the harbour of Belfast covered 68 acres. It now extends over more than 100 acres. About 265 acres of land have also been reclaimed, 165 acres on the Down side, and 100 acres on the Antrim side.

The Belfast Harbour Commissioners are still actively engaged in improving their harbour, and many important works are now in progress.

Before the various improvements were commenced, the income of the Board, which was derived from dues, &c., amounted to £43,160 (in 1863). They now reach an average annual total exceeding £100,000.

The river Lagan, which rises on the northern declivity of the Slieve Croot mountains, in the barony of Kinalarty, county Down, takes a north-westerly direction for about sixteen miles; it then turns to the north-east, and so continues for twenty miles, when it falls into Belfast Lough, at a distance of thirty-six miles from its source. The Lagan is navigable from Belfast up to the entrance to the Lagan Canal, which connects Lough Neagh with the harbour of Belfast by an inland navigation of twenty-eight miles. This communication is continued through Lough Neagh to the Ulster Canal.

Belfast Lough presents a very picturesque sight, and the outer harbour is considered one of the safest in the kingdom. The Lagan, on which Belfast is situated, was originally most tortuous and difficult to navigate, but in consequence of various improvements which were commenced about 1830, a straight channel has been cut from the lower part of the harbour. The channel has been deepened, and large ships can now come alongside the quays, which extend for about a mile below Queen's Bridge on both sides of the river.

The exports from Belfast are very largely conveyed to London, Liverpool, and Glasgow, whence they are transhipped to their destinations; so that the various published returns do not give any idea of the actual foreign trade which is conducted here.

The manufacture of flax has for half a century been gradually concentrating at Belfast. This industry was commenced in 1830 by Messrs. Mulholland, and in 1840, ten years later, there were 240,000 spindles at work. These had increased in 1851 to 561,000, and in 1871 to 930,000, of which number about four-fifths had been set up in Belfast. The export of linen and linen yarn forms a very important item in the trade of the Lagan. The average exports of linen, which, in the earlier times, were about 1,000,000 lb., had in 1865 increased to 16,490 tons, and now amount to (1885) 25,273 tons.

Shipbuilding is extensively carried on at Belfast, the works of the well-known firms, Messrs. Harland & Wolff, Messrs. Workman, Clarke & Co., Limited, and Messrs. McIlwaine, Lewis & Co., Limited, being situated on the Lagan. This industry was originally established at Belfast in 1791 by William Ritchie, a Scot, who combined it with the manufacture of rope and canvas. There are also extensive marine engineering works.

We annex a statement showing the number and tonnage of vessels built on the Lagan each year since 1876:—

Year.	Sailing Vessels.		Steamers.		Total.	
	Number.	Tons.	Number.	Tons.	Number.	Tons.
1876	6	3,208	2	754	8	3,962
1877	8	8,465	1	40	9	8,505
1878	5	5,184	2	3,372	7	8,556
1879	4	3,875	8	7,557	12	11,432
1880	2	1,795	7	7,076	9	8,871
1881	2	199	12	13,694	14	13,893
1882	7	7,398	11	12,800	18	20,198
1883	6	10,021	19	17,402	25	27,423
1884	11	11,247	12	19,366	23	30,613
1885	8	10,866	9	16,890	17	27,756

THE WYRE—FLEETWOOD.

We cannot say positively whether in the remote ages of early history Fleetwood was populated by any of the aboriginal Britons, invading Romans, or piratical Danes, but the discovery, about forty years ago, of a paved Roman road buried deeply in the sand, proves indisputably that there was some traffic at this place at a very early stage of history.

From a very interesting "Account of the Port of Fleetwood," we learn that during the civil wars which culminated in the advancement of Oliver Cromwell to the Protectorate, the Manor of Rossall and the estuary of the river Wyre were the scenes of many exciting episodes. For more than 200 years before the town of Fleetwood was in existence, the river Wyre constituted an important factor in the commercial world. At this time the Harbours of the United Kingdom were far less accessible and convenient than now. From one of the earliest authentic records connected with the river Wyre we learn that "in 1708, during the reign of Queen Anne, William Jennings, collector of customs, received for his yearly services £30 per annum, and five subordinate officers had £75 equally divided among them."

About half a century ago the spot on which the Town of Fleetwood now stands was a vast range of sandhills and warren, belonging to the Rossall estate, and forming a part of the possessions of the late Sir Peter Hesketh Fleetwood, Bart., of Rossall Hall. No habitation except a warrener's cottage existed here, and the only inhabitants of the vicinity were the rabbits.

To Sir Peter Fleetwood is due the credit of having first conceived the idea of converting this desolate spot into a seaport.

The Wyre had long been known as a safe river; in fact, the saying "safe and easy as Wyre water" was a well-known proverb.

As the outcome of Sir Peter's ideas a number of gentlemen, known as the "Preston and Wyre Railway, Harbour, and Dock Company," sought for and obtained, in 1835, the Parliamentary powers necessary to carry out a scheme for establishing a port at Fleetwood. Operations were at once commenced, and on the 15th July, 1840, a railway from Preston to this spot was declared open and ready for traffic. Meanwhile, dwelling-houses, hotels, and a spacious wharf had been rapidly growing over the homes of the rabbits, and in the year 1840 there was quite a town ready to welcome the advent of the railway. The town grew rapidly, and in five years was a large and thriving place.

In 1847, on the 20th September, Her Majesty

the Queen, accompanied by their Royal Hignesses the Prince Consort, the Prince of Wales, and the Princess Royal, passed through Fleetwood *en route* from Scotland to London.

A red-letter day in the history of Fleetwood was Wednesday, the 2nd June, 1869: on this day the first sod of a Dock was cut by H. S. Styan, Esq., the surviving trustee of the estate under the will of the late Sir P. Fleetwood, who died in 1866.

For some reason, which may fairly be conjectured to have been an uncompleted list of shareholders, the Fleetwood Dock Company determined to suspend all operations barely six months after they had begun, and the work was never resumed under the same proprietorship.

Two years later, in 1871, the Lancashire and Yorkshire Railway Company obtained an Act of Parliament to carry out, on a more extensive scale, the undertaking which had been abandoned almost at its birth.

As an instance of the early growth of Fleetwood, the following figures, which we select from an "Historical Account of the Port of Fleetwood," published by the Lancashire and Yorkshire Railway Company, to which work we are much indebted for these particulars, will be of interest:—

Amounts received by the Preston and Fleetwood Railway in each of the following weeks.

Week ending December 14,	1842......	£127 18 6
Corresponding week	1843......	228 13 3
,, ,,	1844......	303 3 5
,, ,,	1845......	379 5 5
,, ,,	1846......	552 17 5

This same authority states that in 1877 the average weekly returns on this railway, with its branches to Blackpool and Lytham, amounted to £2,600. "Nearly the whole of the goods receipts," it adds, "are for merchandise transmitted to or from the quay at Fleetwood, and form a reliable indication of the large amount of traffic constantly being carried on in the loading or discharging of steam and sailing vessels in the harbour." These remarks were made nearly ten years ago, and since then Fleetwood has been yearly growing in importance.

As a seaport Fleetwood occupies an excellent situation, and one which can compare favourably with any site in the United Kingdom for position and accessibility.

Off the foot of the river Wyre in Morecambe Bay there is excellent anchorage called Lune Deeps, where there is a depth of twenty-seven fathoms and good holding ground, and no better roadstead could exist than is found inside the sheltering arms of Morecambe Bay, free from the influence of any treacherous currents.

Fleetwood possessed the distinction of a port in 1839, with customs established by order of the Treasury; subsequently, in 1844, it was ignominiously reduced to a creek under Preston; then, in two years' time, it was elevated to a sub-port; and finally, in 1849, was reinstated in its first independent position.

In 1845 the receipts for dues amounted to £528 9s. 5d., as against £36 2s. in 1835. The year 1845 was the most successful then known; twenty-three ships of large tonnage brought produce from various parts of the world, and took back in their holds goods from the warehouses of Manchester, Preston, and other adjacent towns. In this year the barque *Diogenes* arrived with the first cargo of cotton ever landed at Fleetwood.

The year 1859 demonstrated, principally through the rapid growth of the steamship trade between Fleetwood and Belfast, that more extensive warehouse accommodation was required, and that the progress of Fleetwood was now so steadily growing that it was desirable to secure at once the most approved appliances for handling ships and goods. Accordingly steam cranes were in use in 1863, and gradually the old system of hand labour at the quay-side was superseded by the universal adoption of the more expeditious and economical assistant, steam, and steam subsequently superseded by hydraulics in 1885.

The progress of Fleetwood is clearly shown by the accompanying interesting figures :—

Statement showing the Sailing Craft left on the Register at Fleetwood, at the close of each of the following years.

Year.	Vessels.	Tonnage.
1850	15	560
1880	172	26,407

Coal forms an important item in the list of exports from Fleetwood, as can be seen from the following figures :—

Year.	Coal Exported. Tons.
1870	43,653
1880	134,844

A very important traffic at Fleetwood is that of the Belfast Steamboats. These were first established in 1843, by the North Lancashire Steam Navigation Company, who commenced operations by running two steamers. This fleet now consists of five steamers, with a gross tonnage of 5,434 tons.

In the earliest times of the port an industry destined to become one of the principal occupations at Fleetwood was almost by chance established. A pilot boat arrived in Fleetwood many years ago, and finding but little work the crew provided themselves with a trawl net, and with this turned their idle hours to profitable account. Subsequent to the success thus obtained a fishing company was formed, with half a dozen boats. At the present time there are 70 boats belonging to the port engaged in the fishing trade, which has come to be considered of very great importance.

The accommodation afforded for shipping at Fleetwood consists of a dock 1,000 ft. long by 400 ft. wide, covering an area of 10 acres. The lock is 250 ft. long by 50 ft. wide. There is a timber dock covering an area of 15 acres. There are sheds on the dock quay capable of storing 18,000 quarters of grain. A new grain elevator on the American principle is now complete, and at work. The dimensions are 300 ft. long by 90 ft. wide, and 140 ft. high. Its storage capacity is 30,000 tons of grain, and it is fitted with shakers, blowers, and all the latest improvements required to restore the condition of damaged or heated cargoes. The whole of the elevator, dock quays, and approaches are lighted by the electric light.

Vessels are discharged by means of two shear legs, capable of lifting at the rate of 120 tons per hour each, from bulk.

The harbour at Fleetwood is safe and commodious, one of the principal features being the Canshe Hole, a natural docklike harbour which is formed by and in the river Wyre. Here vessels may lie at anchor or at buoys, as has been the practice for many years, during the lowest tides, without fear of grounding. In addition to this forming part of the channel to the dock, this natural basin is of the greatest use to vessels about to enter the dock. There is also a gridiron 260 ft. by 40 ft.

A ship may enter the Bay of Morecambe on the morning tide, and before night-fall portions of her cargo can be at their destination in Preston, Bolton, Manchester, or elsewhere in Lancashire and Yorkshire.

In the year 1884 several large vessels with cargoes of cotton arrived at Fleetwood direct from New Orleans and Galveston. The cotton was discharged direct into warehouses situated about eight to ten yards distant from the dock side, then weighed and trucked to the railway waggons on the other side, and was at no period exposed to the weather, as is the case at Liverpool. There is a clear saving on cotton imported into Fleetwood as compared with Liverpool of 6s. 8d. per ton, or 1s. 4d. per bale, a saving large enough to amount almost to a bounty.

Large deposits of salt have been found close to Fleetwood, and the mines will, it is expected, in a very few months be in active operation.

The following statement is of interest as indicating the growth of this traffic:—

Year.	Goods. Tons.	Passengers Conveyed.
1855	26,133	20,609
1860	39,714	32,829
1865	57,104	41,206
1870	55,176	40,673
1875	65,357	43,602

THE SEVERN.

The Severn is a river of deep interest. In point of length, it is second in this country to the Thames. As an "industrial" highway it has done duty for ages, and it has also furnished many a poet with food for song. Both historically and geographically, it may be regarded as a stream of numerous noteworthy connections. In days long since, it was at several points, a link between England and Wales, and at the same time, a line of demarcation. Upon its banks the inhabitants of our land have feasted and fought, and the very names of such places as Tewkesbury, Gloucester, Worcester, and Shrewsbury, are sufficient to arouse the sleepiest of readers to the consideration of eventful occurrences in the life of the nation. It may be said that a river 190 miles long, in an old country, would naturally be invested with a great deal of historical interest. We shall not dispute the right of anyone to look at the matter in such a light. We only regret that space will not permit us to give more than an incomplete and passing reference to the remarkable events with which the river, as "Severn," "Hafren," "Sabrina," or "Sæferne," has been associated.

It may be suggested that the Severn has a claim, poetically, at all events, to be known as something more than "sandy." It is a noble stream, notwithstanding the neglect from which it formerly suffered; it breaks over romantic rocks in its passage from Plynlimmon, and it flows in a stately manner through many a beautiful English landscape before it reaches the lower lands, where its sandy aspect is so leading a physical characteristic. Viewed from Cleeve Hill, Cheltenham, from the Cathedral tower at Gloucester, or from numerous other points that might be mentioned, the Severn is seen, on a bright day, wending its way through the ample woodlands and the widespread pasturages, like a silvern thread. May we not call it, then, the Silver Severn? And on the bosom of this fascinating river commerce has been borne from time immemorial, although it cannot be claimed that the facilities offered to trade have been at any time equal to those afforded by the Thames. The Severn, although fairly broad for a considerable distance, was somewhat shallow, and the entrance from the Bristol Channel was very difficult to navigate, owing to the sands, but improvements have been effected in this respect, and even now, when the means of locomotion have been revolutionised by steam, and ships are scarcely great if not leviathan, the Severn is largely used at various points for the purposes of inland trade. What nature does not permit us to do cheaply enough, the art of man at times contrives to encompass, and, if the larger ships of our day cannot easily go up the Severn, where the older vessels used to sail in the care of dauntless mariners, a way has been found whereby the larger craft can yet keep on the line of the Severn, and engage in the competition of these "fast times."

The river contains good fish, the which to catch is the object of many fishermen, who find a living on the banks. Who has not heard of Severn salmon?

The stream rises on the eastern side of Plynlimmon, and drains Montgomeryshire in a north-easterly direction, and after flowing some distance near the borders of Shropshire it enters that county. Then it takes a south-easterly course, and passes through Worcester and Gloucestershires. Having received many tributaries, it finally merges itself with the Bristol Channel, once called Severn Sea.

It is estimated that the surface drained above Gloucester is about 4,500 square miles in extent. Floods have sometimes happened in the Severn, and low-lying tracts of land in Gloucestershire and other counties have been submerged. In 1770 the land was covered to the depth of six feet nine inches. It is circumstantially evident that a great area of land near Berkeley and Newnham has been reclaimed, and Sir R. I. Murchison has supposed that the Bristol Channel, at a remote period, included the Vale of the Severn, with the Malvern and Cotswold Hills as boundaries. Here, it may be interesting to also mention that, in the excavations at Sharpness Docks, a submerged forest converted into peat was discovered near the river bank. According to Mr. W. C. Lucy, who read a paper on the subject before the Cotswold Club, the maximum thickness of the peat bed, which lay in a hollow, was fourteen feet, and the minimum a few inches. Towards the top some hazel nuts were found quite perfect. The trees represented were chiefly oak, elder, beech, and hazel, which lay generally north and south. Where the peat was thickest, and within about two feet of the bottom, were found the fine head of *Cervus elephas*, with the antlers apparently cut off by some rude implement, the antlers and jaw of a small deer, the head of a horse and *Bos longifrons*, the skull of a dog, and the tusk of a boar. The bottom of the peat was about the height of mean low-water mark in the Severn. The bed was found to extend into the river at least 100 yards from the bank, and there is a like bed at Lydney, two miles lower down, on the opposite side of the river. Peat has also been found at Berkeley Pill and Awre. Mr. Lucy inferred that the Sharpness Forest was of great antiquity, that its growth soon followed the glacial period, when the climate began to ameliorate. At that time, in all probability, the whole of the land in that part of the Severn Valley, and also the lias beds of Gloucester, and beyond to Tewkesbury, were eroded, after which a vast forest growth must have gone on for ages, the land being then far higher than at present, what is now the estuary of the Severn being a dense forest, with probably only a rivulet running through it, admitting of passage of some of the extinct animals that inhabited the caves of Glamorganshire and Monmouthshire; while part of the German Ocean may have been at that time forest land connecting this country with the Continent.

The tidal and other deposits of the river are large. The accumulation of mud at South Wales ports on the Bristol Channel itself is a feature which the respective dock engineers have to give constant attention to. Cliffe, writing in 1847, said it might be imagined that the Severn was a very difficult river to improve, a circumstance which probably accounted for its having been left in a state of nature until recently. " The detentions which vessels have sustained have been serious. Large fleets of river craft have often been detained for months together, owing to want of water, and the average extent of detention has been about three months in the year from drought or floods." In 1836 a movement was commenced at Worcester, which does honour to that city, for the purpose of rendering this fine river navigable at all periods of the year. After a long struggle an Act was obtained, in 1842, which placed the river under the control of Commissioners, and gave that body power to adopt means to obtain a constant average depth of not less than six feet between Stourport and Gloucester. This work, regarded as one of a national character, was carried out under the superintendence of Mr. Cubbitt at a cost of £200,000. It was completed in 1846, and toll was then levied by the Commissioners.

The "bore" which comes up to Gloucester is, as is well-known, a tidal incursion of accumulated strength. Owing to the contracted state of the river above the estuary, the waters surge up in considerable volume, and with a roar that can be heard at a distance. Nennius, in his "Wonders of the Island of Britain" (Harleian MS.), says: "When the sea overflows with the tide at the mouth of the Severn, two separate heaps of froth are formed, which strike against each other as if there was a battle between them. Each proceeds against the other, and they attack each other by turns. They then recede the one from the other, and again proceed, and this on the surface of the sea during every tide. This they have done from the beginning of the world to the present day." By means of canals, communication is established between the Severn and the rivers Mersey, Dee, Ribble, Thames, Ouse, Trent, Derwent, Avon, Humber. Generally speaking, it may be considered an arterial connection of four or five hundred miles of inland water navigation in a dozen counties. The canal from Stroud-Water, a branch of the Severn, to the Thames, which passes through a brick tunnel 16 feet high and 16 feet wide, under Sapperton Hill and Hatley Wood (two miles and a quarter) in hard rock, was opened on May 21, 1789, and was considered a great engineering achievement. Our ancestors little dreamt of a South Wales Railway, a Severn Railway Bridge, or a Severn Tunnel. The following letter *à propos* of the "Junction of the Severn and the Iris" was

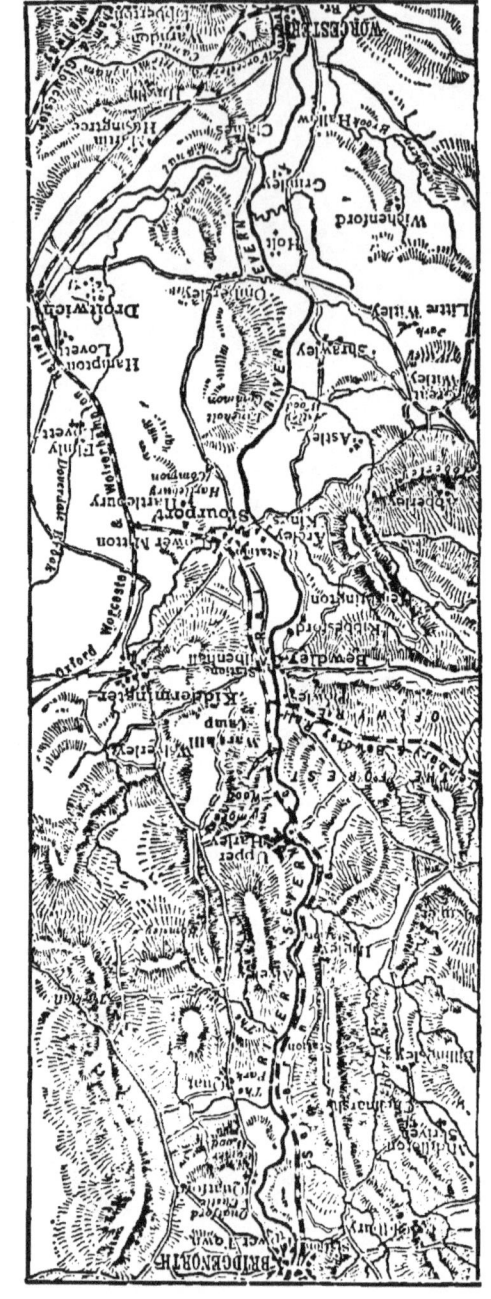

THE SEVERN FROM WORCESTER TO BRIDGNORTH.

written on November 20, 1789: "Sir, yesterday, a marriage took place between Madame *Sabrina*, a lady of Cambrian extraction, and mistress of very extensive property in Montgomeryshire (where she was born), and the counties of Salop, Stafford, Worcester, and Gloucester, and Mr. *Thames*, commonly called 'Father Thames,' a native of Gloucestershire, now a merchant trading from London to all the known parts of the world. The ceremony took place at Lechlade, by special license, in the presence of hundreds of admiring spectators, with myself, who signed as witnesses; from whence the happy pair went to breakfast at Oxford, dine at London, and consummate at Gravesend; where the Venerable Neptune, his whole train of inferior deities and nymphs, with his wife Venus and her train, are to fling the stocking. An union which presages many happy consequences, and a numerous offspring. I mention the lady's name, as the *tendre* came from her, after many struggles with her modesty, and Cambrian aversion to a Saxon spouse. *A Traveller.*" There is no doubt the arts of peace are more satisfactory to all concerned than the forces of war. Old "aversions" are, we believe, fast disappearing, in consequence of the facilities now afforded the people of one part of the country and another to form a more correct idea of what have been supposed to be conflicting characteristics. The inhabitants of all parts of the country may now be counted as one in their desires to avail themselves of the advantages of British enterprise. As to Wales, its mountains and valleys are the home of many English, Scotch, and Irish men; and the Welsh, realising that life is not made up of ideas of descent, more or less fanciful and out of place in this age of cosmopolitan tendencies, are showing a greater inclination to come forth from their mountainous surroundings and greet the "Saxon" as a brother on the lowlands of their remote ancestors. Indeed, as education spreads, Welshmen may be counted upon to develop their inroads on other parts of the country more and more. Welshmen themselves, let us remark, cannot claim to be an absolutely pure race, as they are supposed by some to be. There is strong admixture of blood even in Wales. And the Welshmen in England may not inaptly pause to consider whether there is as much or more Welsh blood in England than there is in Wales. It is a mistake to suppose that Englishmen are as "Saxon," as they were at the time of chronic disturbances centuries ago. England has preserved its old characteristics to a far less extent than Wales, and when we consider the present population of the Principality, and bear in mind that a large proportion consists of non-Welsh residents, surely it is not too much to suppose that the Welsh element absorbed in England is greater than that which is existent in a purer form among the mountains. Otherwise it might be questioned whether the Welsh were ever a strong people, numerically. I rather think the daughters of Wales have had something to do with the question. They have not refrained from reciprocating the admiring regards of Englishmen. And while disputes have been embarked in by the men, women, who usually ignore the logical results of all things, have been making history.

It must be remembered that the Severn, commercially, has not only been of inland benefit, but it has been a great outlet to the Midlands for coast ports. From the Severn and the Bristol Channel vessels could proceed to various points on the seaboard, and to foreign destinations. The lower portion of the river was, and still is, rather shoaly, but the canal between Gloucester and its docks at Sharpness—sixteen or seventeen miles long—has afforded much relief to the Severn navigator. The extension of the Gloucester and Berkeley Canal to Holly Hazel Pill was completed on November 25, 1874. A year or two before, weirs had been constructed above Gloucester, where the Severn flows in two branches. This had the effect of giving a permanent depth of from six to ten feet of water as far as Tewkesbury.

Tides rise to the height of 48 ft. in Kingroad, and at Chepstow (on the Wye, near the confluence of that river with the Severn) as high as 60 ft.

We shall now return to the upper portion of the river, and briefly note a few facts about some of the leading places on the way down.

Newtown, sometimes termed the "Leeds of Wales," is a centre of the Welsh flannel manufacture. A handsome stone bridge crosses the river here, near the upper end of the Montgomery Canal.

Welshpool, where the Ellesmere Canal commences, was, half a century ago, a great market for Welsh flannels, but in 1834 the trade was mostly transferred to Newtown. Communication is had by means of the canal named with the Birmingham and Chester Canal lines. There are some malt-houses and tanneries in the locality. The fall of the river hence to the sea is 225 ft. only.

Shrewsbury, situated, as an old writer says, on the top of " an hill of red earth," is a place of considerable antiquity. It is supposed to have been established subsequent to the destruction of the Roman station, *Uriconium*, and in the reign of Alfred it was one of the chief cities. In after ages it was given with other land by the Conqueror to Roger de Montgomery, who erected the castle, of which some portion still remains. In 1102 the whole locality was forfeited to the Crown. Edward I., in whose reign the Principality of Wales was formally annexed to England, made Shrewsbury at one time his headquarters. On many occasions Parliaments have met here. The town was the scene of many border quarrels between the English and the Welsh, and it gives its name to that very memorable battle in 1403 between the Royal army under Henry IV. and that of the rebel Earl of Northumberland, commanded by Lord Percy (Hotspur). The King was victorious over the opposing forces, which were on their way to join the "irregular and wild" Glendower in Wales. Hotspur was slain, and Northumberland's brother, the Earl of Worcester, was executed on the field. Edward IV., during the Wars of the Roses, raised an army here, and won a victory at Mortimer's Cross. In the Civil War, the inhabitants declared for Charles I., and in 1664 the town was taken by Colonel Mitton and the Parliamentary forces, and the fortifications were destroyed. The museum is a celebrated repository of relics of early British and Roman times. The town also contains some fine churches, and its schools are of almost historic note. In the neighbourhood is Wroxeter, built on the site of Uriconium (Watling Street passed this way), and Boscobell House, where, after the battle of Worcester, Charles II. was concealed by the Penderells, is about twenty-two miles distant. Offa's Dyke passes through Salop. The space between this and Watts' Dyke was anciently regarded by the Saxons and Welsh as neutral territory, and it is related that, in Offa's time, a Welshman who was found on the English side of the boundary was compelled to lose his right hand. There is a valley in the Berwyn mountains called Cwm Llanwenog, from the circumstance of Enog, a Welsh champion, having been mutilated in this manner. The Pass of Graves, Offa's Dyke, was the locality of a terrible conflict between English and Welsh. In the sixth century, Shrewsbury was called Pengwern, and at Baschurch a memorable battle was fought by the Mercians and the Welsh forces of Cynddylan, Prince of Powys, whose chief city was Shrewsbury. At or near the old British hill, Berth, it is supposed the Prince received the "fierce thrust" that proved fatal.

The Severn at Shrewsbury is very circuitous. At that town it is spanned by the English and Welsh bridges, and it flows onward through rich pastoral grounds. Thread and linen yarns are manufactured in the locality.

Lower down, the scenery is very charming. Views can be obtained of the Wrekin, a prominent mountain, and Benthal Edge and Much Wenlock, celebrated points of interest, and within easy reach. Ironbridge, built on a hill slope, is notable for its iron bridge, which, the first of its kind, was constructed at Coalbrookdale in 1795. It has a span of 100 ft. Near here is Broseley, known for its bricks, tiles, &c. At Coalport, where there is another early iron bridge, are large china works. Beyond is ancient Bridgnorth, the site of many furious battles between Saxons and Danes; then we pass through Wyre Forest and come to Bewdley.

Below Stourport, where the Stour joins the Severn, is Worcester. This city, associated commercially with iron-making industries, porcelain, and gloves, is supposed to have been built by the Romans as a menace to the Silures. It was destroyed in 1041 by Hardicanute, the Danish king. In 1113 it was again burnt, this time by accident. The cathedral possesses many features of interest, and the city may claim to be one of the most ancient on the banks of the river. Bohun, in 1688, said: "This town suffered much for its loyalty to Charles I. and Charles II., especially in the year 1651, when after the fatal Battel under her walls she fell into the Hands of the enraged Tyrant, Oliver Cromwell." Boselius is stated to have been the first bishop. He was settled in Worcester by Ethelred, king of the Mercians, in 679. The first Earl of Worcester was Ursus de Abot, created by William the Conqueror in 1087; the second, Waleran de Beaumont, in 1144; the third, Thomas Percy, Lord Admiral in 1397; the fourth, Richard Beauchamp, in 1420; the fifth, John Tiptoft, Lord Treasurer and Lord Constable, in 1449; succeeded by Edward, his son in 1477, who died in 1485; the seventh, Charles Somerset, Lord Herbert, created Earl by Henry VII. in 1514. Henry, the seventh in this line, "for his great virtue and loyalty, was, by Charles II., created Duke of Beaufort in the year 1682." The city has good railway and canal communications, especially with Birmingham. The river was greatly improved by the Commissioners in accordance with the Act of 1842, and on the quays are many warehouses. The county is noted for its hop plantations. Historically, the battle of Worcester, in 1651, will not be forgotten. Cromwell on that occasion overtook and defeated the Scots under Charles I., and gained his "crowning mercy."

Tewkesbury, another old English town, where

interesting specimens of ancient architecture are to be met with—celebrated also for its abbey, recently restored—is near the confluence of the rivers Avon and Severn. It is nearly insulated by the "Mill Avon," an ancient division of the Avon. A cast-iron bridge with a span of 172 feet is thrown over the Severn, a short distance from the town. A town-hall was erected by Sir William Codrington in 1788. The place was famous for its "mustard" and cloth manufactures, but the local trade has decreased. The "Bloody Meadow," a large tract of land, was the site in 1471 of the decisive battle between Edward IV. and the Yorkists and the Lancastrians, with Queen Margaret and her son at their head. The latter, who had been overtaken on their way to Wales, suffered a terrible defeat, thousands of soldiers were slain, the Queen was sent to the Tower, and her son was murdered in the presence of the King.

The Port of the Severn.

But we may not unnaturally regard Gloucester as the key port of the Severn. Other places of importance stand on the river banks, as we have already noticed; but, as a trading place, the old city of "Glevum," commanding Severn imports and exports as it does, by reason of its lower position, and its canal connection with the Sharpness docks in the estuary, cannot well be locally superseded. At the present moment the whole of the navigable part of the Severn and its outlet is controlled to a very large extent by the proprietors of the Sharpness and Gloucester, Worcester, and Birmingham Canals, and the proposed widening of the latter canal, so as to admit of the passage of large ships from Sharpness to the Metropolis of the Midlands, is a project which, if carried out, will still further enhance the value of the Gloucester undertakings.

The city clusters somewhat compactly around the cross, where the four ancient and leading streets, Northgate, Southgate, Eastgate, and Westgate, find a common centre. The cathedral, which is approached from several old courts off Westgate-street, is a magnificent specimen of ecclesiastical architecture. The tower, 225 feet in height, is one of the finest in the country. The origin of the cathedral is due to a very ancient monastic institution. Osric, in the reign of Ethelred, 681, founded a nunnery here, and his tomb is still to be seen. In 767 the establishment, it seems, was dispersed, and the then building got into a ruinous state. It was restored as an abbey for secular Canons in 821 by Beowulph, the Mercian king. The monastery was transferred by Canute in 1022 to the monks of the Benedictine order. The income was valued at £1,550 at the dissolution in 1539. Henry VIII. in 1541 erected the see of Gloucester, and the abbey church, re-dedicated to the Holy Trinity, was now termed the Cathedral. The length of the pile, including the Ladye Chapel, is 423 feet. The south porch, with an ornate front of tabernacle work, restored a few years since, is one among many objects to be noted and admired in connection with this superb structure. Space forbids detailed references, but we may briefly observe that Gloucester is well worthy of a visit on account of its cathedral alone. The areas of the three cathedrals at which the celebrated Triennial Festivals are held, are: Gloucester, 33,000 ft.; Worcester, 30,600 ft.; Hereford, 26,850 ft.

Gloucester was first conquered from the Britons by Ceaulin, king of the West Saxons, in 570. The Danes took it in 878 and did considerable damage. The city was sometime a Danish headquarter. The cathedral was subsequently founded. "This city falling at first into the hands of the rebels in our late Troubles, was besieged August 10, 1643, by the King's Forces, the 18th the King came in person to this Leager, but Essex coming up September 10, the siege was raised: and so for ought I can find it continued in their hands till the restitution of Charles II." (Bohun, 1688). Kings have been crowned and Parliaments held in Gloucester. Near here Elgiva, the beautiful but ill-fated wife of Edwy, was seized on her return from Ireland, hamstrung, and left to die in great misery.

We now go on to the consideration of some of the historical "trade marks" of the port. A wharf was erected on the Severn at Gloucester in the reign of Elizabeth, a fact which drew forth an ineffectual complaint from Bristol to the Royal Council. Bristol has always assumed to dominate the Severn, although Gloucester had more claim geographically to the premier position. In 1764 a line of Gloucester vessels sailed between

Newnham and London, and at that time so great had the importance of the communication between Birmingham and London, *viâ* Gloucester and Newnham, become that additional vessels were added. A week was considered a rapid voyage between London and Newnham. The old people were proud of their means of communication, and the "nightmare" of the "steam horse" had not come to worry them. But if, to the great chagrin of Bristol merchants, "Irish men with their barks" had "found a direct trade to Gloucester to ship away corn," the Gloucester worthies were on the look-out for still bigger things, and, with a view to obviate the dangerous passage of the lower Severn, and to offer inducements to larger vessels to come up, they embarked in the construction of a ship canal about twenty miles long, with an entrance at Berkeley Pill. The plans of Mr. Mylne were adopted in 1794. About four miles of the work had been done from Gloucester, when the company's project fell through, the capital having been fixed too low, £121,500. In or about 1804 the project was revived in a fresh form. Some proposed that the canal be continued for four additional miles, as far as the proposed junction with the Stroud-Water Navigation from the Severn (thus affording access to the Upper Thames and the Metropolis). Mr. Upton, the local engineer, however, advised that the Berkeley Pill entrance lock should be abandoned, and that Sharpness should be selected as the final point of a continuation of the water-way. This scheme was ultimately agreed to, and on July 15, 1818, the Duke of Gloucester, attended by the then Earl Fitzhardinge and Lord Fitzhardinge, performed the interesting ceremony of laying the first stone of the new entrance. In an inscription affixed to the stone the work was prospectively regarded as "a monument of national enterprise, a benefit to the proprietors, and a secure harbour for the commerce of the world." Difficulties again interfered with the due performance of the work, the funds again proved insufficient, the contractors themselves came to grief. Later on the Government was appealed to, and £165,000 was obtained on loan from the Commissioners for the Loan of Exchequer Bills. Telford was put in charge of the affair, and in 1823 the contract for the continuation of the work was let to Mr. McIntosh, and on April 26, 1827—not until then—the canal was opened by the schooner *Meredith*, from Charente, and the barque *Ann*. The large basin at Gloucester, being part of the original work, was, of course, thrown open at the same time. Length of the canal, 16 miles. Then followed the erection of warehouses and the formation of timber-yards at the Gloucester end of the canal.

Regarding the South Wales railway enterprise, that was ultimately to prove so great a benefit to Gloucester, it appears from a railway journal published forty years ago, that in 1824 a railway from Swansea *via* Gloucester to London had been projected, "chiefly for the purpose of conveying coal and other minerals to the London market, as well as passengers, at coach speed." In 1836 a Gloucester company proposed to construct a South Wales railway through Swansea. This was followed by a "paper scheme," the "England and Ireland Union Railway," a northern line having a terminus at Fishguard. The projects fell through, but in 1844 a railway through South Wales was advocated under different auspices. The Great Western Railway Company favoured the idea, and Mr. Brunel took charge of the scheme. It is stated that the Company had the support of all the great mine-owners of South Wales, together with a large majority of the representatives of the South Wales districts, many of whom appeared as members of the provisional committee; also noblemen and gentlemen connected with the South of Ireland. The line was laid out to run near the coast for the chief part of its length, 162 miles; and, as originally proposed, was intended to form a junction with the Cheltenham and Great Western Railway below Gloucester, where it was to cross the Severn by means of a bridge. This part of the project, it seems, was strongly objected to by the Corporation and citizens of Gloucester, and others, who memorialised the Board of Admiralty and opposed the Bill in Parliament. Then, we learn, "the Admiralty sent down a commission to inquire into the subject of the proposed bridge for crossing the Severn, and that commission reported against the company. Several attempts were made in the House of Commons to over-rule the objection of the Admiralty; but they were unavailing, and the Bill, after very great opposition, passed the Legislature, the part for the construction of the bridge having been omitted. The engineer, Mr. Brunel, subsequently proposed to pass the Severn by means of a tunnel, and an application was made to Parliament for that purpose in the following year, but without success." Powers were obtained to continue the line to Chepstow, with a view to a further extension, so as to join the Great Western line at Gloucester. The Bill received the Royal assent on August 4, 1845, and the capital was fixed at 56,000 shares of £50 each. The Great Western Company were empowered to subscribe towards the capital of the South Wales Railway the sum of £560,000. Another Bill was passed for extending the line to a point of junction with the Gloucester and Dean Forest Railway at Hagloe (Gloucestershire), thus affording an "unbroken broad-gauge railway from London to the Irish Channel." The construction of a branch line from the main railway into Swansea town, and another to Haverfordwest, was sanctioned at the same time. The total length of the South Wales lines authorised by the Acts of 1845, 1846, and 1847 was 205 miles. It is also interesting to note that not only had the Severn tunnel scheme been rejected, but the "idea of passing the Severn" had been wholly abandoned. The South Wales line was afterwards taken over by the Great Western Railway Company, an agreement having been made between the two companies in 1847, to the effect that "the Great Western are to pay the South Wales shareholders in perpetuity a minimum interest at the rate of 5 per cent. per annum upon the share capital expended, besides defraying all the current interest on loans taken up, not exceeding the sums mentioned, the lease to commence when the line from Gloucester to Fishguard and the Newport and Monmouth line shall be finished, provided (as respects the latter) the Great Western Company shall also complete their line from Gloucester to Monmouth by the same time, but not otherwise. One moiety of surplus profits at the end of five years after the lease commences is to be divided among the South Wales shareholders in addition to the guaranteed interest.

In connection with the canal an additional basin (or dock) was opened near Southgate-street, Gloucester, in 1848, and the area of the docks at this city now aggregates 12 acres. There are also two dry docks (the old, 113 ft. long, 35 ft. wide at the top, and with a depth of 10 ft. 10 in. on the sill, with the canal water at 18 ft. 6 in.; and the new, 165 ft. long by 56 ft. wide, and a sill depth of 12 ft.), as well as a barge dock in the same connection.

The Midland and the Great Western Railway Companies give direct access to the canal side. The Severn Navigation Commission, to which allusion has been made, devoted especial attention to the river above Gloucester, and they erected weirs at Diglis, Tewkesbury, Maisemore, and

Gloucester, with a view to increase the depth of the water; and towards the expense incurred in the lower works contributions were made by the Canal Company. An improved entrance at the mouth of the canal was now spoken off—trade having shown signs of progress—and a special report on the subject was prepared by Mr. W. B. Clegram, son of a former resident engineer, who dwelt on the annoyance caused by detention of vessels outside the crowded canal basin, and the greater facilities offered by the Bristol Channel ports, and proposed that a new entrance should be made at Holly Hazel Pill. The outer entrance was to be dry at low water, enclosed within open timber piers, running out nearly to low water line, and the level of the rocks was to be reduced to the depth of one foot below the sill at the entrance at Sharpness Point. South Pier was not to extend so far out as the north pier, and the width at the opening of the entrance was to be 300 ft. Then there was to be a tidal basin 700 ft. long by 300 ft. wide, with gates 60 ft. wide, the sill to be on the level of that at the Point, and a lock 320 ft. long, with three pairs of 60 ft. gates—the whole being designed to admit of the through passage to Gloucester of large laden vessels. As many of the largest class of vessels would have wholly to discharge their cargoes at that end of the canal, and others to take out part of their cargo before proceeding to Gloucester, it was further proposed to make a dock 2,000 ft. long, to commence at the lock, with a maximum width of 350 ft., diminishing to 200 ft. Depth of water in the dock 24 ft. for a length of 900 ft., then gradually diminishing to 20 ft. Quay walls and landing-places were incidentally provided. From these new works a cut 720 ft. long, with a top width of 150 ft. and a bottom width of 55 ft., with a depth of 19 ft., was designed as a means of junction with the old canal. The promoters went to Parliament, and, in spite of strong opposition by Lord Fitzhardinge, consent was obtained. Mr. Wythes contracted to execute the work by May, 1873 (the capital consisted of £75,000 subscribed by shareholders, and £125,000 borrowed) but, owing to unforeseen circumstances, and one or two remarkable accidents, the work was not finished until the year following. The dimensions of the undertaking are as follow: Tidal basin, length 545 ft., width 300 ft., entrance 60 ft. wide, mean spring tides on sill 29 ft.; mean neap tides, 16 ft.; lock, length from lower to upper gates, 320 ft., width 60 ft., depth 24 ft.; floating dock, length 2,200 ft., depth of water for 1,000 ft. from 24 ft. to 20 ft.; graving dock, length 350 ft., width of floor 60 ft., width of entrance 50 ft., depth of water on sill 15 ft. It is claimed that the docks are not only connected with the inland centres by means of the canal water-way, but that the Severn Bridge Railway "will open up the Forest of Dean and South Wales coalfields for export at these docks." The idea is a very good one, from a Gloucester point of view, especially now that the Severn Tunnel between Portskewett and the New Passage is available for mineral trains, and will be the means of diverting from the Gloucester route some of the through coal traffic from South Wales.

It need scarcely be said that it was a great day for Gloucester when the extension to Holly Hazel Pill was opened. The event took place on November 25, 1874, and the additional and more suitable accommodation then obtained was contemplated locally with the liveliest satisfaction. Several important Midland counties were in a direct line of canal and river communication from spacious and deep docks, and it was felt that at last something had been done not only to save Gloucester from ruination, but to offer facilities that would in effect be the means of preventing Bristol, Cardiff, and Newport from retaining the whole of the heavier mercantile traffic. Regarding the extension which brought the total dock acreage at Sharpness up to 14 acres, various opinions had been advanced by scientific men, but the work was ultimately carried on in accordance with the designs of Mr. Clegram, resident engineer. Of course the docks at Sharpness have led to the establishment of a little town in the immediate neighbourhood, but the Gloucester connections have been retained, and the seeming division of interests—not so, perhaps, in reality—was better than an absolute forfeiture on the part of Gloucester to be considered a trading port at all. Like every other place, Gloucester had to meet the altered circumstances of the times in the best possible spirit, and it was useless to go on wearing old laurels, or to repine for the lack of trade without going beyond the door, as it were, to look out for fresh opportunities.

It was easy to read the signs of the times. Some of the Bristolians had resolved at length to do something for themselves, and Cardiff and Newport were making great strides. The Gloucester men were not even now in advance of circumstances, because, when the extension was made, it was found that one dock had already been made at the mouth of the Avon, and another was projected also for the protection of the interests of the ancient river port of Bristol; at Cardiff the new Roath Dock Basin had just been built, and at Newport the Alexandra Dock was approaching completion. Gloucester had to make an effort, the effort was made, and about twenty acres of meadow land at Sharpness were converted into a harbour with the necessary canal access. The work, with Mr. Harrison, as referential engineer, was accomplished in four years, and that, notwithstanding many incidental difficulties. A deep water approach from the vicinity of Kingroad was now secured, and the harbourmaster, Captain Calway, became exceedingly energetic. When the opening ceremony took place the spring-tide came up at the rate of ten knots an hour, and the first vessel to arrive at the Pill was the *Tre Fratelli*, an Italian barque of about 600 tons, grain laden, for Messrs. Fox Bros.: the second, the *Vaza*, was also an Italian barque, of about 500 tons. Both vessels were brought up by their tugs, were swung in mid-stream and passed on to the older part of the docks. The Norwegian full-rigged ship *Director*, with timber for Messrs. Nicks & Co., from St. John's, N.B., was the first vessel to tow into the tidal basin. She was subsequently taken by the tugs, *Cambria* and *Vanguard* into the dock. The Canal Company, prior to the opening of the extension, succeeded in purchasing the Birmingham and Worcester Canal, and were thus enabled to secure for ever the navigation from the estuary of the Severn to Staffordshire and the centre of England. Among subsequent developments may be named the opening for goods traffic on August 2, 1875, of the branch Midland Railway from Berkeley road to Sharpness Docks, and in August, 1876, for passenger traffic. The Canal Company in the same year secured the Midland and Great Western Railways in the immediate vicinity of the two docks in Gloucester, for £5,000, and in the year following they acquired 38 acres of land on the west side of the canal, near Llanthony, for improving the width of the canal, and making a timber float, but this site has not yet been dealt with. The Severn Bridge, a fine structure which gives railway access from the western side of the river to Sharpness, was opened on October 17, 1879, and the undertaking was amalgamated with the Severn and Wye Railway. Towards the cost of this great bridge the Gloucester Company contributed over £70,000 the entire capital being £200,000. Several Parliamentary enterprises were subsequently embarked in, but were ultimately withdrawn. In order to more effectually counteract the attractions of the docks at Avonmouth and Portishead (where bonuses had been given to vessels), reductions were made by the directors of the Sharpness Docks on corn and timber to an amount computed to be £6,000 on the year. As a result the undue competition was checked, the rival companies agreeing in their mutual interests to a uniform increase on the suicidal rates which had come to be the fashion. Economy was now the order of the day, and the preference stock, which had for four years been at a dead stand, earned in 1884 a full dividend, while ¼ per cent. was declared on the ordinary stock. The capital of the Sharpness Company now aggregates £1,206,816 (£840,207 in the Gloucester and Sharpness undertaking, £293,833 in the Birmingham and Worcester Canal, and £72,776 in the Severn Bridge).

The income of the canal and the volume of trade may be indicated by the following statements in regard to foreign imports :—

QUINQUENNIAL PERIODS.

		Income.		Tons.
Sept. 25,	1848	£113,083		368,783
,,	1853	127,153		702,354
,,	*1858	110,870		541,453
,,	1863	138,005		860,129
,,	1868	150,644		1,046,787
,,	1873	200,679		1,429,622
,,	1878	270,686		1,794,750
,,	1883	254,984		1,737,613

PAST TWO YEARS.

,,	1884	46,352		331,585
,,	1885	47,778		333,113

* Russian War period.

The foreign exports, chiefly coal and salt, average about 55,000 tons per annum. Imports, mainly corn and timber.

Several efforts have been pluckily made to establish lines of steamers, passenger and otherwise, but the projects were unattended by the success they deserved. A great many passengers were conveyed to foreign parts, but the financial returns did not compensate the shareholders. Shipbuilding has also gone out of fashion at Gloucester, but when wooden vessels were in vogue the state of affairs in this respect was far different. Iron and steel has superseded the old "wooden walls," and Gloucester does not at present construct steamships. We should not be surprised, however, to find the old city waking up to possibilities in this direction, as signs are not wanting of a revival of local enterprise. Great interests are at stake, and Gloucester must not be content to leave the efforts of the past unsupplemented.

Pilotage and pilotage rates have lately occupied the attention of the authorities. On August 27 last, it was notified by Mr. Philip Cooke, clerk to the Bristol Channel Pilotage Commissioners, that private lights "which may be withdrawn at any time without notice" had been placed on the Severn between Kingroad and Sharpness solely for the use of the pilots of the port of Gloucester, and in October, Mr. Dixon, traffic manager of the Gloucester Docks and accessories, intimated that for towage between the Flat and Steep Holms, off

Cardiff, and Sharpness, the following reduced tariff was now arranged :—

STEAMERS.—Assistance from Kingroad to Sharpness, or *vice versâ*. For the first tug £7 10s. ; for the second tug (when required) £6. SAILING VESSELS.—Per registered ton :—From Kingroad to Sharpness and back to Kingroad 10d. ; from Kingroad to Sharpness and back to Holms or Penarth, 11d. ; from Kingroad to Sharpness and back to Newport or Cardiff Docks, 1s. ; from Holms to Sharpness and back to Kingroad, 1s.; from Holms to Sharpness and back to Holms or Penarth, 1s. 1d. ; from Holms to Sharpness and back to Newport or Cardiff Docks, 1s. 2d. One good tug to be deemed sufficient for sailing vessels up to 700 tons register. If second boat required for vessels under that tonnage, or a third boat for vessels between 700 and 1,200 tons register, an additional charge of £6 will be made in each case for the extra boat.

Both at Gloucester Docks and at Sharpness large warehouses have been erected by Gloucester and other merchants, for the stowage of corn and yards for the reception of timber. Salt comes down from Droitwich in considerable quantity, and among local industries may be mentioned that of the Gloucester Wagon Works, an extensive industrial establishment.

The dock officials are :—Mr. Henry Waddy, secretary ; Captain D. Farrant, R.N., dock master ; James Calway, harbour master, Sharpness ; Mr. John Dixon, traffic manager ; Mr. F. A. Jones, engineer.

THE ESTUARY.

In " directions " for crossing the Severn at New Passage, published in the early part of this century, it is set forth that the " passage over the Severn, which separates England from Wales, being of great importance, those who have occasion to use either Aust or New Passage are desired to observe that the time of high-water at the former is nearly the same as at Bristol Quay, and at the latter nearly an hour earlier. The hours of passing at both places are, if the wind be northerly, any time for five hours before, and if southerly or westerly, for seven hours after high-water, at each place respectively." At Aust Passage tradition hath it that Leoline, Prince of Wales, was here summoned by Edward the Elder to cross over and confer with him; but the "haughty Cambro-Briton" declined to accede to the request. When, however, he saw Edward preparing to cross over to him, he threw off his robes, leaped into the water, and exclaimed, "Most wise king, your humility has conquered my pride, and your wisdom triumphed over my folly: I yield myself your vassal." In this century alone great changes have been brought about at this spot. The later "triumphs" have been the inauguration of steam ferry-boats at the Passage, in connection with the main Great Western line (South Wales and Paddington) on the Monmouthshire side, and the railway to the old city of Bristol on the other. And now the river near this point has been "undermined" by the Severn Tunnel, which was opened on September 1, 1886, for mineral traffic, the first coal train passing through from Aberdare. One of the Crawshays was drowned, with other persons, whilst crossing the Old Passage in a sailing boat, in 1840. Forty years ago, when the desirability of promoting the construction of a bridge at the Old Passage was urged, Mr. Walker, Admiralty engineer, who examined the river, reported to his lords that there was, so far as he knew, no great communication in this country so bad, or therefore where an improvement was so much wanted, as at this ferry; and the importance was increased by the fact of there being no bridge below Gloucester, which was thirty miles above the Old Passage, and no crossing below (except the New Passage, which was, he said, inferior to the Old) without going down the Avon from Bristol.

A Severn Bridge (from near Awre to Sharpness) is now an accomplished fact, and the Severn Tunnel, already the scene of extensive mineral traffic, will most probably be opened for passenger traffic before the commencement of 1887. The Severn "defences" will now be likely to receive more adequate attention at the hands of Government.

As as addendum, it may be stated that a special committee of the Gloucester Chamber of Commerce has forwarded to the Town Council a scheme for widening and deepening the Ship Canal between Gloucester and Sharpness, and the approach to Sharpness from the Severn, at a cost of about £100,000. It is suggested that of the capital required, £69,000 shall be subscribed by the city, the citizens to have direct representation on the Canal Board, and a considerable reduction in the canal dues on imports and exports to be effected. Mr. Robert Capper, of

Swansea, read a paper on "The Produce of the Earth, and Canals, Docks, and Waterways," on October 12, 1886, before the members of the local Chamber of Commerce, Mr. Thorpe presiding. He referred incidentally to Mr. G. W. Keeling's scheme for improving the canals between Birmingham and Worcester, so as to render them navigable by vessels of 250 tons, and expressed himself in favour of the scheme, as it would give a practical communication with the sea to Birmingham and the Midlands. His opinion was that the dues then charged at Gloucester were too high, especially as compared with Cardiff, and he " prophesied " that if the needed improvements were made at Gloucester, it would in two or three years have as fine a traffic as could be desired. Mr. Nelson Foster, and Mr. Robinson, M.P., expressed similar views, and other propositions have been advanced on the same subject.

www.ingramcontent.com/pod-product-compliance
Lightning Source LLC
Chambersburg PA
CBHW021942240426
43668CB00037B/486